# Thomas G. Masaryk

## SUICIDE AND

## THE MEANING OF CIVILIZATION

THE HERITAGE OF SOCIOLOGY

*A Series Edited by* Morris Janowitz

# Thomas G. Masaryk

## SUICIDE AND THE MEANING OF CIVILIZATION

*Translated by*
WILLIAM B. WEIST *and* ROBERT G. BATSON

*With an Introduction by*
ANTHONY GIDDENS

THE UNIVERSITY OF CHICAGO PRESS

CHICAGO AND LONDON

Originally published as *Der Selbstmord als sociale Massenerscheinung der modernen Civilisation*, Vienna, 1881.

*International Standard Book Number: 0226-50931-1 (cloth)*
*0226-50933-8 (paper)*
*Library of Congress Catalog Card Number: 74-108777*

THE UNIVERSITY OF CHICAGO PRESS, CHICAGO 60637
The University of Chicago Press, Ltd., London

# Contents

## Translator's Preface

THROUGHOUT THE EXTENSIVE writings of Thomas G. Masaryk (1850–1937), literature serves as a primary key to human nature and culture. This monograph is introduced by a quote from Goethe, whom Masaryk acknowledged to have had a strong influence on his own intellectual development. Masaryk's major study of Russia[1] is dominated by the figure of Dostoevsky, whose novel *The Brothers Karamazov* Masaryk considered one of the great works in all literature. A friend of Tolstoy, whose mystic altruism he severely criticized, Masaryk many times treats the themes of the solipsistic superman image of Faust and the human struggle in the urban setting, an image to which Dostoevsky repeatedly addressed himself. And, since Masaryk had facility in many languages, the range of his literate vision included many ma-

[1]     *The Spirit of Russia*, 3 vols., first 2 vols. (London, 1919), trans. Eden and Cedar Paul from the German edition, *Russland und Europa* (Jena, 1913); vol. 3 (New York, 1967), trans., Robert Bass, ed. George Gibian. The first two volumes analyze the work of Dostoevsky's predecessors and the third devotes about half its text to the work of the great Russian novelist. Though it was written in 1912, Masaryk's involvement in the sweeping events of history did not allow him time to complete or edit the manuscript. After World War II, the manuscript came into the hands of Masaryk's daughters, Dr. Alice G. Masaryk and Mme. Olga Masaryk Revilliod, who founded the Masaryk Publications Trust in 1959 and initiated efforts to publish the work and to make others available in English versions. See Masaryk's own views on the importance of Dostoevsky to the study in vol. 1, pp. vii–x, where he indicates that his series of lectures at the University of Chicago in 1902 "produced the pith" of his work on Russia.

jor and minor thinkers and artists of England, France, Germany, Russia, Austria, Poland, and America.[2]

Illustrative of this centrality of literature as a key to culture is Masaryk's later view of his youthful analysis of suicide. Looking back almost two decades after the original research and writing, he observed:

> This piece of work, written on the battlefield, is itself restless; it has not caught the mood of the time completely, but as a whole I think that I have correctly comprehended the strength and weakness of our century—the century of the despairing Titan.
>
> The problem is the same everywhere: how to fight out one's own fight with the older order, how to work up a consistent view of life, and finally, how to calm one's own soul. . . .
>
> This fight, as it was carried on by Goethe, Byron, Mickiewicz, Krasinsky, Dostoevsky, Tolstoy and all the rest, is a fight about an outlook on the world. It is a fight to get all our knowledge unified and assembled and to put it into harmony with our social system.[3]

While the major figures of literature epitomize the wider struggles of civilized peoples to attain a unified world-view, that strug-

[2]  W. Preston Warren, *Masaryk's Democracy*, (Chapel Hill, 1941), pp. 76–81. This is an excellent critical assessment of Masaryk's philosophical and sociological views and their development.

[3]  *Modern Man and Religion*, trans., Ann Bibza and Dr. Václav Beneš, H. E. Kennedy (London, 1938; first published 1898), pp. 45–46. This work contains Masaryk's essays on "Modern Suicidism" and "Modern Titanism." His mature views on "Suicide and Militarism" and an analysis of German culture—a problem he confronted continuously as scholar and political leader—are contained in *The Making of a State*, (New York, 1927), pp. 335–63. See also *Spirit of Russia*, vol. 3, where Masaryk analyzes Dostoevsky's views on suicide, pp. 35–40, 217–19; Tolstoy, pp. 165–68; and Turgenev, p. 284. George Gibian, the editor, notes in his preface, p. xiii, that Masaryk apparently was "unacquainted with Dostoevsky" when writing his first major work on suicide, "but he came to know him shortly afterwards." This final volume is characterized by Dr. Gibian as a "tract for the Russian public—on the road to take and the road to avoid. Here is a very pro-Western, Protestant, rather nineteenth-century thinker, liberal and rationalistic, who is at the same time similar to most Russians in being an unaesthetic, civic-minded reader of literature as subject matter for social and moral analysis, emerging with a political, cultural, and humane programme for Russia." (p. xxi.)

gle goes to the heart of the problem of suicide, especially the mass phenomenon of suicide. "Suicides," he argues in chapter 5, section 1, of this study, "are the bloody sacrifices of the civilizing process, the sacrifices of the *Kulturkampf*." And in chapter 2, section 2, part 5, he concludes that suicide is directly dependent "on a person's whole outlook on life and the world; it depends on the judgment which the individual can pass on the worth of human life for the universe and especially for mankind; this decision is man's verdict about the world."

W. Preston Warren, in his detailed analysis of Masaryk's thought, notes that

it was with the factor of *cosmic perspective* [italics ours] that Masaryk first began his major philosophic writing, through analyzing out the function of philosophies in life, and in this factor of perspective he found the unity of theoretic thought with practicalities of life. It was in an effort at the diagnosis of our recent social malady of mass suicides that the factor of metaphysical outlook first gained primacy for Masaryk and received therewith an early, clear-cut formulation.[4]

It may be because "the factor of metaphysical outlook" was of importance early in Masaryk's thought and debated in later writings that he has received little or no attention in American sociology. A man so philosophically oriented, so imbued with the search for a unified Weltanschauung, so old-fashioned as to ascribe importance to a religious outlook and to the need for a higher religion, so much addicted to discussing love, science, and democracy in the very same sentence may seem to be more existentialist than empiricist, more literary than scientific. Or the fault may lie in the fact that Masaryk never sought to originate or synthesize a sociological system, but devoted his labors instead to seeking and advocating an integral social philosophy.[5]

4      Warren, *Masaryk's Democracy*, p. 90. A clue to this formulation may lie in Masaryk's observation: ". . . The philosopher who influenced me most strongly was Plato. Primarily through his interest in religion, ethics, and politics and his extraordinary combination of theory and practice." See Karel Čapek, *President Masaryk Tells His Story*, (London, 1934), p. 105.

5      See "Masaryk as Sociologist," Joseph Roucek, *Sociology and So-*

Comparing Masaryk's work with that of Emile Durkheim (1858–1917) reveals that both sought to discover a valid method of social analysis in a common topic, a topic which was of special importance for analysis by individuals representing widely divergent points of view. Though Masaryk did not create "ideal types" of suicide from his data, his empirical analysis establishes the same order of argument as does Durkheim, and in some places uses the same materials.[6] Whereas Durkheim studies social facts, Masaryk analyzes a social phenomenon, and the level of generalization and sharpness of analysis are more abstract in Durkheim's study. For Masaryk, a unified world-view was associated with certain historical principles, such as Protestantism and Catholicism, while Durkheim places less emphasis on history as such and generalizes with respect to the solidarity and integration of any society— ancient or modern, religious, political, or domestic. While Masaryk sought to stimulate the redevelopment of certain traditional values to combat suicide, Durkheim's social remedy consists of a better division of labor so that the organization of the state can be maintained while the individual finds more satisfying relationships in occupational groups.[7]

---

cial Research, 22 (May-June 1938): 412–20, and "T. G. Masaryk, Sociologist," E. E. Eubank, Social Forces, 16 (March 1938): 455–62. These are appraisals written shortly after Masaryk's death. See also Joseph S. Roucek, "Czechoslovak Sociology," in Twentieth Century Sociology, George Gurvitch and Wilbert E. Moore, eds. (New York, 1945), pp. 717–24. In connection with Masaryk's work on suicide, it is interesting that there was a question whether he should be "habilitated" in law, sociology, or philosophy, since sociology was not a recognized discipline when Masaryk first sought academic appointment.

6   Emile Durkheim, Suicide, trans. John Spaulding and George Simpson (Glencoe, Ill., 1951; original ed., Paris, 1897). Durkheim includes Masaryk's work in his bibliography at the end of his introduction (page 53), and interested scholars may compare the bibliographies in both works and the authors cited frequently by both men. A detailed critique of Durkheim's study, including its historical context, is contained in Jack D. Douglas, The Social Meanings of Suicide (Princeton, 1967). Of special importance is the question Douglas examines—the reliability of the suicide statistics used by social analysts.

7   In some respects, Masaryk's sociological thought is closer to that

While it is clear that Masaryk is not a precursor of Durkheim's thought, his importance to sociology lies precisely in the fact that he took an opposite direction in his thinking and interpretation of suicide—and, more importantly, of society. For Masaryk deeply cares about the world and less about a theoretical model. His stress is on the *inner* life of a society, a life that manifests itself in social actions but which is not known except through some understanding on the part of the investigator of this *inner* moral, intellectual, and religious spirit. Masaryk thus places a highly important component of reality in the spirit of the times and sees social behavior reflected in observations but known directly in the manner of Dilthey's "inwardly living through" the individual emphasis of the objective mind.

Our review of more than seventy early studies of suicide by French, German, English, and Italian authors—the earliest dated 1762—shows the wide variety of viewpoints which had already been brought to the topic when Masaryk began his own research.[8] Even today the question remains unsettled, as Louis I. Dublin noted as recently as 1963:

"In spite of the many additional studies that have been made of the incidence of suicide and the impressive advances in psychiatry, the phenomenon is still as baffling as ever. The many factors involved—internal and external—are so intertwined that it is impossible to point to any one as the determining cause of the act. Every generalization is immediately negated by the circumstances of the next case."[9]

---

of the late Pitirim A. Sorokin, whose logico-meaningful models of socio-cultural integration may be seen as mediating the approaches of Masaryk and Durkheim. See *Social and Cultural Dynamics,* vols. 1–4 (New York, 1937–41).

8     Hans Rost, *Bibliographie des Selbstmords* (Augsburg: Haas and Brabherr, 1927). More than 3,500 entries under some 60 classifications are contained here. An updated bibliography can be found in E. S. Shneidman, and N. L. Farberow, eds), *The Cry for Help* (New York, 1961).

9     Louis I. Dublin, *Suicide—A Sociological and Statistical Study,* (New York, 1963), Preface, p. iii. Dublin is referring to the interval between the first publication of his work, *To Be Or Not To Be—A Study of Suicide,* 1933, and the work cited above. However, it is interesting to note,

Since the question remains open, Masaryk's voice is surely among those that deserve to be heard by all contemporary students of suicide.

The stress on suicide as a social mass phenomenon based on the inner spiritual outlook of a culture leads to Masaryk's search for a normative philosophy in which a unified world-view is tied to practices and everyday life in a consistent and practical manner. The remedy lies primarily in a method of education which will prevent the occurrence of unsystematic thinking—of a divorce between the intellect, the spirit and the moral act. Masaryk repeatedly uses the German noun *Halbbildung* ("half-education") and the adjective *halbgebildet* ("half-educated") in this monograph to describe the level of unity in the world outlook of an era.[10] They signify for Masaryk the dilemma of individuals caught in a society experiencing a period of transition in all aspects of thought, feeling and practice. "We surrender our intellects to learning, our feelings to a religion and a church in which we no longer believe and which we no longer trust—that is the single, but atrocious failure of our civilization," he notes in chapter 5, section 1, of this monograph. Finally, Masaryk sees the unstable and transient character of education and a high frequency of suicide as prevalent in those nations where some form of philosophical subjectivism dominates, a subjectivism that leads to fantasy and to a false morality which divorces the individual from responsibility for his acts in the external world. To end this drift and to ease the social mass phenomenon of suicide requires a union of science and rigorously logical thinking with a nonmythical faith.[11]

This emphasis on science and on logical rigor, together with

---

as does Dublin, pp. 180–93, that most suicide prevention efforts are led by people of some religious orientation. Though professional psychiatric care in suicide prevention centers has increased—especially clinically oriented activity—clergymen remain prime movers in these local efforts to "save lives."

10    The translators have rendered these terms as "half-education" and "half-educated." In the German, the prefix "halb" modifies the noun "Bildung," which encompasses culture and its reflection in education, both formal and informal. Chap. 2, pt. 5 of this work contains an extended discussion of this topic and the core of Masaryk's argument.

11    Though Masaryk's work is rarely cited in the American literature

his search for a faith adequate to a new age, began early and remained with Masaryk throughout his long life. For while he searched the literature of civilized nations for keys to their culture, Masaryk was an empiricist of Humean insistence and origin.[12] This work reveals his youthful approach, but he was to detail four years later, in *Versuch einer concreten Logik* (Vienna, 1885), his views of philosophy as a coordinator of scientific knowledge, as a discipline that involves both the concrete and the abstract in valid thinking. Though he sought then to lay the grounds for a scientific philosophy of religion, late in his life, while Hitler ruled Germany and Masaryk defended democracy, he told Karel Čapek:

Progress will have to be by empirical methods: to try to explain how man really does act in particular circumstances; to what extent he can control himself, and his actions, and educate himself; how far he is free and responsible for his actions. I confess that I prefer conscientious statistics, of accidents, say, to a few chapters of Leibniz' *Theodicea*; from statistics I learn what generally is the cause of accidents, and how to deal with them accordingly. If the driver does not drink, mishaps do not happen so easily—ergo don't drink and that's the end of it, and don't try to blame, or justify the Good Lord. Illness —for that there are doctors, and science, so that they learn how to face them. Misery—we are all here to remove that.[13]

He observed in 1896 of his early work on suicide: "My psychological and sociological analysis of suicidism has taught me that the number of suicides is a direct mathematical measure of the

---

on suicide, an exception occurred in the preface to *On Suicide* (New York, 1967), a reprint of the discussions of the Vienna Psychoanalytical Society held in 1910. Paul Friedman, in an excellent essay on the cultural climate in which the 1910 discussions took place, observes, in a footnote on page 20: "Masaryk's assumption that suicide is a product of civilization and did not exist in primitive cultures has been disproved by modern anthropological findings." See also Douglas, *The Social Meanings of Suicide*, pp. 16–20.

12    Warren, *Masaryk's Democracy*, pp. 5–14, 68–70. It must be noted that Masaryk was assisted to this empirical insistence by no less a philosopher than his teacher, Franz Brentano. Masaryk translated Hume's *Enquiry Concerning the Principles of Morals* into German (Vienna, 1883).

13    Karel Čapek, *Masaryk on Thought and Life*, trans. M. and R. Weatherall (London, 1938), p. 78–79

real mood of society, that society is deep down in the depths of its soul excited, perturbed, sick. . . ."[14] But there were many measures of man and society, just as there were divergent forces shaping individual character and mankind's history. Masaryk worked to know and understand these forces, to find these measures, believing that the demands of democracy required men to be moral and to be morally creative, and that "democracy works by scientific method, and its tactics are therefore inductive, realistic and empirical."[15]

The life and work and the outlook of this philosopher-statesman seem to have been smothered by the fall of the small democratic state of Czechoslovakia before the *Machtpolitik* of Hitler's Third Reich. Seven years of Nazi domination and almost a quarter century of Communist rule, however, do not appear to have obliterated the seeds of democracy which Masaryk so realistically sowed and nourished as the founder and first president of the Czech state.[16]

Now, more than three decades after his death, the ideals and the life work of this social philosopher and statesman are beginning to find new life. They seem clearly relevant because some of the tumult of our present age bears notable similarities to those years when Thomas G. Masaryk was seeking to understand the emerging "modern" world. As the nineteenth century ended and the twentieth century began, Masaryk was at the peak of his intellectual powers; yet the zenith of his activities as a political figure was to be reached after his sixty-fourth year of life. To assess his work properly, both as a scholar and as a political leader, Masaryk's contributions to social thought or to social action must be evaluated by comparison with his peers and in reference to that era of history each and all helped to shape.

This monograph on suicide was Thomas Masaryk's first em-

[14]     *Modern Man and Religion*, p. 47.
[15]     *The Spirit of Russia*, vol. 2, p. 515; *Masaryk's Democracy*, pp. 32–62.
[16]     There appears to be some confusion of Thomas Masaryk and his son Jan (1886–1948), Czech foreign minister at the time of the Communist coup of February 26, 1948. Jan's "suicide" remains enigmatic and an event of continuing political importance beyond Czechoslovakia, and the investigation of that "suicide" formed part of the background to the dramatic events of August 1968.

pirical study in sociology. It was submitted in 1878 in application
for a lectureship at the University of Vienna and served as a supplement to a monograph on the principles of sociology. Masaryk
withdrew the original work soon after his return to Vienna from
America, where he had married Charlotte Garrigue on March 15,
1878. He resubmitted it in revised form in November 1878. When
it was published in 1881, it drew some critical attacks but was
praised as a remarkable sociological study. And it did help him receive appointment as lecturer in philosophy at the University of
Vienna—a post with some status but meager income. As one biog-
rapher observes: "It can scarcely be a coincidence that Masaryk's
first lectures at the University were on the subject of pessimism."[17]

Some of Thomas G. Masaryk's later studies, adulatory and critical examinations of his thinking, and several biographical works
are available in the English language.[18] An examination of the
scholarly writings—as distinguished from the political, journalis-
tic or polemical works—clearly reveals a man who anticipated in
important ways some of the most influential contributions to the
sociological knowledge of the present century.[19]

William B. Weist

Lewisburg
Pennsylvania

17    C. J. C. Street, *President Masaryk* (London, 1930), p. 80. See also
Edward Polson Newman, *Masaryk* (London, 1960), pp. 27–28. It should
be noted that a Czech edition of the monograph on suicide did not appear
until 1904. The work caused some stir in other official quarters, as Masaryk
notes: "Though the Russian translation of my first book 'On Suicide' had
been destroyed, it aroused the interest of Tolstoi." See *The Making of a
State*, p. 131.
18    For an extensive bibliography, see *Thomas Garrigue Masaryk, A
List of Works by and about the First President of Czechoslovakia in the
New York Public Library*, Avram Yarmolinsky, ed. (New York, 1941).
19    Masaryk's critical analysis of Marxism, *Die philosophischen und
sociologischen Grundlagen des Marxismus, Studien zur socialen Frage*
(Vienna, 1899; Czech ed. 1898), and of Russia are of special importance
in this respect, for they won him a reputation among Allied leaders. See
his own evaluation in *The Making of a State*, pp. 130–206. The struggle
for modern civilization, *Kulturkampf*, was an issue with which he wrestled
through his long and creative life.

## Acknowledgments

To DR. W. PRESTON WARREN, professor of philosophy at Bucknell University, the translators owe a profound debt, for it was he who taught them the significance of Masaryk's work in the context of a century of social thought. Dr. Richard E. DuWors, professor of sociology, University of Alberta, Canada, was the first to suggest the "classic" importance of Masaryk's analysis of suicide and urged completion of this translation for a wider audience. Dr. Albert Pierce, professor of sociology, San Fernando State College, California, whose expert knowledge of Emile Durkheim's thought and of the history of suicide research helped guide our efforts, contributed the intellectual excitement that makes for persistence on a major undertaking. And it was the late Pitirim A. Sorokin who emphasized to us the need for this work to be made available in an English version. To the directors of the Masaryk Publications Trust we are indebted for their aid in making this translation possible.

To Mrs. Lillian Minnich we are indebted for her translation of our scrawls into a readable typescript.

Finally, we would dedicate our work to three young men, Karl, Kurt, and James, who some day may understand the meaning of such endeavor.

WILLIAM B. WEIST
ROBERT G. BATSON

# Introduction

## I. *Masaryk's Academic and Political Career*

THOMAS GARRIGUE MASARYK was one of the most universally revered liberal democrats of modern times, a man who perhaps came closer than any other to embodying the Platonic ideal of the philosopher-statesman. Masaryk was born on March 7, 1850.[1] He came from a lowly background, the son of a coachman on an estate in Slovakia, then a part of the Austrian Empire. Masaryk's family background is symptomatic of the complicated tangle of cultural and linguistic groups mingling together in the regions which were later to become Czechoslovakia: his mother was Czech, but had attended a German school, and spoke German before later learning Slovak; his father was a Slovak who had migrated into Moravia. Of his father, Masaryk later said, "He was born in serfdom, and remained in it all his life."[2] According to Masaryk's testimony, his mother was the main source of his impetus to intellectual achievment. Masaryk's early educational career was fraught with difficulty. Having left the *Realschule* at twelve years of age, he entered apprenticeship, first to a locksmith and then to a blacksmith. It was only through an unexpected stroke of good fortune, involving the intercession of a former teacher on his behalf, that he was able

[1]  A main biographical source on Masaryk in English consists in his reminiscences as told to Karel Capek, *President Masaryk Tells His Story* (London, 1934), and *Masaryk on Thought and Life* (London, 1938). For the later period of Masaryk's life, the most important source is Masaryk's *The Making of a State,* published as an English translation in 1927 (the original title was *The World Revolution*). The best biography of Masaryk in English is P. P. Selver's *Masaryk* (London, 1940).

[2]  Capek, *President Masaryk Tells His Story*, p. 15.

to obtain a position as a pupil teacher, eventually finding ways and means to reach the University of Vienna in 1872. While there, he supported himself through private tutoring and other occasional work. As an undergraduate he studied a variety of subjects, but concentrated on philosophy, and eventually wrote a doctoral dissertation on Plato. His interests were, however, already largely centered on the analysis of social and historical problems: "In my eyes, philosophy was, above all, ethics, sociology, and politics. . . ."[3] In his early student days at Vienna, Masaryk's political purpose began to take shape: he joined a student society which provided a forum for Czech and Slovak students who were searching for ways to express their cultural identity and their resistance to Austrian domination. When elected president of the society, Masaryk played an active role in organizing lectures for Czech workers in Vienna.

Toward the end of 1877, Masaryk completed a monograph entitled *Principles of Sociology*, which he submitted to the University of Vienna together with an application for a lectureship in philosophy. His position as set out in the monograph, he stated in his letter of application, had been reached on the basis of his reading in classical political theory, together with a later thorough analysis of the writings of Hume, Comte, and John Stuart Mill.[4] He added that he intended to supplement his application by the addition of an as yet unfinished work on suicide. His application was, however, rejected by the university; one reason for the rejection was that objections were raised by the adjudicating professors to the term "sociology" in the title. Sociology, of course, at that time had no official academic status in the Austrian universities, and the term was generally regarded as a barbarous French neologism for a field of study which had no right to existence as a distinctive academic discipline.

Masaryk consequently devoted most of his effort over the subsequent months to the completion of his thesis on suicide, in order to make it the basis of a reapplication to the university. In 1878, prior to submitting the work, Masaryk traveled to America to marry Charlotte Garrigue, whom he had met while she was study-

3    Masaryk, *The Making of a State*, p. 291.
4    Selver, *Masaryk*, p. 86.

ing music in Leipzig. On his marriage, Masaryk adopted his wife's former surname as his own middle name. Having returned with his wife to Vienna, Masaryk completed the monograph on suicide in November 1878, and sent it in to the university in the same month. The work was, however, regarded with only slightly less suspicion than his previous monograph had been; it took a year before Masaryk knew the result of this second application. One of the adjudicating professors thought the work "somewhat socialistic"; another considered that, rather than being sent in to the faculty of philosophy, it should have been submitted to the law faculty. Eventually, after various wrangles the application was accepted, but only on the stipulation that the basis for Masaryk's acceptance was more the capacities he had manifested in his past record as a student than upon the qualities of the monograph itself. The virtues of Masaryk's work were however, recognized, and advocated by Franz Brentano, who had earlier exerted great influence over the direction of Masaryk's thought while the latter was an undergraduate.

In the year 1880, Masaryk underwent something of a crisis of conscience in his religious beliefs. As a child, he had been brought up a Catholic, but had come to reject most the Church's teaching and practice. Political issues were intimately bound up with the relationship between Protestantism and Catholicism in the area which was to become Czechoslovakia: Catholicism was identified with conservative acceptance of Hapsburg domination, Protestantism with the liberal Czech middle class in which were rooted aspirations toward greater autonomy from Austrian rule. Masaryk's rapidly developing commitment to the extension of Czech national identity was therefore part and parcel of his dissociation from Catholicism, culminating in his becoming a Protestant in 1880.[5] At this time he even considered abandoning his nascent academic career and entering the Protestant ministry—but partly because of his appreciation of the significance of Protestantism as a basis of Czech cultural unity.

[5]    Masaryk was instrumental in persuading Edmund Husserl, later to become famous as a founder of existentialism, to become a Protestant. See Selver, *Masaryk*, p. 99.

Masaryk's personal religious struggles are directly reflected in the subject matter of his monograph on suicide. As he states in the work, in his view modern society is in a moral crisis consequent precisely upon the breakdown of the unified world view provided in previous ages by Catholic theodicy. Later in his career, Masaryk made virulent attacks upon the Catholic clergy in connection with particular social and political issues, and was more than once brought to court to defend his views.

*Suicide and the Meaning of Civilization* was published in book form in 1881. Masaryk revised his original monograph considerably prior to its publication. The monograph, which like the published book was written in German, carried the subtitle "A monograph together with prefatory remarks on sociology and statistics." This subtitle was omitted from the published book. The original title of the thesis was *Suicide as a Social Group Phenomenon in the Present Day*, but in the published version the latter phrase was changed to *"in Modern Civilization"* (and, for this present translation, the title has again been changed). On its appearance, the book immediately became well-known outside of Austria. Masaryk wrote: "I am satisfied with its reception. It had favorable notices in German, English, French and Italian learned journals."[6]

On the strength of its favorable reception, Masaryk was offered an assistant professorship at the University of Czernowitz (Chernovtsy, U.S.S.R.). He declined the offer, preferring to remain in Vienna, where he continued, in addition to his academic activities, to involve himself in promoting the cause of Czech separation. Shortly afterward, however, a more attractive opportunity presented itself, at the University of Prague. For many years teaching in the University of Prague had been given in German, but in the year of Masaryk's appointment a separate university was set up in Prague in which all teaching was to be given in Czech, and it was to this institution that Masaryk came as an assistant professor of philosophy. "As a matter of fact", he said later, "I would rather have had a chair of sociology, but that did not exist in Austria".[7]

In his teaching at Prague, Masaryk sought to break away from

6     Quoted by Selver, *Masaryk*, p. 103.
7     Capek, *President Masaryk Tells His Story*, p. 124.

the traditional reliance upon German philosophy which continued to prevail even in the new university, lecturing upon—among others—Descartes, Locke, Hume, Comte, and Spencer. In other ways he followed lines which were, in the context of the established modes of instruction, highly unorthodox. He offered a course in "practical philosophy" dealing with questions of vocational choice, hygiene, and extracurricular activities. Masaryk avoided the dogmatic pedantry characteristic of the older professors, and in his first few years at the university enjoyed enormous popularity among the students.

He was soon, however, caught up in the first of several acrid controversies in which he was involved during the course of his long academic career at Prague. This concerned the issue of the authenticity of two manuscripts on early Czech history which had been "discovered" in 1818, and had been since then generally accepted by Czech nationalists as constituting proof of the long-standing cultural identity of the Czechs as a people. In a journal which Masaryk had founded shortly after arriving in Prague, the documents were exposed as forgeries. (In fact when they first came to light in 1818, some scholars had questioned their genuineness, but their objections were overridden by the strength of popular sentiment in their favor). Masaryk was subjected to a barrage of public criticism and vilification which took several years finally to abate. His answer to his critics was clear and firm; while continuing to stress his Czech patriotism, he held there could be no doubt that the documents were forgeries, and "Our pride, our culture, cannot be based on a lie."[8] When Masaryk first came to Prague, he had been promised a full professorship within three years of his arrival; in the event, his promotion took thirteen years to materialize, and there can be no doubt that the affair of the documents was a factor retarding his academic advancement. Nevertheless, by the time he finally received his promotion, the documents in question were accepted by almost everyone to be forgeries.

Masaryk's stance in the affair aroused admiration as well as rebuke, and with the cooling of hostile fervor Masaryk was elected to the parliament in Vienna as a member of the "Young Czech"

[8]    Quoted in D. A. Lowrie, *Masaryk of Czechoslovakia* (London, 1937), p. 39.

party. In the parliament he made various speeches advocating greater Czech independence and criticizing Austrian policy in the Balkans and elsewhere, and his activities completely reversed the unpopular image he had previously had in some quarters of Prague. During this period he twice visited Russia, where he met Tolstoy.

In the 1890's Masaryk came into direct contact with the socialist movement, lecturing to strikers in Prague and Kladno, and joined with the workers in protest marches. He considered himself a "realist" in both philosophy and politics, and fought romanticism in both spheres, but he could not ally himself directly with any form of Marxian socialism. He once expressed his attitude on this matter as "Always for the workers, very often with socialism, rarely with Marxism."[9] Masaryk's views on Marxism are set out at length in his *Studien zur socialen Frage*, published in 1899.[10] In this work Masaryk declares himself against "historicism" in any form; both he who represses and he who is repressed can base their claims to future dominance on past historical rights. Masaryk's discussion of historical materialism parallels that of virtually all of the major liberal social thinkers of the nineteenth century: concluding that, while historical materialism illuminates certain aspects and certain periods of social development, it cannot be maintained that economic relationships in any sense "finally determine" all major processes of social change.[11] Neither can the modern social order be rebuilt upon a basis of class revolution; while class struggles undoubtedly play a role in history, they do not supply the key to it.

In addition to this work, Masaryk published over the course of his lifetime books and articles on a variety of subjects, academic and political. The *Spirit of Russia*, published in 1913, is Masaryk's most ambitious and highly regarded work.[12] The book consists of a collection of sketches of the main periods of Russian history, to-

9    Quoted in Selver, *Masaryk*, p. 202.
10   Masaryk, *Die philosophischen und sociologischen Grundlagen des Marxismus. Studien zur socialen Frage* (Vienna, 1899).
11   *Ibid.*, pp. 130 ff.
12   Masaryk, *The Spirit of Russia*, 2d ed. (London, 1955), 2 vols., originally published in English in 1919.

gether with long discussions of the development of Russian ethical and social philosophy. A main theme underlying the whole work is that the categories of thought and action derived from Russian orthodoxy have been increasingly challenged by the "philosophy of Protestantism," by which Masaryk means primarily the post-Kantian German philosophers, both idealist and materialist—Fichte, Hegel, Vogt, and Marx. Russia has quite suddenly been opened up to progressivist European thought: "Medieval Russia, the Russia of antiquity . . . was dragged without transition into the European evolutionary process of the eighteenth and subsequent centuries."[13]

In *The Spirit of Russia* one finds combined together all of the main themes and problems which occupied Masaryk's thought: the influence of Protestantism and the break with medieval traditionalism, which ocurred much more suddenly in Russia than in Western Europe; the problem of the moral and institutional "vacuum" which that creates for the modern world, and which is evinced in the growth of melancholy suicide; and finally, the so-called "Slavic question"—the question of the nature of indigenous Russian culture, and what it has or has not to offer as against the culture of Western Europe. Masaryk's conclusions in the book as regards the latter of these issues are that, on the whole, the hopes of the "Slavophiles" are misplaced; that the highest and most hopeful developments for the future of Europe are still centered in the West; and that Russia cannot overcome the passivity of centuries and draw level with the West by telescoping into a few decades what in the West has been the outcome of many years of evolution.[14]

In 1908 Austria annexed Bosnia and Herzegovina, and the Austrian government made a mass arrest of more than fifty Serbs and Croats who were charged with, and found guilty of, high treason against the Empire. Masaryk played a leading role in exposing the machinations on the part of the Austrian Foreign Ministry which underlay the affair, and was in the end instrumental in forc-

---

13    *Ibid.*, p. 556.
14    On its publication in its original form (the work was first written in German, under the title *Russland und Europa*), the book was reviewed —unfavorably of course—by Trotsky in *Der Kampf.*

ing the Austrian Foreign Minister to resign. As a consequence, Masaryk's reputation grew enormously among progressive Czech elements, and by the outbreak of the First World War he was recognized on an international level as a leading opponent of Austrian hegemony. Well before the beginning of the war, Masaryk had become convinced that the Hapsburg Empire was bound to collapse in the near future, and that out of the ruins new independent nations could be born. After the outbreak of hostilities, Masaryk began to play an active part in organizing Czech resistance to involvement on the side of the Germans. In Geneva, in 1915, he for the first time publicly stated his opposition to Austria; he was condemned by the Austrian government as a traitor, his property in Czechoslovakia was confiscated, and his daughter, who had remained in Prague, was imprisoned.

During the war years, Masaryk worked to further the cause of Czech independence, both in writing and actively on a wide variety of fronts. In 1915, having set up in Switzerland the headquarters of an underground movement to operate in Prague, Masaryk came to London, where he accepted a professorship at King's College. He continued, however, his unsparing efforts toward furthering the Czech cause. Following the initial stages of the Russian Revolution in 1917, Masaryk traveled to Russia to organize some fifty thousand Czech soldiers who had either deserted to, or had been captured by, the Russians, and who had subsequently declared themselves ready to fight against Austria. After many difficulties, Masaryk succeeded in forming a disciplined Czech army. In 1918 he went to the United States, where he succeeded in securing vital Allied support for the formation of an independent State of Czechoslovakia on the conclusion of the war.

This was finally put into effect when, on October 14, 1918, in Washington, Masaryk proclaimed Czechoslovakia to be a sovereign state; exactly a month later he was elected as its first President. He served as President of Czechoslovakia for a period of seventeen years, being reelected three times: a special provision in the new constitution stated that no man, save for Masaryk, could serve for more than one term of seven years of office. Masaryk died on September 14, 1937, having preserved his enormous popularity within the country which he, more than any other single individual, helped to create.

## II. *Masaryk's* Suicide *in the Context of Previous Research*

The word "suicide" is quite recent in origin; although constructed from Latin roots, it is not itself a Latin word. The earliest use of the word in English seems to date from 1662.[15] While "suicide" (*suicide, suicidio*) is used in French and Italian, the German word (*Selbstmord*) still keeps the connotations which were attached to "self-murder" in the Middle Ages. Although the term "suicide" is itself a relatively new one, the phenomenon to which it refers makes its appearance in the oldest of written records,[16] and a broad variety of cultural attitudes regarding suicide have been held in different societies and at various periods in history.

The earliest reference to suicide in the Classical Greek literature appears to be that of Epikaste in the Oedipus myth. In Homer's narrative of this episode, there is no indication of a condemnatory attitude toward suicide. Suicides are in fact fairly common events in the Homeric poems, but most of these are of a heroic rather than a melancholy character.[17] The tendency to applaud suicides of a heroic type is found in the writings of many Classical authors. Suicide was apparently never considered an offence under Athenian civil law, although certain religious sanctions probably existed and were practised against attempted suicides.[18]

The leading schools of Greek thought at various periods expressed differing opinions concerning the morality of suicide.

---

[15] Cf. W. W. Westcott, *Suicide, its History, Literature, Jurisprudence, Causation and Prevention* (London, 1885), p. 31. The Latin phrase used to designate suicide was *sibi mortem consciscere*.

[16] As G. Garrisson says, "Suicide appears in the world with society and develops with it" (*Le suicide dans l'antiquité et dans les temps modernes* [Paris, 1885], p. 6).

[17] See A. W. Mair, "Suicide," in J. Hastings, ed., *Encyclopaedia of Religion and Ethics* (Edinburgh, 1921), vol. 12, pp. 26–27.

[18] *Ibid.*, pp. 29–30.

Pythagoras and his followers condemned suicide, primarily on the basis of inferences from religious grounds. Plato and Aristotle both considered suicide a reprehensible act: the former in terms of it being an act against God and man's essential nature, the latter in more secular terms as a threat to the authority of the state.[19] But the Stoic and Cynic philosophers expressed more tolerant attitudes toward suicide.[20]

A positive philosophy of suicide was later more fully elaborated in the hands of the Roman Stoics.[21] In the Stoic philosophy, suicide was free of stigma; the right of an individual to determine the time and the nature of his own death was considered to be unequivocal. According to Mair, for those following this school of thought, "The morality of suicide was no longer in dispute: given such a situation as either from the individual point of view or from the point of view of his relation to the State appeared intolerable, then suicide was the obvious and expected course of action."[22] The literature offers many examples of the calm and rational evaluation of life and death, ending in the decision that death is preferable. "If life pleases you", Seneca wrote, "live. If not, you have a right to return whence you came."[23] According to Roman law, normal succession rights were permitted to the relatives of suicides if the suicide could be attributed to one of a number of factors, including *taedium vitae*, sickness or grief, insolvency, and madness.

The early Christians adopted and extended the Platonic view of suicide, but the history of the early Christian sects provides many examples of deaths which border upon suicide. In describing the martyrdom of St. Perpetua and Felicitas, St. Cyprian recounts how Perpetua placed the hand of the hesitant gladiator to her throat, saying that she could only be slain through her own voli-

---

[19]   K. A. Geiger, *Der Selbstmord im klassischen Altertum* (Augsburg, 1888), pp. 7–9.

[20]   H. R. Fedden, *Suicide. A Social and Historical Study* (London, 1938), pp. 76ff.

[21]   On the Roman Stoics, see W. E. H. Lecky, *History of European Morals* (London, 1869), vol. 1, pp. 223–39.

[22]   Mair, "Suicide," p. 31.

[23]   Lecky, *History of European Morals*, vol. 1, pp. 229–30.

tion, as the evil spirit feared her.[24] In the early history of the Church, instances of deliberately invoked martyrdom, and the ascetic courting of death are common. The attitude of the religious authorities toward these types of intentionally stimulated self-destruction was for some time an ambivalent one. St. Augustine, however, established the absolute sinfulness of every type of suicide through the assimilation of suicide to murder. Suicide was regarded by him as murder of the self and as such comparable to any other kind of murder.[25] Thus suicide was regarded and continues to be regarded within the Catholic Church, from the point of reference of the prohibition against murder given in the sixth commandment. A Council of Arles, held in A.D. 452 pronounced suicide to be of diabolical inspiration; a Council of Bragues several decades later decided that no religious rites were to be performed at the grave of a suicide.

For many years, penalties against suicide were exclusively ecclesiastical in character. Civil action against suicide dates from the late Middle Ages; in English law, suicide came to be regarded as a crime against the state, and entailed the confiscation of the offender's property. Confiscation of the property of suicides was a principle maintained in England until quite recent times. Lecky complained in 1869: "The monstrous injustice of confiscating to the Crown the entire property of the deliberate suicide still disgraces the statute-book. . . ."[26] In England suicide remained a criminal act until very recently; a person who attempted suicide could be subject to criminal proceedings.

While, of course, precise statistics are lacking, historians concur that during the medieval period and prior to the Renaissance suicide rates were probably low in the countries of Western Europe. The *Journal du Règne de Henri IV*, for example, which describes the events of nearly a century in considerable statistical

---

[24]   J. J. O'Dea, *Suicide: Studies on Its Philosophy* (New York, 1882), p. 70.

[25]   See A. Michel, "Suicide," in A. Vacant *et al.*, *Dictionnaire de théologie catholique* (Paris, 1939), pp. 2739–49.

[26]   Lecky, *History of European Morals*, vol. 2, p. 62.

detail, records no more than thirty suicides in that time.[27] O'Dea asserts that "Deliberate suicide seems to have ceased almost entirely with the establishment of Christianity, and to have continued in abeyance until the reign of philosophic scepticism. . . .[28]

The coming of the Renaissance and the growth of secular philosophy eventuated in the appearance of a polemical literature directed against the traditional religious attitudes toward suicide. John Donne, born in 1573, was one of the first modern apologists of suicide. His work on suicide, *Biathanatos*, was published after Donne's death by his son in 1648. Donne discussed examples of suicide in Antiquity, ritual suicide, and Christian martyrdom in his defense of the rights of the individual, in circumstances, to kill himself.[29] Later defenders of the right of the individual to take his own life include Hume and Montesquieu.[30] These apologist treatments of suicide use the writings of the Stoic philosophers, "Suicide", Hume argued, ". . . may be free from any imputation of guilt or blame, according to the sentiments of all the ancient philosophers."[31] An insect is capable of destroying a human life; why, then, may not the reflective individual wilfully dispose of what may in any case be ended through such trivial causes? An individual should not be obliged "to prolong a miserable existence, because of some frivolous advantage which the public may perhaps receive" from him.[32]

These works sparked off a protracted controversy which, albeit in somewhat different form, continues even today; and they provided a stimulus to more objective analysis of the distribution and causes of suicide. A substantial basis of generally accepted fact concerning the distribution, and to a lesser extent the etiology, of suicide came gradually through the eighteenth century to emerge from within the moralistic literature on the subject.

27    E. Lisle, *Du suicide* (Paris, 1856), pp. 422–26.
28    O'Dea, *Suicide*, p. 85.
29    J. Donne, *Biathanatos* (1648).
30    D. Hume, *Two Essays* (London, 1777); Montesquieu, *Lettres persanes* (1901), letter 76.
31    Hume, *Two Essays*, p. 5.
32    *Ibid.*, p. 19.

Most students were agreed that suicide was on the increase; that, as Dumas wrote in 1773: "Suicide is becoming . . . common throughout all parts of the Christian world."[33] It was generally accepted that expanding urbanization on the one hand, and the decline of the traditional social and moral order on the other, were directly connected to the rising rates of suicide. In contrast to the writings of the liberal philosophers of the seventeenth century and of the first half of the eighteenth century, much of the subsequent writing on suicide, until well into the nineteenth century, preserved a strongly conservative moralistic attitude. The increase in suicide was considered to be a reflection of the pathological state of societies which had lost their grounding in a firm moral order. Discussion of suicide here was used in a contrary way to the reasoning of the seventeenth-century philosophers; whereas the latter had used the right to suicide as an attack upon estabished morality, many nineteenth-century tracts on the subject took the rise in suicide to be evidence of the deleterious consequences of the undermining of the traditional order.

Among the generalizations concerning the social distribution of suicide which were fairly well established by the early years of the nineteenth century were the following: that suicide rates tend to be higher in urban areas than rural areas; that rates of suicide among Catholic groups are generally lower than in Protestant communities; that suicide rates are correlated with socioeconomic status, at least as regards the urban occupational structure; that suicide varies with age, sex, and marital status; and that suicides tend to cluster in certain seasons of the year (particularly in spring and early summer) and at certain times of the day. Officially published statistics on suicide, which in some countries began to appear in the late eighteenth century, provided the source material for these correlations.

While there were many specialist studies of suicide produced throughout the nineteenth century, suicide also formed a part of the concern of the "moral statisticians." As statistics published by

<hr>

[33]    J. Dumas, *Traité du suicide, ou du meurtre volontaire de soi-même* (Amsterdam, 1773), p. 2.

government authorities grew progressively more comprehensive, writers on moral issues began to use them extensively as a source of "objective" measurement of the moral state of society. Among the most influential of these writers was Quetelet, who showed that the statistical distribution of "moral phenomena"—including murder, crime, and suicide—was as stable from year to year as demographic phenomena such as birth or death rates.[34] Quetelet, who must be ranked as one of the founders of the tradition of quantitative analysis which has come to form one of the pillars of modern sociology, also provided a theoretical interpretation of the causes of suicide, holding that suicide rates vary in relation to the degree of "moral density" of society. Suicide, in common with other moral phenomena which would at first sight appear to be purely "individual," is in fact governed by the laws of the social system.

During the same period as the statistical study of suicide was becoming well established, a rather different approach was also becoming firmly rooted. In medieval times, madness was considered of diabolical inspiration and in part this attitude was extended toward suicide also, since suicide was condemned by the religious authorities—thus the body of a suicide was commonly subjected to various degradations.[35] When, therefore, the discipline of medical psychiatry began to emerge, it tended to preserve the assumption of a close linkage between suicide and mental illness. Psychiatric studies, based mainly on case material of patients, form the second body of work on suicide from the late eighteenth century onwards. Works by psychiatrists partly overlap with those written in the statistical tradition, in that some works combine both case study material and statistical surveys; but there also developed important lines of theoretical and empirical difference between the two approaches. In part, this clash of opinion was related to the question of the "reality" of the social factors which the statistically-minded students of suicide adduced as explaining the regularity of suicide rates; the psychiatrists, more committed to examining the psycho-

---

[34]  L. A. J. Quetelet, *Du système social et des lois qui le régissent.*
[35]  In France, for example, according to Lecky, the body of a suicide would be dragged publicly through the streets, and then hung upside down. See Lecky, *History of European Morals*, vol. 2, pp. 61ff.

logical antecedents of suicide, were also often committed to an "individualistic" position with regard to its etiology.[36] On an empirical level, this discussion came down to a dispute over the relationship between suicide and mental disorder. For if, as it was widely believed, mental illness is primarily determined by inherited characteristics of temperament, then it seemed there could be no place for the causative role of social factors; if these latter play a part at all, it would be simply that of the situational characteristics precipitating suicide. This view was set out in Esquirol's famous *Maladies mentales*, which was published in 1838.[37]

Among the first comprehensive investigations of suicide in the nineteenth century, Falret's *De l'hypochondrie et du suicide*, published in 1822 was one of the most influential.[38] Falret examined a wide range of material both statistical and psychiatric on suicide in the countries of Western Europe. He identified a variety of different "internal causes" of suicide, stressing the importance of inherited mental illness in this respect. These he distinguished from the "external causes," which explain the variations in the distribution of suicide between different national and intranational groups. In Falret's work there appeared a whole range of statistical generalizations linking suicide to a wide range of social phenomena. A spate of works, some largely statistical in character, others more inclined to the psychiatric view, followed Falret's work. These included, among many others, in France, works by Guerry, Étoc-Demazy and Lisle; in England, by Winslow; in Italy, by Morselli; and in Germany the works of Casper, Müller, and Wagner.[39]

36    For an examination of the importance of this problem vis-à-vis Durkheim and his school, cf. A. Giddens, "The Suicide Problem in French Sociology," *British Journal of Sociology*, 16 (1965) : 3–18.

37    E. Esquirol: *Des maladies mentales* (Paris, 1838), 2 vols. Cf. also C. E. Bourdin, *Du suicide considéré comme maladie* (Paris, 1845).

38    J. P. Falret, *De l'hypochondrie et du suicide* (Paris, 1822).

39    A. M. Guerry, *Essai sur la statistique morale de la France* (Paris, 1833) ; C-F. Etoc-Demazy, *Recherches statistiques sur le suicide* (Paris, 1844) ; E. Lisle, *Du suicide* (Paris, 1856) ; F. Winslow, *The Anatomy of Suicide* (London, 1840) ; E. Morselli, *Il suicidio* (Milan, 1879) ; J. L. Casper, *Über den Selbstmord und seine Zunahme in unserer Zeit* (Berlin, 1825) ; O. Müller, *Der Selbstmord* (Hamburg, 1859) ; A. Wagner, *Die*

Masaryk's *Suicide* built upon all of these. Its originality in relation to the work of these previous authors lies not so much in its statistical documentation of the distribution of suicide—although Masaryk does go into this in some considerable detail—as in Masaryk's attempt to provide a sociological interpretation of the phenomenon on the basis of the crucial importance of religion as a source of moral control in society. Like Durkheim's later work on the subject, the book was conceived by Masaryk to be far more than simply a discussion of the causes of suicide; it "gives in a nutshell a philosophy of history and an analysis of our modern era."[40]

Masaryk opens his work by indicating the prevalence of suicide in modern Europe. According to official statistics, some 22,000 people in Europe kill themselves every year, and if it is the case, as has been suggested, that these statistics are underestimations of real rates of suicide, then the true incidence of suicide may be something nearer to 50,000 cases a year. Masaryk recognizes that suicide has been the object of a wealth of previous studies, but considers that his own work is the first systematic *sociological* analysis of the phenomenon. His work, he states, is scientific and factual, but it nevertheless allows us to identify some of the characteristics of a moral crisis in modern civilization which, in Masaryk's view is definitely a pathological phenomenon.

Masaryk separates "suicide" from what he calls "self-inflicted death." The latter refers to cases where an individual causes his own death, but not in a deliberate, wholly conscious fashion—where a man meets an early end through living a physically debilitating form of existence, or where he adopts a "passive attitude toward the dangers of life." Suicide refers to that more restricted category of cases where a man "longs for death as such," and therefore "intentionally and knowingly ends his life."[41] Both suicide and self-inflicted death, in Masaryk's sense, must be separated

---

*Gesetzmässigkeit in den scheinbar willkürlichen menschlichen Handlungen* (Hamburg, 1864).

[40]  Masaryk, *The Making of a State*, p. 291.

[41]  P. 7. This is similar to what Menninger has called "partial suicide." See K. A. Menninger, *Man against Himself*, (London, 1938).

from self-sacrifice, whereby an individual kills himself in further-
ance of some higher value.[42]

Masaryk follows most previous writers on the subject in distinguishing two main classes of factors which may influence suicide
rates: those in the physical environment (climate, the seasons,
etc.), and those deriving from man himself (biological and social
factors). Masaryk's discussion of the influence of the first type of
factor rather uncritically adopts the characteristic view of most
nineteenth-century alienists that climatic variations, such as
marked rises in temperature, act directly upon the nervous system
so as to produce irritability, depression, and a tendency to suicide.
However, Masaryk concludes, influences from the physical environment at the most can be said to exert a conditional effect upon
suicide: the determinate causes of suicide must be sought in the
biological and social constitution of man.

Masaryk discusses a variety of statistical researches bearing
upon the relationship between suicide and the many factors in
man's biological makeup and social organization which previous
authors have considered as influential in the etiology of suicide. As
Masaryk notes in some detail, numerous relationships can be
demonstrated, such as those showing that suicide varies by sex,
marital status, occupation and age; that rates of suicide are higher
in urban areas than rural ones, decline in times of war and rise in
periods of rapid economic change. All of these show how closely
suicide is connected with the conditions of social life, but these
relationships are actually symptomatic of a more deeply-rooted
malaise in the moral order of contemporary societies which is the
underlying cause of the high rates of suicide characteristic of the
modern age.

That this is so, Masaryk considers, is demonstrated by the close
correlation which exists between suicide and level of education. In

---

[42] This category would include many of the forms of self-destruction
which Durkheim calls "altruistic suicide." Many writers, however, both
prior to and subsequent to Durkheim have concluded that self-sacrifice
forms a separate type of act which must be considered apart from suicide.
See for example, Maurice Halbwachs, *Les causes du suicide* (Paris, 1930)
conclusion.

general, the higher the educational level of a country, the higher its rate of suicide. This is to be explained, according to Masaryk, not in terms of the prevalence or otherwise of intellectual development as such, however, but in terms of the increasing spread of superficial culture (*Halbbildung*: "half-education"). It is all too frequently a result of modern education, in Masaryk's view, that the individual is imbued with a disorganized, heterogeneous set of ideas which, while removing the stable world view given in traditional religious education, provides no secure framework in its place. "Knowledge which cannot be used makes its possessor a victim of fantasy, of hypercritical nonsense, destroying the desire for useful labor, creating needs which cannot be satisfied, and leading in the end to boredom with life."[43] Moreover, intellectual education has largely replaced moral education. Now there can be no doubt, Masaryk argues, that suicide is in a basic sense an "immoral" act, in that the man who kills himself demonstrates a lack of moral courage. Many individuals who do not kill themselves face greater hardship and misfortune than most of those who commit suicide. "The special immorality of suicides therefore rests on their characteristic hopelessness and despair, on their lack of trust, on their belief that the destiny of man cannot be improved, and on their lack of energy to work willingly for the betterment of their destiny."[44]

There is undoubtedly a close connection between mental disorder and suicide. According to Masaryk, "a third of all cases are to be traced back to mental illness." It is true that there is a large hereditary component in the etiology of mental disorder, but it is, Masaryk concludes, false to suppose that mental illness can be explained purely in these terms; only a constitutional disposition to mental disorder can be inherited, and whether or not this becomes activated depends upon the life experience of the individual, and thus also upon the social circumstances in which he exists. Examination of the causes of mental illness shows, in fact, insofar as it results from social influences, that they are the same as those of

[43]   P. 68.
[44]   P. 78.

suicide. Suicide cannot, therefore, be explained in terms of mental illness; rather, both spring from the moral disorder of modern societies.

Knowledge of traditional societies shows us that religion is everywhere the source of morality. Religious beliefs and practices provide, in such societies, both a source of inspiration to men and a basis for courage and hope in the face of adversity. The increasing secularization characteristic of contemporary societies, however, has meant that this secure moral bulwark has been largely destroyed. Thus we reach an understanding of the fundamental cause of the modern tendency to suicide: the decline in religious faith, which is a direct result of the overthrow of the traditional order.

Suicide, according to Masaryk, is virtually unknown in primitive societies.[45] The life of primitive man is relatively restricted, and he has no opportunity to indulge in the reflective self-criticism characteristic of men in more developed societies. Suicide becomes increasingly common with the advance of civilization. Thus suicide in Classical times reflects the development of skeptical philosophy there. On the other hand, the triumph of Christianity in the West, and the dominant position assumed by the Church, meant that suicide rates became negligible in the Middle Ages, "because religion inspired all aspects of life, the masses accustomed themselves to spiritual guidance, and they had in their unified worldview a fixed support for the tragic vicissitudes of life in the Middle Ages."[46] The rise of Protestantism was a reflection in the religious sphere of the advances in science and learning in the fourteenth and fifteenth centuries. Protestantism stimulates the development of free enquiry; it involves a much higher degree of individualism than the Catholic Church, has no hierarchy, and reduces the amount of ritual practice associated with worship. This explains why suicide is more common among Protestants than among Catholics: The Protestant is more easily left open to doubt and despair. But, according to Masaryk, this is by no means the inevitable out-

---

[45] There was much debate among anthropologists in the late nineteenth century over the frequency of suicide in primitive societies.

[46] P. 126.

come of Protestant theology; rather, it is a consequence of the decline in religious belief and practice which has followed on from the spread of Protestantism. That this is so, Masaryk believes, can be seen by the fact that the same tendencies are today invading Catholicism. It is, indeed, only through a revival of religion in a form which is different from both contemporary Protestantism and Catholicism that the moral vacuum can be filled and suicide rates reduced. For Masaryk, neither science nor art can replace the "moral meaning" which belief in a superior being confers.

The general views which Masaryk expresses in the book remained the foundation of most of his later thought, and are clearly evident in the structure of his major oeuvre, *The Spirit of Russia*. As Masaryk says in the latter work:

In my attempts at philosophico-historical explanations I start from the conviction that religion constitutes the central and centralising mental force in the life of the individual and society. The ethical ideals of mankind are formed by religion; religion gives rise to the mental trend, to the life mood of human beings.[47]

The disintegration of the unified system of values and beliefs provided by Catholicism in traditional Europe is the background to the analysis set out by Masaryk in *Suicide*. The book as a whole is an attempt to provide an explanation for the "surprising and terrible fact" of the increase in rates of suicide of the countries of Europe. The rise of this increase leaves no doubt that it is a pathological phenomenon, a resultant of the profound social changes which have occurred in Europe since the eighteenth century. The rapid rise in suicide, and the multitude of states of mental pathology associated with it, are indicative of the fact that modern societies are in a state of transition, a state which Masaryk in another work refers to as a period "of immaturity in the modern outlook on life and of a resulting inadequacy in the organisation of society."[48] In medieval society, Catholic theocracy was the center point of a social and political order which was unified and encompassing; the development of modern forms of society entailed the

[47]   Masaryk, *The Spirit of Russia*, vol. 2, p. 557
[48]   Masaryk, *The Making of a State*, p. 314.

partial dissolution of this order, and the emergence of secular idea systems in the form of science, philosophy, and literature. The revolt against the collective authority of the Church gave rise to individualism and subjectivism in philosophy, and these in their turn led to "egomania and 'solipsism', to spiritual and moral isolation, to general anarchy in place of the earlier systematic Catholicism."[49] Belief and certainty were replaced by the *Angst* of modern man: skepticism, and self-doubt. The anxieties and uncertainties bred by the dissolution of the traditional order have given rise to two apparently contrary sets of phenomena: on the one hand to pessimism and the impulse to suicide, and on the other to aggressive, Utopian fantasies of power. Suicide and murder are psychological opposites which both, however, spring from a state of egregious individualism.

The conception of the "superman," which Masaryk finds to be evident in many aspects of modern European social philosophy and literature, is a primary manifestation of the response to the egoistic uncertainty of contemporary man. One of the first examples of the "superman" is Rousseau' Saint-Preux; Masaryk says that, although Rousseau does not deal in depth with the matter, "he reveals the moral sickness that drives his superman to suicide."[50] Goethe's Faust, one of the first examples in German literature, is averted from suicide only at the last moment when preparing to take poison. In *The Spirit of Russia*, Masaryk analyzes in some detail similar tendencies in Russian literature, where he finds many instances, ranging from Pushkin's Onegin to Tolstoy's Levin, but including above all the novels and stories of Dostoevski. In *The Making of a State* (written after the First World War), Masaryk extends this analysis to comprehend the rise of Prussian militarism.[51] The modern form of militarism must, he stresses, be distinguished from previous types of warfare; only in modern times, and most notably in Germany, has the impulsion to war derived

---

49    *Ibid.*, p. 315.
50    *Ibid.*, p. 316.
51    Thus reaching strikingly similar conclusions to those of Durkheim as expressed in the latter's analysis of Treitschke. See Durkheim, *"L'Allemagne au-dessus de tout"* (Paris, 1915).

from the myth of the omnipotent absolutist state. Similarly, primitive man knows nothing of the modern form of suicide—suicide deriving from pessimism and apathy. Suicide in primitive societies derives from "rage at some affront or at the failure of some vigorous effort"; only men in contemporary societies suffer "from morbid suicidal mania, from lack of energy, fatigue or dread born of mental and moral isolation, of barren megalomania, and supermanishness."[52] Modern Prussian militarism rests upon the equation of "super-man" and "super-state"; it is a collective (and, in Masaryk's view, pathological) response to the egoistic condition of the individual in present-day society: "Indeed, I believe that the moral significance of the World War stands out clearly as an effort to find, in objectivism, freedom from exaggerated subjectivism."[53]

The moral crisis of modern civilization can only be resolved through a religious revival: not a revision to the repressive control the Church exerted in previous ages, but the reawakening of a religiously inspired moral discipline which is integrated with the critical understanding fostered by science. This cannot take the form of a Comtean "religion of humanity," but should be rooted in the Christian ethic of love and duty.

There is today, according to Masaryk, still a vast gulf between the deeply felt need of men for a moral authority on the one hand, and the outworn dogma and ritual of the constituted churches on the other, Masaryk nowhere specifies what institutional form this hoped-for revival of the religious spirit should take; the particular institutional character which it might assume is for him secondary to its content as a moral stimulus: "What we need is faith, living faith in something higher than ourselves, something great, sublime, eternal."[54]

Masaryk's *Suicide* set the stage for the elaboration of a distinctively sociological theory of suicide. The dramatic success of Durkheim's work in this respect has tended to overshadow Masaryk's contribution. However, although it is more systematic and sophisticated than Masaryk's work, Durkheim's *Suicide* shares a number

---

52    Masaryk, *The Making of a State*, p. 317.
53    *Ibid.*, p. 318.
54    Capek, *President Masaryk Tells His Story*, p. 215.

of broad theoretical similarities with it, and Masaryk's conclusions no doubt influenced Durkheim's formulation of his own ideas.[55] For both Masaryk and Durkheim, the rising rates of suicide apparent throughout the nineteenth century indicate the existence of a profound crisis in contemporary societies. Both consider the main social movement which offers the vision of an alternative society— socialism—to be of only limited value in that the remedies proposed by socialists are primarily economic; no economic solution can be found to a set of problems which lie mainly in the sphere of morality. Both authors see the decline in the previously all-encompassing position of religion in society as the major factor in promoting the moral malaise which makes suicidal pessimism a concomitant of social advancement; neither however believe that science itself should be held responsible for this: indeed, both authors are wholly committed to scientific rationalism. The maintenance of rationalism, however, should be integrated with the moral supports which alone give life meaning. Masaryk's views on the future of religion, emphasizing the continuing importance of Christianity, differ in detail from Durkheim's conception of the changing form of moral solidarity, but Masaryk's insistence on the permanent significance of religion in society echoes Durkheim's famous phrase: "There is something eternal in religion which is destined to survive all the particular symbols in which religious thought has successively enveloped itself."[56]

ANTHONY GIDDENS

Leicester
England

---

[55]     Durkheim lists Masaryk's book in his bibliography. See Emile Durkheim, *Suicide* (London, 1952), p. 53.
[56]     Emile Durkheim, *The Elementary Forms of the Religious Life*. (London, 1964), p. 427.

# Thomas G. Masaryk

## SUICIDE AND

## THE MEANING OF CIVILIZATION

Greift nur hinein in's volle Menschenleben!
—wo ihr's packt, da ist's interessant.

GOETHE

## Author's Preface

No MATTER HOW MUCH an individual case of suicide may capture our interest, suicide as a general social phenomenon demands quite special attention. Today, suicidal tendencies are appearing with alarming intensity in every civilized country. Here in Austria, 2,600 suicides are committed each year. In Germany the number is about 9,000, in France nearly 7,000. The annual total for all European countries that publish official reports is at least 22,000.

If what many believe is true—that the statistical data represent no more than half the number of suicides attempted and completed —then some 50,000 people in the civilized nations of Europe now take their lives each year. Imagine what the numbers will be in a decade or a half-century! In Vienna alone there are 200 suicides per year. This is about one for every 1,500 adult inhabitants, which amounts to about one suicide for every 500 men.

The question of the meaning of suicide has been examined from many standpoints. Philosophers have explored its ethical grounds and physicians its pathological causes, while the statisticians have compiled a wealth of sociological materials. No one, however, has yet undertaken a definitive explanation of suicide from the sociological point of view. It is precisely this kind of explanation that most concerns us here, for the question of the causes of suicide involves the very happiness or unhappiness of mankind.

The purpose of this work is to show how suicide as a general or "mass" phenomenon has developed out of and as part of modern culture. We shall discover that suicide as a mass phenomenon appears periodically. It shall therefore be our special purpose to understand and evaluate the nature of this periodic appearance. Important also is the relationship between the modern suicidal tendency and widespread nervous afflictions and mental illness. Consequently, it shall be the task of our psychological analysis to identify in both these trends the sick, pathological condition of the present day, and to conceive it as a unity.

I am quite convinced that I have rightly explained the essential nature of the sickness of our century, and identified its true cultural significance. Still, not every question has been fully answered. Indeed, this work calls for further individual efforts, and it is my fervent wish that many additional monographs on the specific causes of suicide may be published. Detailed studies should be made, for example, of suicide in different cities, in various occupations and social classes, and among different races, etc. Historians, too, should give equal attention to the subject, to insure that in every respect it is accurately researched and described.

Those familiar with the literature may perhaps miss in this work a few of the general doctrines occasionally laid down by many authors in their investigations into the nature of suicide. I, too, should have liked very much to say something about sociology, its methods, and especially its relationship to statistics. This would have been all the more advisable since sociology is still so little known as a science, at least among us. Yet I did not want to further lengthen a study that is already long enough in itself. I have attempted, therefore, to present a sociological monograph that follows the example of natural science. My assumption has been that a specialized study is more scientifically fruitful than either general studies or the premature setting forth of logical systems. The general principle can well be learned and taught from the special case.

One further observation must be made.

This labor has led me—and it could not have been done otherwise—to touch upon many, if not all, the issues that today command popular attention. Let me therefore state explicitly that I view the pertinent subjects from a purely scientific point of view, or at least desire to view them only from this standpoint. I hope that my views will be criticized in the same spirit.

To psychologists and sociologists, social phenomena are simply facts, just as stellar phenomena are simply facts to the astronomer. It is irrelevant to both how the practical politician may interpret and make use of the former, or the poet the latter. If I have examined the religious state of modern civilized nations with scientific detachment and with the freedom that science requires, if I have undertaken sociological inquiries into the character of Christianity and its sects and treated as mere fact much that is of heartfelt concern to many, it is no lack of piety that guided my step, but a striving for truth regardless of the consequences. As willingly as I accept correction where I have erred, so I have also guarded firmly against the indifference and intolerance so commonly practiced in sociological discussions.

Finally, I sincerely thank all those who have given me their most friendly support both in word and deed in the preparation of this work.

THOMAS G. MASARYK

Vienna, January 1881

# 1

# DEFINITIONS

1. DEATH IS USUALLY THOUGHT OF in stark contrast to life. We seldom consider that it is really the natural end result of a continuous process that takes place in the organism from its first cry of birth—and even before that—until its last gasp and beyond. Life and death coexist in every living creature. The whole body and its various parts wear out, and are then renewed, rejuvenated again. Continuous assimilation and organization occur, an incessant struggle for life with death; every step forward is also a step backward. Between the two poles of becoming and passing away surges the movement of life, roaring and foaming in the ocean of life. We may observe how the waves gradually subside and smooth over, yet still we think only of the stark contrast between life and death. In this contrast death appears so terrible that only a few accept its inevitable decree with equanimity; only a few can calmly look death in the face, for it bewilders humanity just as the sun blinds the eye—and yet so many seek it of their own free will!

Just as a constant struggle of life with death takes place in the individual, so life also wrestles with death in all mankind. At every moment men are being born, at every moment they die, as if one were a condition of the other.

2. *The kinds of death are manifold.* If the human body has been deprived of none of the conditions necessary (so far as we know) to its life process, then its death occurs as a necessary end result, and we refer to this as *natural* death. Accordingly, death by war, duel, manslaughter and murder, abortion in a certain stage of the embryo, accidents, execution and, finally, suicide is to be de-

fined as a violent, *unnatural* kind of death, as an exception to the rule.

3. The *concept of suicide* can be interpreted in several ways. In the *broad sense* of the word, it is understood to mean those anomalous kinds of death brought about by an unintentional interference of the subject with his life process, whether by positive, active self-participation or a negative, passive attitude toward the dangers of life. In this sense, for example, the suicide is one who meets a premature death through an immoral or imprudent life, for it would be normal for every man to reach old age (according to Flourens, the normal man ought to live to be 100), and then depart from this world only through the infirmities of his age and life. In the *narrow and strict sense*, on the other hand, the suicide is only he who intentionally and knowingly ends his life, who longs for death as such and is certain that his death will be brought about by his own action or failure to act. The swiftness of death is not the characteristic mark of the act, because one can also seek to die slowly and gradually. Nor is self-participation essential. The negative, passive attitude toward the dangers of life can similarly occur with suicidal purpose. As with every act of free will, it depends on the intention.[1]

Excluded from these two groups, although logically belonging to the first, is self-sacrifice. While the former are morally disapproved, the latter is considered to be the highest human virtue, although in this respect, also, vital energy is sacrificed more often than necessary.

Our distinction corresponds to the legal separation of manslaughter and murder. Henceforth, therefore, we shall understand *self-inflicted death* to mean suicide in the broader sense, while *suicide* shall refer to the deed in the stricter, narrower sense.[2] In this

[1]    It is clear, with respect to this difference, that the duel is not to be treated as suicide in the narrow sense, though some have treated it as such, but as suicide in the broad sense. The duelist does not wish to die; he would much rather see his opponent dead; he endangers his life and his opponent's life and can expect to die or commit manslaughter usually with a 50 percent probability.

[2]    Oettingen speaks of a chronic and an acute suicide; these do not stand, by themselves, as the true definitions of suicide.

way no new terms are created, and, since the analogous separation of manslaughter and murder has already gained acceptance, we avoid infringing the law of logic which looks with disfavor upon the introduction of new definitions.

4. Both self-inflicted death and suicide occur more often in modern society than is generally believed. Accurate observation of men in their daily activities quickly reveals that ignorance and baseness, unawareness of and nonadherence to the practical sciences (hygiene, ethics, etc.) cause very many self-inflicted deaths and as much unrevealed manslaughter, which is not condemned by any court only because it is too common. Statistics can easily demonstrate that the average duration of life is at least a third shorter than it should be.[3] The clever hygienist was almost right, who said that men die from various diseases and . . . stupidity. Men interfere more and more arbitrarily and despotically in their own lives and the lives of others, thereby diminishing their vitality and furthering the kingdom of death. When shall we learn to conserve our vitality?

What is true of self-inflicted death generally also applies to suicide, which could be conceived as a special case of self-inflicted death. The matter of free will and free choice, however, imparts the greatest interest to this particular form of death, which we now therefore turn to for a detailed examination.

[3]    Kraus, *Hygiene*, 1878, p. 243.

# 2

# THE  CAUSES  OF
# THE  SUICIDAL  TENDENCY

1. In general, the social mass phenomenon of suicide is conditioned, just as is any social act that rests upon free choice, by all the varied causes capable of creating such phenomena; thus, on one side, by natural causes, on the other side, by human ones. And one can organize these causes as follows:

  I. Effects of nature:
     A. terrestrial
     B. cosmic
 II. Effects of the physical and cultural organization of man:
     A. physical conditions of bodily organization
     B. general social conditions
     C. political conditions
     D. economic conditions
     E. conditions of spiritual culture: intellectual, moral and religious cultivation: outlook on life in general.

2. This classification, as every classification, has its value only for a distinct purpose. The problem is to present as comprehensively as is possible the great number of causes that condition suicide. This is not a simple task, however, since social conditions are highly complex; the following schema should achieve our purpose, if only approximately. A related problem arises: the causes should be ordered according to their effect. Therefore, we begin with what is secondary and advance by degrees to what is primary, seeking first to isolate and identify the minor causes in order to compre-

hend the true efficacy of the major ones. Only in this manner can we clearly discern the nature of suicide and evaluate its great significance for contemporary social life.

## Section 1. The Effects of Nature

1. That heaven and earth affect mankind and influence human decisions has long been recognized and, today, is almost generally accepted; but it is very difficult to measure the influence of nature and to determine accurately its effect. Without engaging in a methodological discussion, we wish at least to present several general statements in order to show how we can understand the effects of nature on voluntary death.

Nature can be analyzed into these different factors:

  I. Earth:
   A. climate (latitude, temperature, dampness and dryness of the air, etc.)
   B. land (form of surface, terrain, etc.)
  II. Cosmic influences (sun, moon, etc.)

The analysis of these different factors should show whether they have a constant, periodical, intermittent, or ephemeral effect, should show the difference between the direct and indirect effects, and—what is most important—should avoid in the actual explanation all mystic notions, generalities, and mere ingenious combinations. The effects of natural forces on body or mind must always be truly perceived and presented. They are as follows: (a) physical, (b) physiological (morphological), pathological, (c) psychological.

Whatever one considers to be the relation between body and soul, the separate effects of natural forces on the human spirit are given facts and must be taken as such. The old question of the interaction of body and soul must receive a precise formulation through research into the effect of nature on humanity; determinism in the physical and social realms must be completely understood. But it is obvious that the various social phenomena cannot be explained only by the effects of nature; on the contrary, it is most important that we achieve an explanation of the remaining conditions in which man finds himself. This is evident from the psychological nature of the phenomenon itself, and only as a last resort does one turn to the effects of nature: sociology cannot be constructed out of natural history or geography. In terms of this analysis, we therefore ask ourselves how and to what degree the tendency to suicide is produced by the influence of nature.

2. *Climate.* The geographical distribution of suicide may be easily presented, and even represented graphically, if one simply collects the statistical data. In general, it is world-wide, but it appears most frequently in Europe, with the highest rate in the northwest; toward the south (east and west), it diminishes. In individual European countries, the north also exceeds the south, as, for example, in Austria, Italy, France. But this is not a general rule: in England and other places the situation is quite different. However, it is evident that we will attain no insight at all into the causes of suicide from the geographical locations alone, and that we must, therefore, examine the remaining factors of climate.

3. *Seasonal forces.* All estimates generally agree that most suicides occur in the early summer. The maximum occurs in the months of May, June, and July, the minimum in November, December, and January; spring exhibits a greater number than autumn.

No decisive regularity appears. For example, the maxima for our military forces from 1872–75 occurred in November, August, June, and May. In Vienna, the highest proportion of cases occur in May, the fewest in February. Falret even presents different maximal months for each sex. April for men, August for women; but newer and more reliable data show that in this respect both sexes are approximately equal.

Now, what is the cause to which we have to ascribe this regularity in the appearance of suicide? Naturally, it cannot be the season itself, or one would also have to admit the existence in social life of a predestined date or time, such as is used on the stage.

One may be initially inclined to recognize temperature—that is, heat—as an effective cause, and indeed it is so: what must be more accurately determined is how and to what degree warmth affects an increase in suicide. That warmth alone does not condition suicide follows from the fact that suicides are committed in all seasons. Therefore, the absolute degree of summer heat is not the cause. We also know that in southern European countries, where it is warm for longer periods, suicide appears less often than in the northern, colder regions. Prolonged periods of warmth relax the organism; in milder (and more fertile) countries, living is less difficult because food, clothing, and shelter are more easily obtained; the whole way of life is more pleasant, more comfortable, and easier—all factors working decisively to diminish suicide. It could be asserted that men in our regions are more robust in summer than in winter, a circumstance which must be understood as more favorable to life than unfavorable. Therefore, it is not the absolute degree of warmth, but the relative: if the thermometer rises, Boudin believes, suicides also increase, and Fodéré and Duglas actually consider it dangerous when the thermometer goes above 22° Réaumer.* The statisticians Wagner and Morselli also find that it is the unusual warmth which must be recognized as a cause; thus the suicide index rises in spring and summer, decreases in fall, and continues to decrease in winter. The unusual heat specifically affects the nervous system, stimulating and exciting it; bodily weight, correspondingly, decreases in spring and summer—increases in winter—secretion becomes pronounced in spring and reaches its maximum in summer. The primary causes of suicide must then be more effective in this state of great stimulation than when this stimulation is not present, other things being equal.

The validity of this explanation is undoubtedly demonstrated by the following facts:

The effects of extremes, excesses, and irregularities of temperature obviously are completely unfavorable to human life. For example, in 1803, compared with other years, there were many suicides in Vienna as a result of the unusually great heat; in that year the inhabitants said that they were overcome by such an inclination to suicide that to commit it would be as involuntary as is sneezing. Similarly, the French troops under Napoleon in Egypt had numerous suicides because of the unbearable, unusual heat, and in

* [The freezing point of water is 0°; the boiling point, 80°R.—Trans.]

Russia because of the unusual cold. It has also been observed that the sirocco effects an increase in suicide. Thus, suicide is similar to natural death: a higher than normal temperature in summer increases mortality; a lower than normal temperature decreases it.

This deleterious effect of an unusual rise in temperature is best seen in the fact that suicide, as a result of mental illness, is committed more frequently in spring and summer than in other periods of the year. Mental illness generally is more likely to occur in the warm than in the cold seasons of the year. Physical suffering drives more people to suicide in summer than in winter, which is further evidence of a dangerous excitement of the nerves by warm temperatures. The practical experiments in acclimatization show the same facts: the unusual heat of the tropics stimulates terrible agitation and leads frequently to mental illness according to Boudin,[4] Negroes in America commit proportionately twice as many suicides as whites, as a result of the unusual climate. Boudin also states that in the expedition of General Bugeaud, conducted in temperatures of 72° C., eleven suicides and 200 brain congestions occurred in a few hours among only a few thousand troops.[5] Tropical regions are said to harbor a disease—calenture—associated with an inordinate desire to throw one's self into the sea.[6]

Finally, it should be noted that most crimes against the person are committed in summer and, according to Boudin, most duels also take place then; lastly, it should not be forgotten that in summer most crimes of fornication appear and that the months of greatest conception obviously fall in this season. (As a rule, only adults commit suicide.)

The above facts completely verify our explanation: the unusual summer heat produces despondency or, under certain circumstances, behavioral outbursts. The effect of the seasons on suicide is all the more certain because, apart from this, the act is committed by physically and psychically more or less affected indi-

---

4     *Ann. de hyg.*, 1849, p. 53.
5     Boudin, *Traite de Geogr. et de Statist. méd et des maladies endem.*, p. 397.
6     Brierre de Boismont considers a similar tendency among sailors during winter. *Du Suicide*, p. 20.

viduals who are influenced more frequently and decisively by the forces of nature than are the healthy.[7]

Statistics must answer another problem for our purposes: it must identify accurately the month in which the most suicides are committed. Some have said July, but as demonstrated by Guerry, Kolb, et al., it may, in general, be June. I say "in general," because an absolute constancy is impossible for a cause that is only indirect, disposing, and secondary. But the following facts point to June. In our regions, January is the coldest month, July the hottest; in May the warmth increases most rapidly, reaching a maximum in the middle of July.[8] Now, the standard for our explanation is not the absolute, but the relative maximum heat; May should be, accordingly, the real month for suicide, but this is not quite so, because the effect of the unusual warmth manifests itself only after a period of days. In like manner, the severest cold occurs in January but the greatest mortality occurs in February; the greatest warmth in July and the least mortality in August. The influences of nature on the organism, both pernicious and curative, need to work for some time before they are manifested in greater suicide and as greater or lesser mortality. Because of this, most suicides should therefore appear in June.[9]

4. *Damp weather.* Several researchers believe damp weather

[7]    Oettingen correctly states therefore that the seasons exercise a greater influence on the appearance of the suicide tendency if physical suffering and illness grow out of them than if assignable mental and moral motives prevail.

[8]    July has the character of being the hottest month all over the earth. Kloeden, *Handb. d. phys. Geogr* (3rd edition), p. 879.

[9]    Kolb—as do Boudin and others—asserts that the length of the day "marks" the greater appearance of suicide, and he reproaches Wagner for not reducing the months to an equal number of days. If one makes such a reduction, the maximum number of suicides does in fact occur in June, but even with this the length of the day is still the proper ground; there must be a cause which operates on longer days, since length of day, of itself, cannot be a cause. Wagner could therefore be correct as well as Kolb V. Kolb, *Handb. d. vergl. Stat.*, 1875, p. 15. Cf. Schimmer, *Biotik d. k. k. osterr. Armer*, p. 54: the length of the day exerts a substantial influence on the number of suicides in the military. (Because the fewest suicides are committed at night, more cases could occur, other things being

favors the tendency to suicide in a very special way. For this reason, Montesquieu has disparaged the English as the truly suicidal people, and November is commonly considered even now as the suicide month.[10] However, one must go beyond this. Holland is much damper than England—there are 150 rainy days per year and the weather changes continually, two to three times a day—but, it shows comparatively less suicide than the less damp countries. Constant dampness here has as little influence as constant warmth, and therefore one must say: unusually damp weather effects an increase in suicide; an unusually gloomy sky darkens the spirit and very damp weather attacks the nerves. Cabanis and Esquirol also believed that they had found the most cases in a wet autumn which followed upon a dry summer; and that the appearance of gloomy weather often signaled more suicides than a period of bright, beautiful days.[11] But, on the whole, the effect of dampness is not so unfavorable as is usually assumed.[12]

5. *Wind.* The wind and suicide are already related in the popular belief that strong winds rise whenever someone hangs himself. In any case, certain winds are pernicious, as for instance, the sirocco; Cheyne claims the fall and west winds are responsible for suicides in England, and Osiander makes the same assertion for northern Germany. But how hot, drying winds, or cold and damp winds exert their unfavorable effects is evident to all. Think, for example, how the drying winds of America cause a degeneration in the glandular system, which causes the striking difference between the Yankee and his Uncle Bull and also in part his irritability.

6. The choice of day of the week is also obviously not accidental; but no generally valid data about this exists yet. Morselli

---

equal, during a longer day than during a shorter day. But this is quite consistent with our explanation.)

10    In Switzerland and in England, November is called "the month of hangings."

11    A modern novelist attributes the numerous suicides committed in Paris to the thick haze and smoke which lies over the city, seldom permitting Parisians a clear view of the sky.

12    Cf. Kraus, *Hygiene*, p. 480.

attributes the maximum to Wednesday, Thursday, and Monday, probably keeping in mind Oettingen's interpretation: the fewest suicides appear on Saturday because on this day the workers are paid, that many are committed on Monday and Tuesday as the result of the painful consequences of days of celebration spent in reveling; that one is most needy on Thursday, while Friday brings new hope for the approaching pay day. This explanation clearly assumes that the working class, paid weekly, supplies the greatest number of suicides, which is not correct, but this interpretation nevertheless is a good one and can be confirmed in many cases.

Women, it is said, choose Sunday with relative frequency, no doubt for religious reasons; Saturday, as housecleaning day, allows them no time for dissatisfaction with life; Monday is also supposed to be very unpleasant for women.

7. With respect to time of day, most suicides are generally committed during the day, the fewest at night. Night has something soothing, life-giving, and restorative about it; also, most men are born at night, when the fewest deaths occur. The bright day excites and stimulates, while the darkness of night leads to understanding, peace of mind, and sleep. One may meditate at night upon the act he will perform, but it will only be executed during the day, when we customarily carry on all our affairs. Tissot rightly observes that premeditated suicides occur early in the morning, the unpremeditated during the course of the day; Morselli states that the morning hours from 6 to 12 are the maximal hours.

More accurate estimates have no great worth. The maximum is estimated to fall from 10 to 12 in the morning, and from 4 to 6 and 6 to 8 in the afternoon and evening, among others. The minimum is said to occur from 12 to 2 at night. No suicides are believed to appear during the noon hour.[13]

---

[13]    One might ask, among other things, whether the choice of time of day is the same for all seasons. Of interest would be an investigation whether the relative daily temperature is related to the number of suicides. The following pattern of daily temperature changes is important: the surface of the earth becomes warmer from sunrise until noon through the sun's radiation, and the temperature of the air increases; the maximum temperature is reached when the sun's radiation and the earth's surface

8. We pass over the remaining climatic factors because their effect on the appearance of the tendency to suicide is minute. Many and quite artful deductions might be contrived in detail, but in doing this our work would become highly confusing. The sociologist proceeds as does the mathematician: minimum quantities are omitted without loss in calculation.

9. *The effect of the land.* The constant effect of the land in shaping all conditions of human life is certainly very great, and the economic and political life of peoples are especially influenced by this natural factor. However, because we have to investigate these conditions in more detail, we abstain here from deduction, for only in this way can our mind remain open, there being almost no materials for induction. Anyone may compare a geological map with estimates of the extent of suicide. Petit, for example, states, with respect to France, that every department which is flat shows the most suicides, but mountainous and primitive regions show the fewest cases.

10. Of all the factors involving the influence of land, place of residence has long been of special interest, particularly the relationship between the city and the provinces.

Suicide is relatively higher in all cities than in the provinces; today it is everywhere, reaching the remotest areas, but the cities, especially the metropolis and cosmopolitan cities are very strongly represented. For example:

| City | Year | Per 100 Suicides in the Nation: |
|------|------|---------------------------------|
| Vienna | 1876 | 320 |
| Berlin | 1872–74 | 143 |
| Copenhagen | 1876 | 112 |

The morbid tendency to suicide usually spreads like a contagious disease from the city into the provinces, in that it more strongly influences the surrounding countryside than the more dis-

---

radiation are equal. This occurs approximately at 2:00 P.M. in summer and about 1:00 P.M. in winter. Of course, this maximum can be reached before noon in some situations, as is the case, for example, on many sea coasts in the torrid zone.

tant areas; for example, approximately 1.86 cases occur per 10,000 inhabitants in lower Austria, including Vienna; in lower Austria alone, 1.51, but throughout the entire nation, at most, 1.0; Vienna itself, 2.63 cases. It should not be thought that all countries with a high urban population also show the most suicides. England, which has the most cities and highest urban population, shows significantly fewer suicides than Germany, France, and Austria. It is not the cities that spread the tendency to suicide throughout a country; rather, other more general causes must bear the guilt. Cases are also generally more frequent in the country when the cities represent a large contingent of the population. The city conditions a greater disposition to suicide than the provinces; it effects an increase in suicide, but does not generate it.

Brierre notes the fact that of suicides occuring in Paris, the majority are residents who have migrated to the city and not native-born Parisians. In like manner, the majority of crimes committed in the city are traced back to the same migrants coming from the provinces to the city, therefore that the city cannot have a more unfavorable effect than the provinces. But that is a negative and incorrect objection: the modern city in its rapid growth owes its character, in largest part, precisely to the circumstance that the provincial populace and the migrants are moving to the city, giving the city a fluctuating population, now smaller, now larger. Conditions in these newly settled areas, which produce deleterious effects on their inhabitants, had appeared, and these can appear only in the city, however they operate.

The growth of the urban population in relation to the increase of rural population is discussed in Chapter 2, Section 2, Part 2, No. 1.

Cities, in contrast to the provinces, show great variation. To call special attention only to what is most important, the seasons exercise a lesser and different effect on the urban population than on the rural; lesser because the city offers greater protection, different because the economic conditions are different than in the provinces. For example, the periodic summer travels of the wealthier classes may exercise a regular, cyclic, deleterious effect on the poorer population. Further, there are differences with regard to sex (chap. 2, sec. 2, pt. 1, no. 4), and similarly with age (chap. 2, sec. 2, pt. 1, no. 4).

Finally, there is the interesting observation that the increase of the suicide tendency in the cities is not, generally, so rapid as in the provinces. (chap. 4, no. 5).

11. The most effective and most visible influence of the land might be, in the final analysis, its influence on the necessities of life, and several luxuries should be of particular interest among these. The unfavorable effect of alcoholic drinks we will treat later (see Drunkenness); concerning the influence of coffee, tea, and tobacco, there is still no agreement. I am inclined to attribute to all these luxuries, if they are immoderately used, an unfavorable influence due to their nerve-exciting power; also, I do not believe that these stimulants are necessities as a result of the spiritual demands of the present. Moreover, this and similar investigations are, for our purpose, more interesting than necessary, and I mention them only to satisfy a more logical than substantive requirement.

12. Concerning the *cosmic influences* on the development of the tendency to suicide, there is little to be said. In and of themselves, they may be analyzed only with difficulty, because they are present with and given in the terrestrial factors; also, their efficacy is, in fact, not so great as many poetic heads like to imagine. On the whole, we will do best if we keep our eyes fastened on primary causes and overlook the secondary and less relevant causes, always being mindful that our earth is only an insignificantly small part of a greater galaxy, and that Paris, as someone has said, is not the capital of the universe.

13. Relative to what we have said about the seasons, for our purpose the significance of the sun as a source of warmth is clear; naturally, the light of the sun cannot be separated from warmth. It is well understood, for example, that the loss of the usual light of day is disquieting and can be a disposing cause of suicide. There are tales of how whalers of the North become very sad when the sun has disappeared and then frequently take their lives.

We have already considered damp weather.

14. The effect of the moon is certainly relevant, but, at this time, not measurable. We know that the moon excites certain ner-

vous and psychotic persons, that in the tropics illnesses are conditioned more by the phases of the moon than among us, and, finally,
that the amount of rainfall is related to the wax and wane of the
moon (cf. Damp Weather).[14]

15. The facts brought out in the previous 11 sections concerning the influence of the forces of nature on the genesis of the suicidal tendency clearly show us that *this tendency cannot be derived
from the influences of nature on mankind. The influences of nature
are real and observable, but their effect is merely weak, indirect,
and disposing; usually they occur in an indirect pathological way,
through physiological and morphological changes of the organism
itself.*

For this reason statistics is not able—as some have thought—
to uncover any "terrible constancy" and regularity in the appearance of suicide in different seasons of the year, etc. It is able to
establish only empirical laws, not natural laws that could act with
immutable necessity.

It is therefore possible that among the urban population, in
spite of their greater protection from natural influences, suicide is
committed more frequently than in the provinces, where men are
less protected from the influence of nature.

And even further: among uncivilized peoples, among the primitives, suicide does not appear at all, yet it is these very people who
have been most exposed to the influences of nature. On the contrary, we find it associated with civilization and only with civiliza-

---

[14]    In Prussia one finds:

| Phase | Suicides | | | |
| | *Male* | *Female* | *Total* | *Per 1000* |
| New Moon | 614 | 151 | 765 | 246.8 |
| First Quarter | 644 | 149 | 793 | 255.8 |
| Full Moon | 604 | 134 | 738 | 238.6 |
| Last Quarter | 640 | 162 | 802 | 258.8 |

According to Boudin, more rain falls during the waxing of the moon;
there are more clear days during the last quarter and more rainy and
gloomy weather during the second eighth. It may be that the amount of
light is unfavorable, insofar as it disturbs sleep and excites morbid
fantasies.

tion, particularly the Europeans. But civilization consists for the most part in the subjugation and utilization of natural forces. Man can certainly be overwhelmed by nature, but he is not necessarily governed by it; everything happens to him according to the laws of nature, but no human action occurs without recognition of these laws. Man cannot escape the totality of natural law, because he cannot transcend the totality; but he can free himself from individual laws; he can help himself by using one against the other; he can use this against that as the means to his purpose. Through recognition of laws we have been promoted to the position of becoming lords of nature; we are able to protect ourselves from its influence when it is harmful, and to arrest its influences or guide them in other paths. The primitive trembles before lightning and prays to it out of his fear, as a powerful divinity or as a divine messenger: science takes possession of the raw power of nature and then utilizes it as the effective means for commerce. Nature, Mill says, ruthlessly affects man; it does not spare him; it makes no exceptions. All praise of civilization, of art, or of skill, is just so much a reproach to nature, a confession of imperfection whose perpetual improvement and melioration are the problem and the profit of man. But what is valid for civilization in general is also valid in particular, and so one can derive from this general principle the law that the tendency to suicide of civilized peoples is also not conditioned by the influences of nature to any great or pronounced degree. Our investigation shows the correctness of this derived law, however, by the most striking facts.

Finally, it must still be observed that the tendency to suicide in various countries and peoples has increased through the course of time and continually increases. That does not lessen the evidence that this social mass phenomenon is produced not by the constantly and uniformly effective powers of nature, but by completely different causes. But, since man outside of nature can be effected only by intrinsically human conditions, the real causes of the suicidal tendency must be sought in these conditions, since we have recognized the limited effectiveness of the great factor of nature.[15]

15    I stress all these things because a great confusion of ideas exists in this area of thought. Most conceptions are hazy as to how nature gen-

## Section 2. The Effects of the Physical and Spiritual Organization of Man

PART 1. PHYSICAL CONDITIONS OF BODILY ORGANIZATION. 1. Our research concerning the effects of bodily organization on the origin of the suicide tendency is a natural outgrowth of our studies on the influences of nature, for, strictly speaking, man's body does indeed belong to the external world, and the question concerning the influence of nature on man is only another form of the old question concerning the reciprocal interaction of body and soul. But it is not our task to solve this problem here; on the contrary, we gladly avoid it and confine ourselves simply to the given distinction between the physical and psychical, without concerning ourselves with such questions as to the possible limits of each. However, we will deal in this part with bodily condition (state of health), sex, and age.

2. *Bodily constitution and state of health.* To be able to live successfully under the given conditions of life, a significant physical strength and agility, which obviously only exists in a normal and healthy man, is necessary for individuals and, consequently, for society. The suicide tendency will not originate generally with a normal and healthy man.

The results of the newer anthropometric research are, at present, too meager and too faulty to compare them usefully with the data of suicide statistics. We know, for example, such facts as that the weight of a man exceeds that of a woman, and that the maximum weight of a man is reached at about age forty, for a woman at about age fifty. Concerning the rate of growth, we know that in very hot and cold climates growth ends sooner than in temperate climates, that the city dweller is generally bigger than the rural dweller, that prisoners are retarded in development behind others,

_____

erally affects man. Many theorists, following a false scientific method, derive all social phenomena from the laws of nature and are able to integrate determinism and choice in the most trivial events. Moreover, nowhere today are such foggy notions so used as in the innumerable researches on suicide.

and that children who work in factories are particularly stunted. With respect to muscular strength in the various nations, plus other items of interest, we know practically nothing; therefore we must content ourselves with what little information we possess in order to deduce, in given cases, the physiology which has lead to this morbid tendency.

*Physical illnesses* frequently dispose to and determine suicide. Pain in all circumstances is an evil from which everyone endeavors to be freed. One is most likely to choose death when severe and incurable illnesses rob one of the lust for life, banishing serenity of the spirit and erasing vitality. Especially unfavorable are those illnesses (brain, nerve, liver, and abdominal) which darken the disposition and lead to a more or less pronounced psychosis.

Whether epidemics produce unfavorable effects, cannot be determined with certainty. If we look at cholera, we must conclude that it has had an unfavorable influence on present generations— directly through great fears, terrors, and mourning which indirectly affect the coming generation, to the extent that it impairs their education and infects their physical health already in germ— through conception.

The relation of *morbidity* to the tendency to suicide is important. Morbidity, with respect to climate, has previously been investigated in detail only with reference to a few especially acute ills (e.g., yellow fever); general data are lacking. With respect to the seasons, autumn, followed by summer, appears to be more favorable than winter and spring; morbidity is greater in cities than in the country. Women are overcome by illness more frequently than men, but their illnesses are less destructive than those of men. With respect to age, morbidity is greatest from 0–4 years, least from 5–15 years; from then on it increases with advancing age, but the high age brackets—not too high!—withstand illness better than the younger. Occupation must also be considered; but apart from expressly dangerous occupations, the remaining conditions (way of life, morality, etc.) have more of an effect than the occupation itself; industrial workers show a greater morbidity than country dwellers. The needy and impoverished become ill more easily than the rich and well-to-do. The situation naturally is different in this respect among various nations, but we do not know exactly how. For example, the tolerance and endurance of physical and spiritual sorrows certainly differ for various peoples as with different individuals. It was observed in the Crimean War that, among an equal number of troops, the French suffered many more wounded than did the English; and this is in accord with the greater general tendency to suicide among the French. The suicide data of different nations also indicates to what degree bodily illnesses appear as causes of suicide; unfortunately, the estimates are still unreliable. Because physical suffering often is a cause of suicide, those individuals and peoples who possess less vitality and endurance and who fall ill more frequently and more easily, other things being equal, must be more susceptible to boredom with life than those who possess greater physical stamina and endurance.

Finally, it will be worth noting whether morbidity is to be understood as increasing or decreasing; both positions have advocates, but there is no precise evidence for either argument. Some authors declare that mortality decreases with the progress of civilization; accordingly, the causes of death, and above all severe and fatal illnesses, must now possess less power. On the other hand, some point to "medical care" and complain that the progress of medicine is preserving the lives of the diseased and the weak; humanity degenerates, becomes weaker, bodily illnesses have increased—above all illnesses of the nervous system and the digestive system, anemia, hemorrhaging, among other things. It is difficult to decide who is right; certainly the suicide tendency is increasing and mental illnesses are also becoming more frequent; perhaps, in looking back on the data in question, an answer can be sought along these lines: with progressive civilization the organism itself becomes so much more refined that a disorder is able to enter it more easily and more frequently than in the more barbarous nations.[16]

[16] Many pathologists believe that illnesses have changed their character in the course of time and that the patients of today carry away no more efficacious treatment than earlier. Dr. Elam (*Lancet* 1869, nos. 17, 23, 24) indicates that especially in England recovery from illness does not increase in the same proportion as does skill in treatment, and that

As morbidity stands in direct relation to mortality, so *mortality* has an even closer relationship to the suicide tendency.

Climate naturally exerts a great influence on mortality; the most deaths occur in the cold period of the year and during the day; the city shows a greater death rate than the provinces, the male sex a greater rate than the female. The years of childhood are most dangerous and, obviously, old age; for men the first twenty years are also destructive (because of the dominance of passion?). Married persons show a lower mortality than do single; likewise, mortality is proportionately high among illegitimate children and prison inmates. Certain kinds of occupations are naturally more dangerous than others, and poverty and need also have a bad effect; to be sure, the industrious dependable, and regular workers live longer than the rich and prominent, namely the nobility. On the whole, as Süssmilch has already discovered, civilization influences vital energies more than do natural effects, and mortality therefore also decreases as civilization progresses. The same causes which lead to death at one point can lead to suicide in another, causing death indirectly, as it were; but while mortality by and large is decreasing, the suicide tendency is progressively increasing. But this shows that men must have a special reason for their dissatisfaction with life.

3. *Sex*. Men commit proportionately more suicides overall than women. The relationship is different in various countries and never quite constant; on the whole, one may say that approximately three times as many men as women take their lives.

The seasons do not affect both sexes equally; females are more easily overcome by heat than males and, therefore, it may be possi-

---

the mode of treatment in 1869 was of little more profit than that of thirty years past. He supports this with the following data:

>1838–66 there were 2242 deaths for 100 cures
>1860–66 there were 2261 deaths for 100 cures
>1863–66 there were 2348 deaths for 100 cures

Not medicine, but the great social malady is to blame for this phenomenon.

ble that the maximum for women occurs in May; with respect to the choice of days of the week, see Chapter 2, Section 1, No. 6.

The relationship between suicides in the city and the provinces is interesting. In the first place, Cazauvieilh and more recently Morselli have asserted that in proportion to the number of males, more cases appear in the provinces than in the city. There may be a greater similarity between males and females in the provinces, where women develop more nerve and muscular strength than in the city; thus, in the provinces the difference is also smaller, as it is everywhere in this special case. On the other hand, it can be argued that the urban female is even more similar to the male than in the provinces and that the relationship in both places will be similar; or, it can also happen that urban females are more strongly represented than rural women, as was the case, for example, in Vienna (1868–78). The question has not yet been accurately answered.

Concerning the relationship of the urban to the rural female, it generally follows from the general preponderance of the city over the provinces, and that urban females also show proportionately more suicides than rural females.

Concerning the effect of marriage and family life on both sexes, see Chapter 2, Section 2, Part 2, No. 2; unfavorable economic conditions have a worse effect on men than on women.

Nationalities also condition differences; however, these have not yet been recognized. In particular, more young women among the Austrian Slavs kill themselves than among Germans. According to Casper, during his time suicide appeared most frequently among French women because the wife in France plays a more prominent public role than in other nations.

Motivation for suicide is different for men and for women, in accordance with their character. Her more delicate character shields the weaker sex from ennui more than the coarser and stronger man. Pangs of conscience, shame, and fear of disgrace (because of illegitimate pregnancy) affects the feminine disposition more strongly than the masculine. Woman is more passionate and unrequited love and jealousy disturb her more than man, whereas men are destroyed more by ambition than by love. Females commit suicide more frequently than males as a result of mental illness. Women in most countries remain at a distance from the agitating activities of politics; they aim less at acquisition of property and therefore are less troubled by ruinous financial conditions, poverty, and need than men. As has been said: "Man must go out into hostile life—must work and strive, sow and create, deceive and acquire, must gamble and dare, to seize his fate." The female is more moral and religious, and therefore, despite her weakness, she more easily finds a support in life than the stronger man.

Finally, there remains the question as to whether the tendency to suicide is increasing equally among both sexes. I am of the opinion that in the contemporary striving for justified or unjustified "emancipation," women are threatened relatively more than men; for the more women allow themselves to compete with men in all fields, the more frequently they encounter unusual situations and are hurt, while men are already accustomed to the harsher competition of life (chap. 4, no. 5).

4. *Age*. As men and women mature and as they begin to assume the burdens of life, the tendency to suicide rises and generally grows in direct proportional relation to age. Various maxima[17] have been reported, but the estimates are mostly useless because they are based upon insufficient induction. The critical period for both sexes certainly begins at the age of puberty; but the trials and tribulations of youth do as much damage as the years devoted to the establishment of a household, when the cares and needs of family life scarcely allow man or woman any peace. This perilous period lasts through one's continuing development, or until fifty years of age for both sexes. With the coming of age (climacterical periods for man and woman), new cares and needs are born which affect one's disposition; loneliness appears, which shows man even more the helplessness and hopelessness of his life. Both youth and the middle-aged lay plans for life and approach their goals vigorously, even if they are nebulous; they are often fated to be deluded; but the aged have fewer fantasies, suffer from no illusions, and thus are, in their natural infirmity of body and spirit, easily bored with

17     Esquirol states that it is 20 to 25 years, Tissot 20 to 30 years; the most dangerous years for women, according to various estimates, are: 24 to 35, or 15 to 25, or 21 to 30, or 40 to 60 years, etc.

life; on the other hand, they possess in just this realism an effective antidote against the pessimism of suicide.

If one wishes a more exact statistical estimate, Morselli has offered one: from 21 to 50 years of age the tendency to suicide continuously increases and reaches the maximum from 40 to 50.

Naturally, several differences of city, sex, nationality, etc., exist, but on the whole the law which gives us the influence of age alone is definitive for all Europe. According to Morselli, the following countries lose a greater number of men in the given age brackets:

| | |
|---|---|
| Hungary, Italy | from 21 to 30 |
| Denmark, France | many over 50 |
| Sweden, Bavaria, Denmark | from 30 to 40 |
| Württemberg, Belgium, Switzerland | from 40 to 50 |
| Denmark, Bavaria, Prussia | from 51 to 60 |
| France, Austria, England | from 44 to 55 |

for the female sex:

| | |
|---|---|
| Sweden, Denmark, Bavaria | from 20 to 30 |
| Prussia, Saxony, England, Austria-Hungary | from 35 to 45 |
| Remaining countries | over 41 |

This agrees in part with Wagner's estimate that among the German peoples the proportion of men and even more of women in the first half of life, up to 40 years of age, is perhaps relatively greater and, in the second half of life, relatively smaller than among the Romance peoples. For the tendency to suicide among Slavic girls, see paragraph 3.

Esquirol in his time, and after him Falret, have asserted that the characteristic of advanced *old age* is that the very old person, who approaches closer to death each day, must entertain a strong wish to stay alive and therefore will not commit suicide. Lisle has shown statistically, however, that this deduction of Esquirol is false, and Casper similarly bemoans the fact that so many very old people commit suicide. More recent statistics confirm Lisle's research: according to Legoyt, suicide increases until the period from 60 to 70 years of age; according to Oettingen, for both sexes the advanced age between 60 to 70 years contains the highest number of suicides.

Here one may also find various deviations from the general rule. According to Oesterlen, suicide in England continuously increases until 45 to 55 years, in France until 70 to 80; according to the most recent estimates, a decrease is supposed to appear among men in England, but not among women after the eightieth year.

According to Brierre, among 192 cases of suicide from 70 to 80 years of age, the following were given as motives:

|  | Men | Women |
|---|---|---|
| Psychoses, boredom with life | 34 | 14 |
| Physical suffering, weakness | 35 | 12 |
| Poverty, loss of wealth, business disturbance | 25 | 10 |
| Domestic cares, loss of dear ones | 22 | 4 |
| Drunkenness | 12 | 5 |
| Unknown causes | 10 | 9 |
|  | 138 | 54 |

Finally, we must devote special attention to the *suicide of children*. Casper and Heyfelder have held that the great increase in suicide among children is a manifestation of their time, and more recent data from all countries show the horrible fact that our delicate, "innocent" youth is constantly becoming less satisfied with life. Above all, suicide among children has increased in the cities.[18]

There are suicides who are barely five years old, who barely have the physical strength to take their lives! And the motives of youthful suicides are not childish: unsatisfied ambition, jealousy, unrequited love, fear of punishment, bad treatment, a life of misery, poverty, and need. Besides inherited psychoses, onanism is also to be adduced as a partial cause; only neglected and ill children can take their lives!

5. We summarize: the physical conditions of bodily organization have a disposing effect; however, illness can also have a determining effect. But this disposing effect does not explain the

[18]   The data for Austria can be found in: Platter, "Uber den Selbstmord in Oesterreich in den Jahren 1819–1872," *Statist. Monatschrift II*, p. 97; for Saxony: *Zeitschr. des k. sächs. statis. Bur.*, 1877, p. 32; for cities: Morselli, *Il suicido*, 1879, p. 329; cf. Durand-Fardel, "Etudes sur le suicide chez les enfants," (*Ann. med.-psych.*, 1855, Jänner).

appearance of the suicide tendency, because bodily organization, like the rest of the remaining external world, can only be comprehended as a secondary cause of physical and social phenomena.

PART 2: GENERAL SOCIETAL CONDITIONS. 1. *The census in relation to the frequency of suicide.* The more inhabitants a country has, the more suicides it can, but need not necessarily, have; this much is clear. The statistical estimates of suicide frequency in various countries are related to the absolute number of the population and serve, in general, for a more or less accurate comparison of individual regions and countries.

If more exact comparisons are desired, one must give special consideration to several conditions. Above all, one must know the *age distribution* in the various nations; one should know how many adults (approximately 15 years and over) there are because the tendency to suicide appears, as a rule, only among adults. For example, knowing the following percentage of youths from one to fifteen years, allows one to draw many conclusions: France, 44%; Germany, 52%; Prussia, 53.38%; United States, 59%. France has fewer children than Prussia; if for both countries approximately the same number of suicides are indicated per one million inhabitants, then the tendency in Prussia can nevertheless be more intensive. Further, in France (1874), 11.6 percent of its inhabitants were more than 60 years of age, while here in Western Austria there were only 6.6 percent; this clearly alters the estimates of suicide among the aged, etc.

The *statistics on the sex of adults* must also be considered. For example, after the war the difference between the sexes in Germany amounted to 755,075—in France, only 137,899—which surely throws some light on the tendency to suicide among women in the respective countries.

Concerning *population density*, one might be inclined to assume that suicide appears more frequently the more concentrated a population. It could be argued that the cities with their more concentrated population show a greater suicide frequency than the less densely populated rural areas; the parallelism between population density and suicide frequency in several countries is also apparent.

Austria, for example, has the densest population in Lower Austria, Silesia, Bohemia, and Moravia, which at the same time also have the highest suicide frequency. Saxony in Germany, apart from the free cities, has the densest population and the most suicides.

The more dense a population is, the more intimate is its social life, the greater the complexity and mutual dependence, the more manifold and richer is its private and social life and activity. Competition, the struggle for survival, is all the more severe, the means of subsistence are more sparsely distributed. In short, boredom with life can be more easily developed and be more easily diffused than in a less dense population. The situation may be analyzed in this way, but *one errs if one assumes that the parallelism between the density of a population and its tendency to suicide rests upon an absolutely valid law.* It can easily be shown that a dense population does not everywhere exhibit the greatest suicide frequency; for example, it does not in Holland, England, and the Rhine Valley. A dense population can be an indication of physical and moral strength or weakness. In one country the dense population may be reasonable, clever, powerful, industrious and orderly, while in another country unreasonableness, weakness, laziness, and disorder may keep the population dense but without endurance. A dense population under different conditions can be either happy or—bored.

A few items remain for special consideration.

No single country in Europe at the present time is *overpopulated,* according to the national economists; but the great desire to emigrate and the high suicide frequency certainly point to a relative overpopulation. The evidence of suicide indicates that the economic crises for several years past has had a very deleterious effect. As men now are—and one can only deal with that—overpopulation does in fact disturb them in individual areas; in this respect one must consider not only material need, but also intellectual and moral imperfection.

An *underpopulation* country under certain conditions can exhibit many suicides; that follows from the above.

The *speed of population growth* can favor the tendency to suicide insofar as this increase results in material and moral abuses.

In Europe the rapid growth of population is most visible in England (including Wales), Saxony, and Prussia; it is least rapid in Portugal; in the former countries, suicide is frequent, in the latter, infrequent. Inversely, the population of France is increasing very slowly, is even decreasing here and there, but the tendency to suicide progressively increases. The parallelism here is therefore again not decisive.

The growth of cities in relation to the increase in rural population must be specially noted. According to Wappaus, the relationship takes the following form:

| Nation | Increase | |
|---|---|---|
| | *City* | *Rural* |
| Denmark | 2.46 | 0.94 |
| France | 1.53 | 0.35 |
| Saxony | 1.46 | 0.81 |
| Norway | 2.00 | 1.02 |
| England, Wales | 1.87 | 1.00 |
| Holstein | 1.63 | 0.76 |
| Sweden | 1.50 | 0.81 |
| Belgium | 0.78 | 0.31 |
| Hanover | 0.39 | 0.05 |
| Holland | 0.81 | 0.74 |

That which we have seen concerning the influence of the city explains to us why the suicide frequency so apparently stands in direct relationship to the growth of the urban population in the countries cited.

The *decrease of population*, if it signifies a physical and moral degeneration, could also exhibit mass suicides as a concomitant cause and symptom of decay: Ancient Rome and other decaying nations show us this process. Concerning morbidity and mortality, see Chapter 2, Section 2, Part 1, No. 2.

For several European countries, emigration is a powerful cause of population decline and this raises the question whether emigration has a favorable or unfavorable effect for our study. Emigration is highest in England and Germany; following these are the Scandinavian countries, Italy, Switzerland, and Belgium, etc. The following reasons have been cited for emigration: need, dissatisfaction with social and political conditions, particularly with military duty. One could say that the mere possibility of emigration, hope for an improvement in material conditions, has a favorable influence, and the country is freed of its dissatisfied elements.

For example, if the suicide frequency in Germany is very high despite extensive emigration, then from this standpoint the suicide tendency would be higher in this country than in France, which exhibits almost as many suicides, but from which very few emigrate although it is just as densely populated as is Germany.

On the other hand one must also consider that only those who have the necessary means for the long journey usually emigrate and, which is especially important, that precisely the strongest and sturdiest people leave the country, while the impoverished, degenerates, weaklings, and invalids remain at home. While the possibility of emigration is therefore advantageous for those who can emigrate, it does not help those who remain, indeed helps them even less the greater is the emigration. Therefore one must probably say that emigration has an unfavorable effect in the mother country.

2. *Marriage and family life.* The previous statistical estimates for married and unmarried suicides and for the influence of married and family life on suicide in general are of little worth because the concepts have not been clearly defined. But we shall seek to discover how marriage and family life affects:

A. Parents: in first, second, third marriages; the condition of the unmarried, of divorced persons, widowed persons, those living in concubinage; the position of man and wife; how the number of children reacts on parents. B. Children: in first, second, third marriages; of widowed persons, of divorced persons, of parents living in concubinage or not living together (illegitimate children); orphans.

A. A very favorable effect on the physical and moral growth of married people is generally attributed to *married life*; compared with the unmarried, it has been noted, the married are healthier, have greater endurance, and their life expectancy is greater, but the favorable effect is more evident for husbands than for wives.[19] Accordingly, it may be expected that marriage, in general, must influence a decrease in suicide. Many statisticians verify this deduction, but there are also, on the other hand, those who seek to prove the opposite. In this respect also, the situation is different for each sex: Falret and Tissot report that most women who kill themselves are married, most men, unmarried.

Obviously, the shared life of marriage can have a wholesome influence only if the marriage results from a true affection and proves and confirms this affection, and if married life is rational and moral; this is not a result of marriage, but must rather be brought into marriage. Marriage improves one's ways, but it, in and of itself, does not make for good in all things. Marital happiness and its beneficial influences, above all, depend upon the intellectual and moral attributes of the people and is regulated by certain places, certain times, and to a great degree by the economic conditions of the country, since married life also requires bread. *In and of itself, marriage can therefore have both a favorable and unfavorable effect; it can restrict or contribute to the tendency to suicide, according to circumstances; it does not have a decisively beneficial effect.*

Considering that suicide is usually committed in maturity, that employed men kill themselves more frequently than women, that for years economic conditions have been depressed, and remembering that the sanctity of marriage is declining, one will have to admit that *today marriage has little or no beneficial influence, perhaps may even have a harmful one.*[20]

[19]    V. Bertillion, *Gas. med. de Paris*, 1861; cf. *Med.-chirug. Rundschau 1870 II*; Farr, *Influence of Marriage on Morality*, Natl. Assn. for the Promotion of Soc. Science, 1858. Contrast Spencer, *Studies in Sociology*, p. 115.

[20]    The suicide data from the different countries can be compared in the following table:

There are approximately these percentages of unmarried individuals in the following countries (from 16 years of age and above):

| France | 33.1 | Holland | 41.5 |
|---|---|---|---|
| England, Wales | 37.2 | Portugal | 43.6 |

It is not clear whether those who are married, who have more children to support, take their lives more frequently than those who have fewer responsibilities; in a few instances which I was able to investigate, the former was the case.

I have no inductive facts concerning childless spouses; I also have nothing new to say about second, third, or fourth marriages.

The *widowed state* is decidedly unfavorable to life, more unfavorable for men than for women;[21] widowhood makes the woman stronger, wiser, and more masculine.

Still more unfavorable is the situation of the *divorced*; here, also, more unfavorable for men than for women.[22]

| | | | |
|---|---|---|---|
| Italy | 37.5 | Switzerland | 44.3 |
| Denmark | 39.3 | Belgium | 44.9 |
| Germany | 39.9 | Ireland | 45.0 |
| Norway | 40.8 | Iceland | 48.7 |
| Sweden | 41.2 | | |

It appears that there are fewer unmarried individuals in the southern Romance nations than in the northern Germanic nations.

The correspondence with the suicide frequency is strikingly illustrated in the following table of [percentage of] married persons from 41 through 50 years of age:

| | | | |
|---|---|---|---|
| Saxony | 84.0 | France | 77.5 |
| Denmark | 82.9 | Italy | 76.9 |
| Prussia | 81.9 | Alsace-Lorraine | 74.9 |
| Norway | 80.8 | Bavaria | 74.5 |
| Germany | 80.3 | Baden | 73.9 |
| Hesse | 80.0 | Belgium | 73.0 |
| England, Wales | 79.2 | Ireland | 71.6 |
| Sweden | 78.5 | Switzerland | 69.6 |
| Holland | 77.9 | Portugal | 69.1 |
| Württemberg | 77.8 | Iceland | 67.5 |

(In general, marriage prevails from approximately 30 years of age on.)

21     On the average, there are twice as many widows as there are widowers in all countries (because a man marries at a later age, leads a more dangerous life, and many more widowers than widows remarry); on the whole, the surplus of widows parallels the surplus of women.

22     There were frequent suicides among the wives of priests separated

Relatively twice as many divorces occur in the city as in the provinces: periods of need have an unfavorable effect in that they completely break up unsettled relationships. Divorces occur in most all cases from base motives; the irrational and immoral end to marriage is the rule and not the exception. It has been proved that the educated classes practice marriage most morally. Divorced women remarry much more easily than divorced men. (Indicating an extra-marital inclination on the part of the woman?)

Temporary or lengthy separation from her spouse appears to affect the wife unfavorably. Historically recognized are the suicides of military wives during the absence of their husbands caused by war. A few such cases are also known to me. (The motive would therefore be longing for the departed man: analogy with unrequited love.)

Women living in *concubinage* show a suicide frequency three times as large as men. The explanation is apparent.

B. The effect of family life on *children* may generally be described by the proverb, "The apple doesn't fall far from the tree." Good and virtuous parents bring up good and virtuous children, bad bring up bad.

It is difficult to say how multiple marriages affect the natural- and step-children. Separation and concubinage certainly have evil influences. Orphans, those with no or one parent, may face equally unfavorable conditions. Contemporary statistical inductions are lacking for all these important conditions; similarly, I find no estimates concerning the suicide of illegitimate in relation to legitimate children.

It can be conjectured that illegitimate children have a higher proportionate suicide frequency than legitimate children, because the illegitimate are neglected in almost every respect. They already lack mother love and still more, following birth, they are without necessary physical care; and only in the fewest cases can one speak of true intellectual and moral schooling. These unfortunate para-

---

from their husbands by Gregory VII's vigorous execution of the policy of celibacy among the priesthood; but, the finality of separation from the spouse is quite evident in this example.

sites of society for this reason may show a proportionately high crime and suicide frequency, as they also succumb in high degree to mental illness.

The question whether the countries that exhibit many illegitimate births also have a high suicide frequency is to be answered thus. Those of illegitimate birth probably have a proportionately higher suicide frequency but, because the mortality of these unfortunates (especially in the early years) is exceedingly great, the number of suicides among the illegitimate is lost in the absolute number of others. So far as unmarried parents are concerned, they commit suicide with relative frequency since illegitimate cohabitation can very easily condition the tendency to suicide. It not only indicates sexual excess, but also manifests irregular economic and social relationships, generally a great coarseness and immorality.[23]

23     There is no agreement whether or not standards of morality concerning illegitimacy shall prove to be effectual. Hausner is pro, Engel, Mayr, and Oettingen are con. I believe that the illegitimately born are the surest sign that a certain number of unmarried individuals will be and can be possessed by violent passions; that is decided by a deficiency in their sexual life, but no absolute or general immorality follows from this. It is true that we are accustomed to think particularly or exclusively of sexual indiscretion as "immorality," but such a position is not entirely correct: one can commit different sins against and without regard for the sixth commandment. Inadequate laws of courtship (Bavaria until 1868), paternity, diet, the shame of defloration, inept agrarian conditions, etc., have been reported to supply the numbers of illegitimate children, and that there are therefore no standards of morality. In opposition to this position, I might mention that no one has shown that all or a majority of cases of illegitimacy will be caused by these factors; and, if they do cause illegitimate birth, does such an explanation of illegitimacy allow room for forgiveness? I do not think it does; at most, it will suffice to provide reserved judgments in certain cases—but not all!

The following shows that illegitimate children are not to be attributed to constant and uniformly effective laws, customs, and similar things. For two decades, illegitimate births have increased in all the states of Europe. Hard times have restricted their frequency. Statisticians further bemoan the increase in drunkenness, idlers, the disruption of family bonds, crimes against morality—illegitimate births, correctly understood, are in fact a standard of the prevailing morality.

*Therefore, on the whole, there does appear to be a parallelism be-*
*tween the frequency of illegitimate births and suicides, but it will*
*be less determinate the more one accurately investigates individual*
*countries by smaller areas.*

One might make these observations: cities have a significantly
higher number of illegitimate births than the provinces; for example, Vienna was notorious for having, in 1862, 1.1 illegitimate for
every legitimate birth (probably including abandoned children in
foundling homes); among all capitals, London evidences the most
favorable conditions. With respect to nationality, we have, according to Hausner's calculation, for each illegitimate birth, the following number of legitimate births:

| | |
|---|---|
| Among the Slavs | 18.3 |
| Among the Romance countries | 16.3 |
| Among the Germanic countries | 8.6 |
| Among      Germany alone | 6.5 |

This agrees with the data on suicide frequency, also with the
following estimates concerning confession: per one illegitimate
birth, there are the following number of legitimate births:[24]

[24]    For every illegitimate birth there occur the following number of
legitimate births in the various nations of Europe:

| | | |
|---|---|---|
| Netherlands | 1860–62 | 24.61 |
| Italy | 1863–68 | 17.04 |
| Spain | 1868 | 17.18 |
| Belgium | 1867 | 14.16 |
| France | 1867 | 13.14 |
| England | 1868 | 12.13 |
| Preussen | 1864 | 10.66 |
| Austria | 1867 | 6.08 |
| Württemberg | 1857–61–63 | 5.10 |
| Baden | 1859–63 | 5.04 |
| Bavaria | 1858–62 | 3.33 |

Bodio states that the number of illegitimate births relative to the total
number of births to be:

| | |
|---|---|
| Holland | 3– 4% |
| Switzerland | 5– 6% |
| England | 5– 6% |

|                        |       |
|------------------------|-------|
| Among the Greek Church | 20.40 |
| Among the Catholics    | 11.15 |
| Among the Protestants  | 10.35 |

*Illegitimate births* are increasing in all countries just as suicide is more frequent.

3. *Effects of imprisonment.* Prison life disposes very strongly to suicide, as the relatively high suicide frequency among prison inmates indicates; solitary confinement has an especially depressing effect on man; isolation and the more or less unusual treatment, in and of themselves, produce a bad humor; most criminals are also physically and psychically altered by their past life; their desire for self-preservation, says Lombroso,[25] is suppressed. Finally, their continual desire for freedom, their hopelessness, and remorse and shame for many have a most unfavorable effect.

---

|         |          |
|---------|----------|
| Italy   | 6– 7%    |
| Belgium | 7%       |
| Hungary | 7– 8%    |
| Austria | 12–14%   |

These tabulations have not been compiled in the same manner; illegitimate births should also be compared in relation to the frequency of marriage, with the number of available virile men, and especially with the number of women, married and single.

Schimmer supplies interesting data for Austria (*Statist. Monatschrift,* 1876); he comes to the following conclusions:

1. A trade and industrial population has more illegitimate births than an agricultural population.

2. Great estates with large staffs of servants, in countries where the division of wealth is disproportionate, are conducive to illegitimacy; children become legitimate through subsequent marriages.

3. The higher the number of women of child-bearing age, the higher the number of illegitimate births.

4. The higher the number of births to youthful parents, the lower the number of illegitimate births.

5. The Germans, with respect to nationality, have the highest number of illegitimate births. The Jews, where they live together in large numbers, are no exception.

[25]     *Uomo delinquente,* 1878; *Über den Selbstmord der Gefangenen,* p. 97 ff.

Therefore, prison inmates show a greater mortality and more suicides than free men.

It has been observed that suicide appears more frequently among those who have committed petty crimes; wicked and hardened sinners, thieves, murderers, etc., take their lives less frequently because they are not susceptible to the agitation of remorse, shame, and pangs of conscience.

A similar explanation may be made as to why those arrested for the first time commit suicide more often than the perennial inmates of prisons. (Mortality among those imprisoned for the first time is also greater than among repeated offenders).

Imprisoned women seldom commit suicide, but often become mentally ill.[26]

The suicide index for prisoners rises in the same proportion that it increases from year to year in the general population.

4. *Occupation.* Statistics on occupation have been seriously compiled only in recent years, and therefore we can not yet define conclusively the suicide tendency for different occupational groups, especially since the suicide statistics in this category are faulty.

The type of occupation tends to correspond to personal character, for occupation rests on free choice, upon one's own or that of other responsible persons. Occupation, in turn, stamps the individual and entire levels of society with a very definite character; occupation indirectly conditions the economic, political, and social position of men; rank, station, caste, and social class, with their corresponding modes of life, are defined for the individual and the whole by type of occupation.

Labor maintains life—labor destroys life and vitality: health, strength, and success depend upon occupation. For example, that the grinders of Sheffield have the most dangerous occupation is evident to everyone who knows the nature of this work; one can

[26]   Some claim that women prisoners must use too harsh a means to commit suicide and, therefore, do not kill themselves. Others believe that women prisoners commit fewer crimes in prison than men, particularly suicide, because they are more active and do not brood upon any one thing.

also understand why cobblers with their squatting way of life often have gastric complaints and, not infrequently, become mentally ill, showing a talent for poetry and political and religious reveries; similarly, hypochondriacs, visionaries, and theosophists are said to develop among weavers, etc.

In certain areas, the tendency to suicide, like morbidity and mortality, will also depend upon occupation; but this dependency is not to be exaggerated. Occupation does not determine the moral character of man; it is only a means to an end by which the choice whether to be or not to be will be influenced only indirectly. An example will make this clear. It has been reported that wine merchants commit suicide relatively frequently because in their occupation they are easily led to drunkenness, which, in turn, frequently leads to suicide; but not all wine merchants are intemperate; they do not necessarily fall into the vice of drunkenness through their occupation, but rather they can indulge in this vice more readily because of their occupation—if they are weak in character. The situation is the same or similar in all cases.

We have seen that the city shows more suicides than the provinces; from this we may conclude that the agricultural population exhibits a lower suicide frequency than the occupational groups which are represented in the city; but one must further conclude that the rural manual laborer, businessman, etc., also show a lower frequency than their urban colleagues. It is not the urban professions as such—this I want to emphasize—which condition the greater tendency to suicide, but rather the total social life and activity of the city. In any case, the agricultural population has the lowest suicide frequency.

For the remaining special occupational groups, according to Wagner, the following assertions can be made with some certainty. Suicide has the greatest relative frequency among domestic servants on the whole, differently for each sex; almost the same frequency occurs among soldiers (cf. Militarism, chap. 2, sec. 2, pt. 3, no. 6); therefore it is most frequent among the classes whose individual freedom is most restricted. Liberal professions and more highly educated classes show a somewhat higher than average frequency; those without occupations and persons who lead a more or less suspect life fall into the first category. The frequency of the business and trade classes falls in part below the general average.

Wagner believes:

Insofar as an average occupational level can be established, those classes which can be defined primarily as those of half-education—domestic servants, soldiers, and those without occupation or vagabonds—show the highest suicide frequency. Persons who may be rated just above or below half-education present a favorable picture, but the most favorable picture is presented by the relatively uneducated classes.

I call attention to the following in detail.

A very low suicide frequency appears among clergymen of all forms of worship; poets, artists, and men of genius are often seized by the tendency to suicide. Crowned heads commit suicide not infrequently; professional beggars almost never.[27]

An accurate estimate of motives for individual occupational classes is lacking at present, but the little we do possess warrants the assumption that, with few exceptions, almost the same motives have strong, relatively equal effects in all types of occupations. But that is explained in that occupation has only a disposing effect, and that the actual causes and motives are, in fact, not to be found here.[28]

For every 10,000 persons enumerated in 1869 by particular occupational class in Vienna, the following average number of suicides occurred, 1869 to 1878:

| | |
|---|---|
| Civil servants | 6.0 |
| White-collar workers | 20.9 |
| Students | 3.3 |
| Attorneys, doctors of law | 25.6 |

[27]    Daniel Langhaus, *von den Krankheiten der Hof-und Weltleute*, 1776. Cf. St.-Fare Bontemps, *Tableau stat. et comp. des qualités distinctives des souverains de diverses nations depuis l'origins des empire jusqu'a la fin du XVIII siécle*. Of 2,542 rulers, from 64 different countries, 20 committed suicide (1 for each 127) and 11 (1 for each 221) were mentally ill.

[28]    The following report of Italy for the year 1874 offers the facing table:

| Occupation | Total | Loss of wealth | Boredom with life, domestic misfortune | Unrequited love, jealousy | Causes Fear of punishment and harm | Drunkenness | Physical Illness | Mental Illness | Unknown |
|---|---|---|---|---|---|---|---|---|---|
| Land and Forest wardens | 290 | 29 | 14 | 4 | 5 | 1 | 131 | 57 | 49 |
| Businessman, industrialist | 213 | 55 | 21 | 14 | 8 | 4 | 29 | 29 | 53 |
| Trade, transport | 98 | 29 | 11 | 3 | 1 | 2 | 12 | 14 | 26 |
| Landlord, rentier | 90 | 12 | 10 | 5 | 2 | — | 15 | 23 | 23 |
| Servants | 31 | 3 | 5 | 2 | 5 | — | 2 | 4 | 10 |
| Soldiers | 50 | — | 18 | 2 | 5 | — | 1 | 3 | 21 |
| Officials | 41 | 10 | 7 | 2 | 6 | — | 3 | 4 | 9 |
| Ecclesiastics | 4 | — | — | — | — | — | 1 | 2 | 1 |
| Lawyers | 6 | 2 | 1 | — | — | — | 1 | 2 | — |
| Sanitation workers | 10 | — | 3 | — | 1 | — | 2 | 2 | 2 |
| Teachers | 14 | 1 | 5 | 1 | — | — | 1 | 3 | 3 |
| Musicians, artists | 5 | 2 | 1 | — | — | — | — | — | 2 |
| Other persons with higher education | 25 | 11 | 2 | 1 | 2 | — | 2 | — | 7 |
| Itinerant professionals (musicians, etc.) | 8 | 3 | 1 | — | 1 | — | — | — | 3 |
| Day laborers | 29 | 3 | 1 | — | 1 | 3 | 6 | 2 | 13 |
| Dependent persons | 79 | 12 | 4 | 4 | 4 | — | 17 | 15 | 23 |
| Unknown occupation | 22 | 2 | 1 | — | 1 | — | — | 2 | 16 |

If we take the frequency of suicides among land wardens as a norm, then the loss of wealth plays a forceful role among businessmen, industrialists, tradesmen, and transporters; the same is true for officials and other categories: in general, loss of wealth is a strong cause. Servants, soldiers, and officials have a relatively greater fear of punishment and harm; many motives which are effective among other groups are entirely lacking among ecclesiastics.

| Gold and silver smiths | 5.0 |
| Carriers and shipping agents | 9.9 |
| Blacksmiths and locksmiths | 3.7 |
| Inn-keepers | 2.5 |
| Butchers | 3.5 |
| Bakers | 3.6 |
| Carpenters | 2.1 |
| Day laborers | 9.4 |

5.  Summary. General societal conditions have only a disposing and indirect effect on the appearance of the tendency to suicide; their effectiveness is not great enough to derive the social
evil in question from them in whole or even only in greatest part.
Compared with the causes treated previously, however, the conditions of man treated here are demonstrably more proximate
causes of the tendency to suicide.

PART 3: POLITICAL CONDITIONS. 1. *Race.*
Although civilized people in general commit suicide, it can be
stated that this social evil is particularly a burden of the Caucasian race; suicide also frequently appears among the Chinese
and Japanese, from which it might be concluded that the Mon-
golian race, the second most civilized following the Caucasian,
must also suffer from the evil. With regard to other races we shall
have more to say below about primitive peoples (chap. 5, pt. 1,
no. 2).[29]

We have no data concerning the mixtures of different races.
Several investigators consider the mixed races more vigorous than
the colored races, indeed, even more vigorous than the white race
itself, suggesting that the mixed races, so far as the factor of race
is concerned, will have more power of endurance than their
progenitors.[30]

2. *Nationality.* According to Wagner, there are the following
number of suicides per each million inhabitants:

[29]    An evaluation of what has been said about nationality must be
made by those who wish to divide races not according to Blumenbach, but
according to others, such as Desmoulins.
[30]    We will soon discuss the Magyars, who have a strong admixture of
Caucasian blood.

| | |
|---|---|
| Germanic nations | 100 |
| Romance nations | 80 |
| Slavic nations | 34 |

and in particular:

| | |
|---|---|
| Scandinavians | 126 |
| Germans | 112 |
| English | 65 |
| French | 105 |
| Italians | 20 |
| Portuguese | 7 |
| Eastern Slavs | 47 |
| Russians | 28 |

Morselli reports that there are at present the following average number of suicides per million inhabitants:

| | | |
|---|---|---|
| Group I: | Italians, Spaniards, Rumanians, Portuguese, | |
| Group I: | Corsicans, Swiss in Tessin | 31 |
| Group II: | Russians, Slavs, Croatians, Dalmatians | 40.0 |
| Group III: | Magyars, Finns | 45.0 |
| Group IV: | Scandinavians | 127.8 |
| Group V: | French | 130.0 |
| Group VI: | Czechs, Moravians, Poles | 130.0 |
| Group VII: | North Germans, English | 148.0 |
| Group VIII: | South Germans | 165.0 |

In particular, the indices show the following numbers:

| Nation | Period | Number of suicides per one million inhabitants |
|---|---|---|
| Spain | 1866–70 | 17 |
| Russia | 1873 | 27.0 |
| | 1875 | 30.0 |
| Italy | 1871 | 31.0 |
| | 1877 | 40.6 |
| England | 1871 | 66 |
| | 1876 | 73 |
| Norway | 1871–3 | 73 |
| Sweden | 1871–5 | 81 |
| Austria | 1873–7 | 95.6 |
| Prussia | 1871–5 | 133.1 |
| France | 1871–5 | 150 |
| Denmark | 1871–6 | 258 |

As a comparison let us look at other figures, newer and older. Bodio gives:[31]

| Nation | Year | Suicides | per one million inhabitants |
|--------|------|----------|------------------------------|
| Saxony | 1877 | 1114 | 391 |
| Switzerland | 1877 | 600 | 216 |
| Prussia | 1877 | 4563 | 174 |
| Bavaria | 1877 | 650 | 127 |
| Austria | 1877 | 2648 | 121 |
| Sweden | 1877 | 430 | 96 |
| Belgium | 1877 | 470 | 87 |
| England, Wales | 1877 | 1699 | 69 |
| Norway | 1877 | 99 | 55 |
| Ireland | 1875 | 75 | 16.2 |

Morpurgo calculates per 100,000 inhabitants:

| | |
|---|---|
| France | 13.40 suicides |
| Sweden | 7.43 suicides |
| England, Wales | 6.56 suicides |
| Belgium | 5.36 suicides |
| Italy | 3.25 suicides |
| Spain | 1.35 suicides |

Block[32] lists the following proportions of suicide per million inhabitants for the period 1856–65:

| | |
|---|---|
| Denmark | 288 |
| Saxony | 251 |
| Prussia | 123 |
| France | 110 |
| Norway | 94 |
| Bavaria | 73 |
| England, Wales | 67 |
| Sweden | 66 |
| Austria | 64 |
| Belgium | 55 |
| Russia | 26 |
| Spain | 14 |

---

[31]    Bodio, *Introduzione al Movimento dello stato civile 1862–1877*, Rome, 1878–79.
[32]    *Traité théor. et prat. de Statistique*, 1878.

Brierre asserts the following series, per million inhabitants:

| | | | |
|---|---|---|---|
| Saxony-Altenburg | 303 | Baden | 119 |
| Denmark | 288 | Norway | 94 |
| Kingdom of Saxony | 251 | Bavaria | 73 |
| Schleswig | 209 | England | 69 |
| Holstein | 173 | Sweden | 66 |
| Mecklenburg (Schwerin) | 159 | Belgium | 55 |
| Lauenburg | 156 | Austria | 43 |
| Oldenburg | 155 | Scotland | 35 |
| Hanover | 128 | United States | 32 |
| Prussia | 123 | Spain | 14 |
| France | 120 | | |

One may also compare the figures for several cities, suicides per 10,000 inhabitants, 1876–78:

| | | | |
|---|---|---|---|
| Leipzig | 4.87 | Vienna | 2.85 |
| Breslau | 3.69 | Berlin | 2.78 |
| Dresden | 3.65 | Munich | 1.76 |
| Paris | 3.59 | New York | 1.48 |
| Brussels | 3.53 | London | 0.84 |

The following series, arranged by individual nations and provinces, shows the frequency in Austria (1819–72) in decreasing order:

Lower Austria
Bohemia
Moravia, Silesia
Galicia, Bukowina
Upper Austria
Styria
Carinthia, Carniola
Tyrol, Vorarlberg
Maritime District (Trieste, Istria, Görtz)
Dalmatia

We have no reliable data concerning the incidence of suicide in Hungary.[33] The Magyars have a relatively low suicide rate; I draw this conclusion from the high number of crimes against the person committed in Hungary: Koneg's criminal statistics for Hungary from 1873 to 1877 record an annual average of 10,851 persons indicted for murder, manslaughter, and serious physical

[33]   Schwicker, *Statistik des Königreichs Ungarn*, 1877, p. 122.

assault, 2654 persons for attempted murder; *that was 44 percent of all crimes* in 1877, in Austria only 26 percent. Where many murders and especially crimes against the person are committed, suicide is relatively low.[34] For Germany Wagner notes the following frequencies of suicide per million for each tribe:

| | | | |
|---|---|---|---|
| Saxons | 219 | Slavo-Prussians | 71 |
| Lower Saxons | 174 | Czecho-Germans | 67 |
| Slavo-Saxons | 168 | Westphalians | 66 |
| Hessians | 134 | Rhinelanders | 62 |
| Alamannians | 108 | Bavarians | 52 |
| Franks | 93 | Yugoslavo-Germans | 29 |
| Swabians | 85 | Rhine Province | 27 |
| Frisians | 79 | | |

For every 100,000 inhabitants, Stricker calculates:

| | | |
|---|---|---|
| Saxony | 1856–60 | 24.5 |
| Mecklenburg | 1856–60 | 16.2 |
| Hanover | 1856–58 | 13.7 |
| Electorate of Hesse | 1856–60 | 13.4 |
| Prussia | 1856–60 | 12.2 |
| Baden | 1856–60 | 10.8 |
| Nassau | 1856–60 | 10.2 |
| Württemberg | 1856–60 | 8.5 |
| Bavaria | 1856–60 | 7.2 |

Finally, if the data cited are compared with the evidence regarding religion (Confession, chap. 2, sec. 2, pt. 5, no. 8) and the increase of suicide in all countries (chap. 4, no. 4), one can then assert the following with certainty. Suicide is most frequently committed by the Germanic peoples, less often by the Romance peoples, and least by the Slavs; among the Germanic nations, the Danes and the Germans are first, among the Romance nations the French, and among the Slavs the Czechs and Poles. The evil frequently appears among the Danes, Germans, French, and Austrians, seldom among the Spaniards, Portuguese, Yugoslavians, Irish, and Scottish, moderately in England, Sweden, Norway, and the United States.[35]

[34] Concerning this important law, see chap. 5, sec. 1, no. 2.

[35] The statistical data especially are inadequate in so many ways. We lack accurate figures concerning nationalities in Austria because the official figures are collected only by the state; thus, for example, we know

The Jews, of the remaining nationalities, must be given special note because of their low suicide frequency; it is high among the Indians, Japanese, and Chinese.

Information *about mixtures of various nations* are understandably lacking. It has been said that mixtures are hardier than pure nationalities and, in this respect, England, Northern Germany, and other countries are usually singled out; Brierre de Boismont actually recommends interbreeding as a means against the increasing tendency to suicide. Certainly in Europe there is practically no large nation which has not been mixed with others; but not all peoples resulting from interbreeding must become powerful and hardy, and, in contrast, one can see no reason why unmixed peoples—for example the Jews!—should not have vitality: it will depend upon the peoples who are mixed and on other factors which, were we to speak of them accurately, would be subjects of scientific ethnography and anthropology.

---

nothing positive about the proportion of Slavs and Germans in Bohemia, Moravia, and other places. The data are also inaccurate for Germany because the computation of Slavic, French, and Danish minorities are contained only in reports of the provinces. Saxony's high suicide frequency surprises Ossiander, and Casper has already substantiated that it is lower in the Rhine region than in the other provinces of Prussia.

The official French data are very reliable; however, these also overlook the differences between the Celtic, the Germanic, and the other remaining races. Belgian statisticians neglect the Flemish.

The data from England are defective in this respect because the differentiation of nationalities—according to some authorities four, others six—is neglected. Heretofore, it has been believed that the English have the largest number of suicides and mentally ill; but Burrow has shown (*Inquiry into Certain Errors Relative to Insanity*, 1820) this view is not tenable.

The data from Italy are good; we possess almost no data for Spain and Portugal; likewise reports from the United States are deficient. (In Spain, in 1847, suicide was almost unknown; Ford, *Handbook for Spain*, p. 337; de Tocqueville says that suicide is infrequent in America but that mental illness is common).

We have no accurate estimates for Russia; but in recent years one often reads of many suicides, particularly among the educated classes. The reports from Turkey and the Balkan Peninsula are, in general, totally inadequate.

The effect of *the renunciation of one's own nationality*, whether or not it involves interbreeding, is interesting to observe. Many individuals renounce their nationality for base and immoral reasons, and there then appears that very characteristic incompleteness which we can note in the many countries of the Austrian Empire, especially Bohemia, Moravia, and Hungary, and which is quite certainly is favorable to the appearance and diffusion of the suicide tendency.

The overall affect of nationality should not be overestimated. It is unbelievable but true—in spite of the magnified role which nationality today plays, we still have no scientific definition and research concerning its character (and that of race). Thus it is very difficult to draw conclusions on this subject. The following observations must therefore suffice. The tendency to suicide among a given people increases or decreases in relation to religion, educational level, place of residence (city or province), time of year —in short, all individual, social, and natural conditions. Further, the suicide tendency shows a constant increase among all civilized peoples. From this it follows that national characteristics exercise only a slight, disposing influence on the development of the suicide tendency, insofar as one understands by nationality only the basic physical and psychical characteristics and not education, morals, or the total condition of a contemporary people. For us, nationality is however, the basic physical and psychical character, taken as a whole, which every individual possesses.

The same is true to an even greater extent of race.

3. *Constitution.* Since every government has a very great area of activity, its direct and indirect power is extensive. It can cause man every conceivable evil, if it is bad, and even a good government can cause many evils. Every government can produce, directly and indirectly, a dissatisfaction with life that can, under certain conditions, grow into boredom with life. The exercise of justice, the administration and police, the system of finances, etc., are able, if they are misapplied, to completely undermine the standard of living of the subjects of the state, to directly and indirectly contribute to the rise and spread of the suicide tendency.

*We find the suicide tendency among peoples with the most*

*varied forms of government; but, on the whole, it is higher in free states, and smaller in enslaved states.* Winslow believes suicide to be more frequent in republics, because fantasies there are stimulated by the state of general equality, through which a general striving for innovation appears; under tyranny, however, everyone is obedient and remains in his appointed place. One must consider, with respect to representative forms of government, that the officers of government are elected, for the most part, and that over the course of time, therefore, an imprudent governmental structure would not be elected, since the people themselves are good and prudent on the average. Disturbances may appear for a time, but lasting mis-government, if such exists in Europe, means the whole society is corrupt and ignorant. In social life, there is an inward consensus of all individuals, an active reciprocity among all parts. The defects of society are the defects of government; therefore, the governments of the countries concerned on the whole really bear no more and no less blame for the prevailing tendency to suicide than the society itself.

4. *Political crises, revolutions, agitations.* Under certain conditions a politically unstable society has a great tendency to *tedium vitae.* For example, a suddenly instituted tyranny can bring many citizens to suicide; on the other hand, the suicide frequency can likewise rise where there appears, precipitously and without preparation, a too liberal form of government. Political crises undermine order and security, ruin the economic base, and kindle passions and immorality, naturally bringing about many suicides.[36]

Many believe that relatively few suicides are committed during times of revolution. I am of the same opinion, although it can be objected that such times make the census unreliable. Attention is directed in entirely new directions, and *tedium vitae* partially forced into another form; all the dissatisfied elements assemble around the revolutionaries, and many find death in battle who

---

[36]    Des Etang, *Du suicide politique en France depuis 1789 jusqu'à nos jours,* 1860. There existed in Paris a suicide club which defined the suicide method for its members. A similar club existed in Berlin, and even in Egypt during the restless times of Cleopatra.

would otherwise have taken their own lives. Thus considered, revolution appears as an indirect mass suicide, as a sort of powerful purification of the weariness with life.

It should also be noted that in revolutions the number of mentally ill does not increase.[37]

The general agitation and nervous excitement of revolution obviously devolve on its heirs, and a whole generation then becomes more susceptible to the suicide tendency. In any case, the great revolution of the previous century has had this effect, because, since that time, political excitement has persisted in all European countries.[38]

Naturally, every agitation has an unfavorable effect, because it excites men and in this way disposes to *tedium vitae*. Political agitation is especially destructive because it often produces an exultation that directly and indirectly leads to suicide.[39]

[37]    Of 76 chairmen of the Paris Convention, three took their lives, four became mentally ill, eighteen went to the guillotine, almost all found a tragic end. Descuret, *La médicine des passions*, 1841, p. 584.

[38]    It has been observed that the population which was born in France from 1791 to 1811 shows a relatively greater crime rate than the younger generation.

It is also known that the revolution of 1848 flooded Europe with bastards.

[39]    The following table gives an idea of how much more active and exciting political life has become for us in recent years:

The following number of newspaper pages was printed in the countries represented in the Reich Council:

|  | 1860 | 1870 |
| --- | --- | --- |
| Lower Austria | 30,851,210 | 54,189,034 |
| Upper Austria | 533,177 | 1,486,340 |
| Salzburg | 65,457 | 118,441 |
| Styria | 2,156,391 | 4,464,985 |
| Carinthia | 2,000 | 109,264 |
| Carinola | 91,500 | 427,880 |
| [Küstenland] | 1,293,571 | 1,364,074 |
| Tyrol, Vorarlberg | 876,000 | 1,791,234 |
| Dalmatia | — | 149,600 |
| Bohemia | 3,916,324 | 12,119,585 |
| Moravia | 1,110,098 | 2,431,223 |
| Silesia | 94,057 | 165,407 |

Winslow ascribes to the socialists part of the blame for the spread of the suicide tendency.

5. *War.* War, especially on a large scale, has a salutary affect on suicide for the moment, in that attention is generally directed toward another object, but it is very deleterious in its results. The people are impoverished, are physically and psychically weakened and demoralized, and experience so much suffering that the effect of a war, won or lost, is equally unfavorable in this respect. A glance at the table (chap. 4, no. 4) shows how in fact during all great wars the suicide frequency decreases in the first years, but rises rapidly and strongly in many cases after the war.[40]

6. *Militarism.* In all countries, soldiers show a greater tendency to suicide than civilians.

Wagner states that the following number of military suicides occur per 100 male civilian cases:

| | | |
|---|---|---|
| Austria | 1851–57 | 643 |
| Sweden | 1851–55 | 423 |
| Prussia | 49 | 293 |
| France | 1856–60 | 253 |
| Württemberg | 1846–50 | 192 |
| Saxony | 1847–58 | 177 |
| Denmark | 1845–56 | (98?) |

More recent figures for 1862–71 read:[41]

| Nation | per 1000 males |
|---|---|
| England | 0.379 |
| Belgium | 0.45 |
| France | 0.49 |

| | | |
|---|---|---|
| Galicia | 1,082,131 | 2,569,790 |
| [Bukowina] | 3,539 | |
| | 42,075,485 | 81,383,857 |

In Hungary, 100 years ago, only 2 (German) newspapers appeared; in 1850, only 3 political newspapers appeared, in 1860, 6 dailies and 6 political weeklies; by 1870, there were 10 and 28; in 1871, 14 and 37.

40    Concerning degeneration through war and militarism in general, see Häckel, *Natürl. Schöpfungsgesch.*, 1874., p. 153 ff.

41    "Die österr. Militärstatistik," Schimmer, *Biotik der k. k. österr. Armee im Freiden*, 1863; more recent data can be found in *Militärstatistik Jarb. of 1870.*

| | |
|---|---|
| Prussia | 0.64 |
| Austria | 0.85 |
| 1870 | 0.95 |
| 1871 | 0.82 |
| 1872 | 0.90 |
| 1873 | 0.82 |
| 1874 | 0.96 |
| 1875 | 1.14 |
| 1876 | 1.28 |

Absolute numbers for suicide in the commissariat are as follows:

| | Austria | Prussia |
|---|---|---|
| 1867 | 147 | 103 |
| 1868 | 131 | 155 |
| 1869 | 229 | 160 |
| 1870 | 243 | 171 ⎱ war |
| 1871 | 199 | 105 ⎰ years! |
| 1872 | 213 | 138 |
| 1873 | 197 | 200 |
| 1874 | 242 | |
| 1875 | 292 | |
| 1876 | 330 | |

Among the Austro-Hungarians:

in 1874   69.4% were born Austrian, 30.2% Hungarian
in 1875   66.4% were born Austrian, 33.3% Hungarian

With respect to branch of service, the infantry, cavalry, and military police show a larger number than the artillery, the Royal Engineers, and the miners and sappers.[42]

[42]   Among us in 1870–75 there was the following relation between the average branches of service in percentages (Austria):

| Year | Abso- lute no. | Rifle- men | Line infantry | Quarter- master | Cavalry |
|---|---|---|---|---|---|
| 1870 | 243 | 1.42 | 1.27 | 0.78 | 0.69 |
| 1871 | 199 | 1.27 | 1.09 | 0.44 | 0.75 |
| 1872 | 213 | 1.04 | 0.97 | — | 1.21 |
| 1873 | 197 | 0.96 | 0.89 | 0.98 | 1.15 |
| 1874 | 242 | — | 1.08 | 1.93 | 1.28 |
| 1875 | 292 | — | — | — | — |

With regard to rank, junior officers and senior officers contribute a relatively higher number than noncommissioned officers.[43]

Among the military the number of attempted suicides is significant; in Austria there were:

| | | | |
|---|---|---|---|
| 1870 | 39 | 1873 | 67 |
| 1871 | 38 | 1874 | 63 |
| 1872 | 38 | 1875 | 64 |

It is to be noted that the noncommissioned troops also show a smaller percentage of attempted suicides.

During war, suicide seldom occurs among soldiers.[44]

What is the cause of such a great suicide tendency among the military?

Nature can have an unfavorable affect on the military in a state such as Austria, with its varied climate, if soldiers are transferred to a new climate they are not used to. But states like Saxony and others, which have a uniform climate, also show a high suicide frequency among the military, and one can therefore safely assert that, on the whole, the influences of nature are no more unfavorable for soldiers than for civilians. While climate may still have an unfavorable effect on the military, there are other condi-

| Year | Border infantry | Artillery | Sappers | Royal Engineers | Sanitation Corps |
|---|---|---|---|---|---|
| 1870 | 0.54 | 0.38 | 0.38 | 0.21 | — |
| 1871 | — | 0.34 | — | 0.17 | — |
| 1872 | 0.34 | 0.59 | — | 0.15 | — |
| 1873 | — | 0.38 | — | — | 0.65 |
| 1874 | — | — | 1.06 | — | — |
| 1875 | — | — | — | — | — |

[43]    Oesterlen, *Handb. d. med. Stat. 1865*, p. 734.

In Austria, per 1000 males, there are:

| Year | Staff Officers | Junior Officers | Troops |
|---|---|---|---|
| 1870 | 1.35% | 2.91% | 0.71% |
| 1871 | 1.69% | 1.36% | 0.59% |

Among 242 suicides in 1874, there were 27 officers, 84 junior officers, 131 soldiers. Among 292 suicides in 1875, there were 18 officers, 89 junior officers, 185 soldiers.

[44]    Oesterlen, loc. cit., p. 851.

tions which favor it. Military service takes the ablest, strongest, mentally and physically healthiest young men. The soldier has no concerns about food, clothing, shelter; he is afforded good medical treatment in case of illness. We are assured that military service strengthens and shapes a man—why then the great suicide tendency?

Many young soldiers are homesick, and moreover most hate military service, which tears them from their accustomed living conditions and places them in unfamiliar circumstances. One result is that the most suicides are committed by youthful soldiers rather than by older professionals. The years from 20–24 are the most dangerous,[45] and the fear of punishment is a frequent cause of suicide. Dipsomania and perhaps mental illness have a proportionally greater effect on soldiers than civilians.[46] The severe hardships and in many countries insufficient nourishment have an unfavorable effect.[47] Finally, the military is more immoral than civilians, and this is the primary issue. It is the military "spirit" which causes the high suicide tendency of the military. This "spirit" promotes only the surface, not the inner qualities of character. Ambition and obedience are the sole virtues; skills are demanded and taught, but not morality. Barracks life is as unfavorable as imprisonment, only the latter takes the immoral while the

[45]    The hatred of military service also makes its appearance as numerous self-mutilations which are mostly committed by non-commissioned officers. In Austria, there were the following self-mutilations among troops:

|      |    |      |    |
|------|----|------|----|
| 1870 | 66 | 1873 | 92 |
| 1871 | 54 | 1874 | 82 |
| 1872 | 43 | 1875 | 70 |

[46]    Concerning the high frequency of mental illness among the military, see Kraus, *Hygiene*, p. 932; cf. *III Hauptst.*, sec. 5, no. 15.

[47]    The mortality rate of soldiers is greater than that of civilians; but one must remember that only men serve in the military, and that men show a higher mortality than women even though they are strong and healthy. On the other hand, children, who show a high mortality rate, are counted as civilians.

former creates them. The tendency to suicide is equally great in both.[48]

Considered from this point of view, the general obligation of military service appears destructive, because all men are exposed

[48]　Kolb, *Statistik*, p. 843, "Über die Sittlichkeit des Militärs." Wagner correctly notes that the absolute suicide frequency among the military of various countries points to a cause which, in general, affects troops; he believes it to be the hardships of military service.

Suicide motives among civilians and military in Austria and Saxony (per million) according to Schimmer and Wagner:

|  | Austria | | Saxony | |
|---|---|---|---|---|
|  | *Civil* | *Army* | *Civil* | *Army* |
| Mental illness | 447 | 430 | 367 | 146 |
| Weariness with life, cares, illness, unrequited love | 238 | 349 | 196 | 154 |
| Need and debts | 114 | 52 | 138 | 20 |
| Mishandling and conflict | 38 | 6 | 36 | 114 |
| Drunkenness | 82 | 23 | 125 | 168 |
| Crime, fear of punishment | 81 | 140 | 138 | 396 |

Among Austrian troops since 1870–75 in percentages (so far as the motives are known = 47 percent):

| Causes | 1870 | 1871 | 1872 | 1873 | 1874 | 1875 |
|---|---|---|---|---|---|---|
| Fear of punishment | 17 | 13 | 12 | 19 | 41 cases | 61 cases |
| Insanity or mental illness in general | 6 | 8 | 6 | 7 | 24 cases | 9 cases |
| Debts, otherwise disrupted pecuniary conditions | 5 | 5 | 6 | 6 | 20 cases | 14 cases |
| Dislike of service | 4 | 6 | 5 | 7 | 5 cases | 20 cases |
| Sorrows of love | 4 | 2 | 4 | 7 | 10 cases | 13 cases |
| Weariness with life | 4 | 4 | 5 | 6 | 18 cases | 16 cases |
| Homesickness, drunkenness, disrupted family relations, incurable illness, impaired ambition | 7 | — | — | — | — | — |
| Incurable illness | — | 4 | — | — | 5 cases | 1 case |
| Homesickness | — | 3 | — | — | 2 cases | 5 cases |
| Disrupted family relations | — | 1 | — | — | 2 cases | 9 cases |
| Impaired ambition | — | 1 | — | — | 3 cases | 8 cases |
| Drunkenness | — | 0.5 | — | — | 4 cases | — |
| Superstition, etc. | — | — | — | 8 | — | — |

to the demoralizing atmosphere of military life for long periods of time. Statistics show us that, at present, military manpower has almost reached a maximum. It is therefore not by chance that many great military states—Germany, France, Austria—show a high suicide frequency, while England, the United States, and others have neither many soldiers nor a high suicide frequency.[49]

7. *Summary.* Political conditions have at most a disposing rather than a determining effect on the appearance and spread of the suicide tendency. The effect is not strong enough to explain the intensity and magnitude of the evil. Political conditions, so far as they are of a social nature, are really the result of certain social forces which lie more deeply and which at the same time regulate the appearance of the suicide tendency as well as many political institutions; to a certain extent suicide tendency and political conditions are functions of the same social situation.

PART 4 : ECONOMIC CONDITIONS. 1. *Unsettled conditions of wealth, need, misery, poverty, riches.* To want to live a man must be able to satisfy his wants; if he is not able to do this, then life loses its worth for him, he becomes dissatisfied and unhappy and he finally seeks death of his own free will. Obviously it depends on the standard that is applied to the means of satisfaction, since the need alone cannot be the correct standard. It is a matter of the value which our understanding and our moral feeling assign to the economic good.

[49]    Compare the data for the rise in suicide tendency with the following statistics on the rapid enlargement of the military forces in recent times:

| *Nation* | *1859* | | *1874* | |
|---|---|---|---|---|
| | *Total Forces* | *Offensive Armies* | *Total Forces* | *Offensive Armies* |
| Austria | 634,400 | 443,800 | 856,980 | 452,450 |
| Germany | 836,800 | 483,700 | 1,261,160 | 710,130 |
| Russia (European) | 1,134,200 | 604,100 | 1,401,510 | 665,890 |
| France | 640,000 | 438,000 | 977,600 | 525,700 |
| Italy | 317,650 | 156,450 | 605,200 | 322,000 |
| Sweden, Norway | 134,900 | 46,300 | 204,510 | 54,910 |

A few means of satisfaction are absolutely necessary for the maintenance of bare existence, but the majority of goods that the civilized man requires are originally not absolutely necessary but only become so through habit over the course of time.[50] Several true and moral necessities correspond to these goods; on the other hand, some are imagined, be it that necessities are not recognized or are falsely presumed, or that goods are ascribed false qualities, or, finally, that ignorance applies to goods as well as necessities.

The nonsatisfaction of needs leads to frustration, unhappiness, and weariness with life. If the needs required for sustaining life are not satisfied, vitality decreases, and we know only too well what a sad picture pauperism presents; a pauper's average length of life is less than that of the classes that are better provided for, his morbidity and mortality are higher, and his immorality is practically frightening. Some can brush starvation aside; others are confronted by it and commit suicide. Poverty often disposes one to and determines suicide.[51] But the nonsatisfaction of needs that are not absolutely necessary also leads to weariness with life and suicide. In this respect the rich, the well-off, and those who are poorer are on the same level as the poverty-stricken, because, since conceptions of a standard of living are relative, *an imagined need has the same effect as an actual need on the appearance of the suicide tendency*, whether the imagining depends on an error of the understanding or on moral imperfection. For example, the French at the end of the reign of Louis XIV were very poor, while they are generally envied today because of their wealth, and yet suicide seldom occurred among them in the earlier period, while

50    Tucker compares: necessities, comforts and conveniences for the respective conditions of life, grand and magnificent elegancies and refinements; Boisgiulbert: necessities, comforts, delicacies, luxuries, extravagances.

51    Instead of the usual declamations concerning "poverty," one should read the basic work of Drysdale: "Concerning the Mortality of Richer and Poorer." (Contained in a publication of the London Medical Society, 1879, Oct. 27, *Memorabilia*, 1880): in England and Wales alone, poverty destroys 142,130 lives annually.

the number is now extremely high.[52] It is precisely a matter of values and the change with the times. The very same means of gratification can create satisfaction or dissatisfaction with life, depending on changes in the standard of values.

2. Statistical reports blame dissatisfaction with one's financial situation for about 20 to 30 percent of suicides, and it therefore appears that unfavorable economic conditions are a powerful cause of the high suicide frequency.

Poverty has a decidedly unfavorable, disposing, and determining effect; it creates a pathological, psychotic state, and suicide then appears as the final link in a long chain of unbearable afflictions. The devastating effects of pauperism appear mostly in large cities and industrial districts, not only among "workers," but also in the "better" classes of the population, such as civil servants.

Poverty can be borne with dignity, if a man is rational, does not take the rich as his example. Today, it happens only too often that the poor man has no desire to restrain himself, but then he sinks into such a state that only death can rescue him.

The wealthy also commit a large number of suicides, so that we can say that, with the exception of the impoverished, economic state in and of itself has a favorable or unfavorable effect; we must allow that the middle class, here as everywhere, has the best advantage.

3. Abnormal changes in economic conditions have an especially deleterious effect, particularly unfavorable changes, although even a healthy economy does not make everyone fortunate.

But not every unfavorable financial change has an equally strong effect. A poor harvest, for example, generally causes no perturbation. The farmer, who is the first to be affected, has learned to expect a poor harvest now and then. Businessmen, who are second in line to be affected, likewise can make adjustments because the blow does not come suddenly and unexpectedly, and

[52]   According to Vauban's calculation (*Dime royale*, p. 34), one-tenth of the entire population must beg, five-tenths are very close to misery, three-tenths have very little upon which to live, and only the remaining one-tenth possess some wealth; on the other hand, in this country of millionaires some 6 percent of the population live off rents.

because it does not affect only one or a few, but everyone. Shared misfortune is only misfortune in part or no misfortune at all. Under certain conditions a poor harvest can also have a deleterious effect. But *every sudden, unexpected, and abnormal disturbance of economic conditions is definitely unfavorable* because in most cases one's intellectual and moral education is not able to bear the misfortune. Loss of wealth has an especially deleterious effect when only a few are involved. For example, the great crisis of 1873 had precisely this effect, and in Vienna from 1869 to 1873 economic disturbances caused 13.8 percent of all suicides; in 1874–79, there were 16.6 percent for the same reason.[53] Naturally, a crisis can be very intensive and long-lasting and thus work unfavorably for a longer time. In this way Laveleye views the crash of 1873 as a definite crisis which will lead to a better mode and manner of speculation and production.

Like all crises, every uncertain speculation has an unfavorable effect; to a professional gambler, winning or losing is synonomous with life or death, and one will have to observe that the incidence of suicide often rises after a lottery drawing.

4. If one were to compare the *statistical estimates concerning the suicide frequencies of various nations with their corresponding economic conditions,* he would arrive at the formulation of no generally valid law. Comparisons of suicide data with estimates of the national debt give no results at all; Spain has the largest national debt and a very small suicide frequency; Denmark has a small national debt and a very high suicide frequency, etc. It depends rather on the way in which the debts have arisen. Next to the national debt, the wealth of the people must be taken into account. The wealth of the urban population also leads to no positive result.[54]

The correspondence is closer if one considers the means of communication. It may be said that to a certain degree the tendency to suicide is relatively higher in those countries where communications are most active—the more railroads, telegraphs, post

53     See table, chap. 4, no. 4.
54     Spain has very poor cities, England very wealthy cities; then, in order of wealth, come Germany, France, Italy and Austria.

offices, newspapers, correspondence, etc., that a country exhibits, the higher is its tendency to suicide. However, it should not be forgotten that the means of communication serve not only economic communication but serve even more that general communication which is the exchange of ideas, and the latter is of great importance for the appearance of the suicide tendency.[55]

5. The type of work, of business and industry, has a certain

[55]    Railroad mileage at the end of 1877: per 10,000 inhabitants:

| United States | 32.9 km. | Austria | 4.8 km. |
|---|---|---|---|
| Sweden | 10.8 | Norway | 4.4 |
| Switzerland | 9.3 | Spain | 3.7 |
| England | 8.1 | Italy | 2.9 |
| Denmark | 7.6 | Russia | 2.8 |
| Germany | 7.1 | Rumania | 2.4 |
| Belgium | 6.8 | Portugal | 2.3 |
| France | 6.3 | Turkey | 1.6 |
| Netherlands | 4.8 | Greece | 0.08 |

In 1876 there was one telegraph station:

| Switzerland | for 2,519 inhabitants |
|---|---|
| England | for 6,254 inhabitants |
| Sweden | for 6,980 inhabitants |
| Germany | for 7,015 inhabitants |
| France | for 8,300 inhabitants |
| Denmark | for 8,420 inhabitants |
| Belgium | for 8,810 inhabitants |
| Norway | for 9,260 inhabitants |
| Cisleithania | for 9,260 inhabitants |
| Netherlands | for 11,371 inhabitants |
| Italy | for 15,839 inhabitants |
| Transleithania | for 17,025 inhabitants |
| Greece | for 21,968 inhabitants |
| Turkey | for 22,522 inhabitants |
| Portugal | for 29,878 inhabitants |
| Rumania | for 31,314 inhabitants |
| Russia | for 43,973 inhabitants |
| Spain | for 60,000 inhabitants |

In connection with the telegraph, it depends upon whether it is used preponderately by the public, as in Switzerland, or by the government, as in Russia.

Concerning the postal system and similar matters, see pt. 5, no. 2.

disposing influence on weariness with life; we have already evaluated this in connection with occupation. The rural population engaged in agriculture shows a smaller suicide frequency than the business or urban population. It is not so much a matter of the kind of work itself as of the surrounding conditions that it creates for the worker, primarily the intellectual and moral power of endurance required of men in various economic conditions. Business and industry, in and of themselves, are not less favorable than agriculture; rather it is the whole way of life of the former, as contrasted with the latter, the social conditions that develop with and in part from economic conditions. Wagner is correct in not making the prevailing economic character of a country (region, place) responsible for the relatively higher suicide frequency. For example, England, with her industrial and business activities, shows a lower suicide frequency than France and Austria, where agriculture is much more important than in England.

6. Theoreticians usually assert that society is progressing economically, that the peoples are becoming wealthier, but statistics show that these same peoples manifest a higher suicide frequency from year to year: Is it not true, let us ask, that we are economically better off than our forefathers, or is the higher suicide tendency actually conditioned by the increase in wealth? To be able to answer this artful question, we must remember that poverty and misery as well as wealth also permit the suicide tendency to appear, and that the statistical data of suicide frequency may not therefore be used as an absolute measure of the economic situation.

Certainly, civilized peoples are wealthier now than before and their wealth is progressively increasing, but I do not believe that a just division of wealth yet exists. Considering the contemporary means for the exchange of ideas and for social agitation, both the just and unjust complaints of individuals are quickly spread. Those who believe themselves to be disadvantaged can easily associate and organize themselves. Thus, one can understand why, despite the increase of wealth among the peoples, dissatisfaction with the economic and social situation must be more widespread than previously, although in prior eras the general situation was no better. Modern peoples now strive to logically mold according to their own insight all their social conditions which have previously developed only spontaneously, so to speak. Besides the many other phenomena that spring from this striving, socialism in its more varied forms then appears in the economic sphere. But, along with this, a great, material striving is taking place all over, and this very striving is again and again animated anew by the great progress in the economic sphere. Animated, not born, because the entire economic work of mankind is only the external result of an inner spiritual development. Modern times unquestionably have become materialistic and pleasure-seeking. Unselfishness, moderation and ideals have become rare. In such a time, in which the material plays so great a role, men can not feel happy, must sooner or later become desolate and stagnant.[56] Thus a general dissatisfaction must develop as a necessary result of the contemporary economic situation, which, in many cases, becomes intensified into boredom with life. But, on the whole, it is not need or wealth, but the immoral evaluation of goods which makes the present age happy. The whole "social question" is the question whether we really want to become moral and reasonable.[57] Neither the wealthy nor the poor, neither the employer nor the worker is solely responsible for the contemporary situation. We are all to blame, and we must all atone and make amends for our general guilt.

PART 5: CONDITIONS OF SPIRITUAL CULTURE: INTELLECTUAL, MORAL AND RELIGIOUS EDUCATION: OUTLOOK ON LIFE IN GENERAL. *

1. On the previous pages we have studied and examined all the

---

* [Masaryk introduces here his notion of "Halbbildung," which we discussed in our preface, at n. 10.—Trans.]

[56]    Lecky (*Gesch. d. Geistes d. Aufklärung in Europa*, p. 455) finds our age mercenary, venal, and unheroic; Maudsley (*Phys. u. Path. d. Seele*, German trans., Bohm, p. 218) says: "The practical religion of daily life, the true standard gospel of life is money-making; the religion which we profess is Christianity." Cf. Lange, *Gesch. d. Materialismus*, II, p. 453 ff.

[57]    Funck-Brentano, *La Civilization et ses lois*, p. 358 ff.

causes of the suicide tendency with the exception of the conditions of spiritual culture, and we have found that they do not provide a sufficient explanation of the phenomenon in question. *The true causes of suicide must lie in the conditions of spiritual culture.* We have seen again and again that most conditions in fact have merely a disposing and little determining effect, but that in both cases their effectiveness is relatively weak. Now it is time to ask what is disposed and what is determined? Man.

Every freely chosen action springs from the character of man and is the more characteristic, the more important it is for the individual. Now there can hardly be a more important decision than whether to be or not to be, and it is therefore clear that suicide arises from the whole character of man in a special way. It directly depends on a person's whole outlook on life and the world; it depends on the judgment which the individual can pass on the worth of human life for the universe and especially for mankind; this decision is man's verdict about the world. How terrible this decision reads if one thinks of the enormous number of suicides at the present time!

Next to this, what are all the cries and jeers of the pessimists à la Schopenhauer!

The most proximate cause of suicide is always a misfortune that the victim considers so terrible that he no longer can bear life; therefore, the statistical evidence concerning the number of suicides is a measure of human misfortune; this measure is certainly not perfect because it tells us little or nothing concerning the intensity, frequency, duration, and extent of misfortune; nevertheless, it says enough.

The misfortune that a man experiences can be real or it can be imagined, depending on his intellectual and moral constitution. For those affected it is certainly always decisive, always great enough to surrender life; but in most cases the objective observer sees that the cause was trivial in relation to the loss, and he is astounded that small and insignificant causes often produce such results. He soon perceives that an intellectual or moral defect has almost always darkened the suicide's judgment. Not without basis does suicide appear incomprehensible and frightful to normal human understanding, because in fact every halfway normal and reasonable man does not commit it. Every healthy outlook on life and the world ascribes a high value to life and seeks to maintain it, following the natural drive for self-preservation. We understand perfectly, for example, why a prisoner can stubbornly bear the most terrible tortures thinking of the gallows to which his confession would bring him, but we are horrified that a man should willingly end his life.

> The weariest and most loathed worldly life
> That age, ache, penury, and imprisonment
> Can lay on nature, is a paradise
> To what we fear of death.

It is our task to examine the present outlook on life and to discover how it happens that in spite of all the progress in almost every area of practical life, men feel not happier, but, on the contrary, unhappier. We must investigate which conditions of spiritual culture are inimical to life to such a high degree.

2. *Intellectual education.* From the fact that the tendency to suicide increases each year in all civilized countries, while the education of the people and their instruction is everywhere improving, one sees that a greater education in any case does not impede the appearance of the suicide tendency. One can reach the same conclusion from a comparison of the city and the province. But the great correspondence of the suicide frequency of entire countries and in certain areas with the general state of education, the fact that among uneducated peoples suicide is less frequent than among the educated, leads one to expect that a casual connection exists between education and suicide tendency.

Statisticians must answer the question whether criminality rises or declines with increasing intellectual education, and many have spoken for and many have spoken against the idea. From the beginning it is clear, with respect to this question, that intellectual education in and of itself does not necessarily influence criminality and morality, and statistical induction in fact shows that certain crimes increase; murder, crimes against morality, rape, infanticide, general moral relapses increase in the most highly educated nations; similarly, crimes become increasingly frequent which require lying, treachery, deceit, and fraud for their execution, the so-called "refined crimes," while the grosser crimes become less frequent. From this we see that higher level of education suppresses only certain crimes, and contrariwise, that it permits others to occur more readily and with greater frequency. We should have to discuss this at length were we to decide what is our position; at this time we can only affirm that *intellectual education brings with it a certain refinement but not improvement nor higher morality*; intelligence can be both good or evil.

The situation is similar in our case. A higher intellectual cultivation does not, as such, lead more readily to suicide; but it refines man, makes his life richer and many-sided, brings him into new and more difficult situations, and through this, confronts him sooner with the question to be or not to be than the less refined person who, because of his narrower horizons, loves life through his simplicity and diffidence, and the question to be or not to be never enters his head. Now, higher intellectual education does not mean proper and true intellectual education; on the contrary, we may expect that between the extremes of noneducation, as is represented in our states by the simplest peasant, and the high education of a university professor, there exists a middle education or, more properly, a half-education of the most manifold gradations and shadings. And in fact it is so, but this half-education is dangerous if, as is mostly the case, it is identical with inharmonious, disunified, and unmethodical organization of the mind. If one closely examines the "educated" and asks of what use their public school, high school, and university education has been to them, the conviction grows that the incompleteness of education stands in direct relation to the degree of schooling. Men know much, very much, but their knowledge has not nearly the influence of their lives that it should; and therein lies the great defect: *we learn much too much for school and not enough for life*. Therefore, half-education disposes to the suicide tendency, entirely overlooking for the moment that intellectual education at the present time is acquired at the expense of moral education.

We can say, ceteris paribus, *the suicide tendency is greatest in those countries and nations where unmethodical and imprac-tical half-education is greatest.* Knowledge which cannot be used makes its possessor a victim of fantasy, of hypercritical nonsense, destroying the desire for useful labor, creating needs which cannot be satisfied, and leading in the end to boredom with life.

In suicide statistics we have then an approximately correct measure of half-education. I say approximately correct because for a definite judgment and comparison of various areas, nations, regions, and classes of people, all conditions which more or less influence the suicide tendency anywhere must be considered. The suicide frequency is a good measure but not the only one. If one compares the known data with the evidence concerning schools, libraries, art collections, presses, book trades, means of commerce and communication for the exchange of ideas in general, finally the results of all these means of education, and examines wherever possible not only quantity but also quality, one sees how the suicide data generally agree with these statistics. Even trivial things agree with this result; for example, the reported use of paper. To illustrate the foregoing, we shall use public school education; according to Levasseur's report to the International Exhibition at Vienna in 1873, there were the following number of students per 100 inhabitants:

| | | | |
|---|---|---|---|
| United States | 18 | Ireland | 8 |
| Kingdom of Saxony | 17.5 | Russia | 7.5 |
| Baden | 16 | Italy | 6.5 |
| Württemberg | 15.5 | Greece | 5.5 |
| Denmark | 15 | Argentine Republic | 5 |
| Germany | 15 | Chile | 4 |
| Prussia | 15 | Uruguay | 3.7 |
| Sweden | 13.7 | Portugal | 2.5 |
| Bavaria | 13 | Serbia, Rumania | 2 |
| Netherlands | 13 | Mexico | 2 |
| France | 13 | Peru | 1.5 |
| Norway | 12.5 | Ecuador | 1.3 |
| England | 12 | Brazil | 1.2 |
| Belgium | 11.9 | Turkey | 1 |
| Austria | 9 | Venezuela | 0.3 |
| Spain | 9 | Egypt | 0.3 |

This and similar data for popular education corresponds, on the whole, with the data for the suicide frequency of peoples everywhere; they cannot completely correspond, because—assuming both sets of data were complete—popular education in and of itself is not the major cause of suicide.

It is difficult to measure popular education, especially its quality, and though I hesitate to express my opinion, it must be done. After reflection I have come to the following conclusion.[58]

Education in the schools is best organized and most uniform in Germany, where the state is responsible for all schools and sees

[58]    1. In rank order of peoples with developed school systems, Germany has the fewest people who do not have an education, particularly in Saxony, the classical land of formal schooling; Prussia, in 1871, had 13 percent of its population with no formal education. Public education in Switzerland is excellent. In 1870, there were 17.15 percent men in the total population of the United States and 23.05 percent women without any formal education; this group was composed mostly of the immigrants from Ireland, Scandanavia, and Bohemia. In 1866, 32.84 percent of the total population of France could neither read nor write; in 1872, in France, 23.89 percent of those between 6–20 years of age were completely uninstructed, of those over 20 years of age 33.37 percent of both, an average of 30.77 percent. In Austria, the following percentage of conscripted recruits from 1872–74 *could* read and write:

| | | | |
|---|---|---|---|
| Lower Austria | 94.2 | Tyrol | 53.4 |
| Silesia | 91.2 | Carinthia | 52.6 |
| Salzburg | 88.5 | Croatia | 42.3 |
| Upper Austria | 85.7 | Maritimes | 29.5 |
| Bohemia | 84.7 | Galicia | 15.2 |
| Styria | 73.7 | Carniola | 7.3 |
| Moravia | 71.4 | Bukowina | 6.2 |
| Hungary | 59.9 | Dalmatia | 1.6 |

In 1875, 58 percent of those over 6 years of age in Hungary could neither read nor write.

In England, in every 100 marriage applicants, the following *could not* write:

| | | |
|---|---|---|
| 1875 | England | 17.2 bridegrooms, 23.2 brides |
| 1872 | Scotland | 10.4 bridegrooms, 20.5 brides |
| 1875 | Ireland | 30.3 bridegrooms, 36.7 brides |

In 1877, of 3,154,973 children compelled to attend school in England and Wales, only 1,976,899 remained in school until the legally required minimum education was attained. In 1861, only 40.52 percent of those between 6–12 years of age in Italy attended school, and only 57.27 percent from 1875–76; there were still 19½ million illiterates in 1871, some 67.5

to their administration; but education in school does not replace the practical education which man can and should acquire throughout his life. In Germany, however, life in relation to the school

---

percent of those over 10 years of age, 68.2 percent of those over 6 years of age. In Spain, in 1860, only 3,129,921 could read and write, or one-fifth of the population; Kolb draws attention to the following: in 1850, children were limited entirely to no other text than the Catechism—papal bull; Ferdinand VII closed the universities because he considered education to be dangerous, and instituted a school to teach the art of bullfighting.

2. Secondary and intermediate education is best in Germany, Switzerland and Austria; the universities in these countries are at least genuine centers of learning.

3. The Germans are very fond of writing; 13,925 books appeared in Germany in 1877; the French and English write far fewer books.

4. England and the United States have the most newspapers.

5. In 1875, each person in the total population received:

|  | Letters | Newspapers |
|---|---|---|
| Great Britain |  | 34.5 |
| Switzerland | 27.3 | 17.2 |
| Germany (Imperial Postal District) | 15.6 | 8.0 |
| Württemberg | 13.3 | 14.0 |
| Bavaria | 11.5 | 15.5 |
| Belgium | 13.0 | 12.5 |
| France | 10.2 | 4.8 |
| Austria | 10.6 | 2.9 |
| Hungary | 4.4 | 1.8 |
| Russia | 0.5 | 0.5 |
| Turkey | 0.2 | 0.1 |

6. European paper consumed by each person in:

| United States | 14.0 kg. | Scandinavia | 5.0 kg. |
|---|---|---|---|
| Switzerland | 6.3 kg. | France | 3.6 kg. |
| Germany | 6.0 kg. | Austria- | |
| Belgium | 5.1 kg. | Hungary | 2.5 kg. |
| Great Britain | 5.0 kg. | Italy | 1.4 kg. |
| | | Russia | 0.9 kg. |

7. Transportation of persons on railroads in 1875:

| Austria-Hungary | with 38 millions, | 41,396,384 persons |
|---|---|---|
| Germany | with 43 millions, | 202,372,930 persons |
| France | with 37 millions, | 116,546,175 persons |
| Great Britain | with 33½ millions, | 506,975,234 persons |

teaches very little: life and school go their separate ways. The student learns a great deal, but does not apply it to life, especially in the military; the entire educational policy of Germany is aimed at the training of an intelligent army. Germany has very many and very great scholars; they stand high above the people, writing not for the people, but for themselves; the German people themselves think and learn much but only too frequently that which is useless and impractical.

The situation is similar in Austria; among us also one sees more attention paid to diplomas than to true and practical, useful knowledge.

In England, the education in the schools is defective; Dickens has described unforgettably in his writings the methods of the private schools. But life outside the school offers rich education, and the English people, although less learned than the German people, are more rational and put their knowledge to better use, applying it more to all conditions of life. Many times have I heard Germans say that a simple English workman understands more than a German university graduate; and this observation is correct insofar as it can also be said that a solid education is not obtained through school attendance alone. Among us in Austria, at least, one has almost no further theoretical interest beyond his schooling just because theory and practice are not one.

The United States is the opposite of Germany. There knowledge is ignored unless it can be applied, and people seek to educate themselves as much as possible outside of school. There are few scholars, but, to make up for this, education is more uniform and more widespread; knowledge and life are one.

France only recently has begun to plan for good school instruction; heretofore, education was acquired more in the salon than in the school and thence diffused. Italian schools are poor, but better than the Spanish and Portuguese.

The schools in Switzerland and Holland are good; in Russia and the Southern European countries, the dawn of education has just appeared.

The following groupings may be made in terms of what has been said:

a. Germany, Austria, Denmark, Sweden, Norway

   b. Switzerland, Holland
   c. England, United States
   d. France, Italy
   e. Russia, Yugoslavia, Rumania
   f. Spain, Portugal

It is clear that where school and life most widely diverge, half-education, in the bad sense, must be most widespread, and that suicide can appear relatively most often in these nations.

Finally, more specific attention must be given to the parallelism between education and the suicide tendency for individuals. With respect to both, the urban surpasses the rural population; the male sex surpasses the female; and professions that require greater intellectual education contribute more suicides. Concerning confession, Protestants are more highly educated than Catholics; the Greek Church exhibits the least education except for non-Christian followers of the Koran.

3. *Moral education.* Man not only possesses intellect, he also possesses will; to correctly interpret human action requires recognition and evaluation of not only the influence of intellect, but also the moral factors of will. The question of the moral education of suicides is therefore no less important than the above mentioned study of their intellectual education. For as the whole man is an enduring unity of intelligence and morality, we will attain a clear understanding of the social mass phenomenon of suicide only when we have recognized the moral atmosphere from which the tragic phenomenon springs.

To this end I introduce several tables as they appear in older and more recent documents, the most important of which is the list drawn up by Wagner according to the French classification.[59]

[59]    The value of these tables is not lessened by their age. The phenomenon of suicide remains essentially the same everywhere, and therefore the older and oldest reports of causes and motives do, in fact, provide equally valuable material. The value of the tables does not decrease, however, to the extent that the classification is not appropriate to the data. (Wagner believes that the French classification is apparently correct, because the numbers in the particular annual columns are repeated with great regularity, but this actually means only that the same type of cases, and no [or few] new ones appeared.)

| Causes and Motives of Suicide | France 1856–61 | | | Saxony 1847–58 | | | Belgium 1840–49 |
|---|---|---|---|---|---|---|---|
| | Men | Women | Total | Men | Women | Total | Total |
| 1. Unknown | 1768 | 371 | 2139 | 531 | 100 | 631 | 616 |
| 2. Weariness with life | 772 | 179 | 951 | 302 | 49 | 351 | 63 |
| 3. Mental illness | 4912 | 2509 | 7421 | 1152 | 599 | 1751 | 851 |
|   a. Insanity | 3931 | 2115 | 6046 | 318 | 177 | 495 | 751 |
|   b. Melancholy, Hypochondria | 273 | 94 | 367 | 834 | 422 | 1256 | 2 |
|   c. Monomania | 266 | 95 | 361 | — | — | — | 7 |
|   d. Derangement | — | — | — | — | — | — | 71 |
|   e. Brain fever | 210 | 98 | 308 | — | — | — | 10 |
|   f. Imbecility, idiocy | 232 | 107 | 339 | — | — | — | 10 |
| 4. Passion with accompanying derangement | 10 | 14 | 24 | 6 | 2 | 8 | 1 |
|   a. Religious ecstacies | 3 | 13 | 16 | 6 | 2 | 8 | 1 |
|   b. Political exultation | 7 | 1 | 8 | — | — | — | — |
| 5. Bodily affliction | 2031 | 620 | 2651 | 280 | 96 | 376 | 32 |
| 6. Passions | 424 | 321 | 745 | 190 | 74 | 264 | 224 |
|   a. Violent anger | 8 | 5 | 13 | — | — | — | 2 |
|   b. Anger, despair | — | — | — | 123 | 47 | 170 | 174 |
|   c. Unrequited love | 330 | 271 | 601 | 67 | 27 | 94 | 38 |
|   d. Jealousy | 86 | 45 | 131 | — | — | — | 10 |
|   e. Ambition | — | — | — | — | — | — | — |
| 7. Vices | 2417 | 315 | 2732 | 608 | 29 | 637 | 171 |
|   a. Drunkenness | 378 | 41 | 419 | — | — | — | 104 |
|   b. Dipsomania | 1261 | 166 | 1427 | 594 | 29 | 623 | — |
|   c. Dissipation | 716 | 105 | 821 | — | — | — | 67 |
|   d. Gambling and losses from gambling | 37 | 1 | 38 | 14 | — | 14 | — |
|   e. Idleness | 25 | 2 | 27 | — | — | — | — |
| 8. Sorrow and grief over others | 231 | 100 | 331 | — | — | — | — |
|   a. Loss of relatives | 208 | 93 | 301 | — | — | — | — |
|   b. Homesickness | 14 | 2 | 16 | — | — | — | — |
|   c. Other similar cases | 9 | 5 | 14 | — | — | — | — |
| 9. Discord and anger over relatives | 1973 | 627 | 2600 | 88 | 41 | 129 | 193 |

| Causes and Motives of Suicide | France 1856–61 | | | Saxony 1847–58 | | | Belgium 1840–49 |
|---|---|---|---|---|---|---|---|
| | Men | Women | Total | Men | Women | Total | Total |
| a. Filial ingratitude | 74 | 39 | 113 | — | — | — | — |
| b. Wrath of children against parents | 51 | 17 | 68 | — | — | — | 1 |
| c. Clash of interests in family | 42 | 7 | 49 | — | — | — | — |
| d. Children of vice | 1 | 1 | 2 | — | — | — | — |
| e. Domestic discord | 1762 | 551 | 2313 | 88 | 41 | 129 | 192 |
| f. Domestic quarrels in general | — | — | — | — | — | — | — |
| g. Strife with, rebuke from, the head of household | 43 | 12 | 55 | — | — | — | — |
| 10. Financial distress | 2447 | 317 | 2764 | 594 | 46 | 640 | 197 |
| a. Poverty and fear of it | 897 | 171 | 1068 | 396 | 45 | 441 | 110 |
| b. Disrupted financial conditions | 1108 | 74 | 1182 | 198 | 1 | 199 | 66 |
| c. Loss of wealth | 153 | 16 | 169 | — | — | — | 1 |
| d. Loss of business | 88 | 19 | 107 | — | — | — | 7 |
| e. Unemployment | — | — | — | — | — | — | 4 |
| f. Loss by law suit | 27 | 7 | 34 | — | — | — | — |
| g. Other losses for like reasons | 115 | 18 | 133 | — | — | — | — |
| h. Remorse over bankruptcy | 34 | 3 | 37 | — | — | — | — |
| i. Unfulfilled hopes (financial) | 25 | 9 | 34 | — | — | — | — |
| 11. Dissatisfaction with situation | 200 | 53 | 253 | — | — | — | — |
| a. With social position | 13 | 6 | 19 | — | — | — | — |
| b. With military service | 67 | — | 67 | — | — | — | — |
| c. Other circumstances | 120 | 47 | 167 | — | — | — | — |
| 12. Remorse and shame | 43 | 115 | 158 | — | — | — | — |
| a. Pangs of conscience | 43 | 18 | 61 | — | — | — | — |
| b. Shame, fear of scandal | — | 97 | 97 | — | — | — | — |
| c. Illegitimate pregnancy | — | 97 | 97 | — | — | — | — |

| Causes and Motives of Suicide | France 1856–61 | | | Saxony 1847–58 | | | Belgium 1840–49 |
|---|---|---|---|---|---|---|---|
| | Men | Women | Total | Men | Women | Total | Total |
| 13. Fear of Punishment | 1332 | 196 | 1528 | — | — | — | — |
| a. Fear of judicial investigation | 1091 | 176 | 1267 | — | — | — | — |
| b. Fear of Execution or punishment | 120 | 20 | 140 | — | — | — | — |
| c. Fear of military disciplinary punishment | 121 | — | 121 | — | — | — | — |
| 14. Suicide after murder, etc. | 153 | 12 | 165 | — | — | — | — |
| Total | 18713 | 5749 | 24462 | 4317 | 1180 | 5497 | 2428 |
| Total without the Unknown Cases | 16945 | 5378 | 22323 | 3786 | 1080 | 4866 | 1812[60] |

60  The following relative estimates of the number of each type per 1000 cases may serve as a more convenient survey of the thirteen classes cited above:

| Causes | France | | | Saxony | | | Belgium |
|---|---|---|---|---|---|---|---|
| | Male | Female | Both sexes | Male | Female | Both sexes | Both sexes |
| 1. Weariness with life | 46 | 33 | 43 | 80 | 45 | 72 | 35 |
| 2. Mental illness | 290 | 467 | 333 | 304 | 555 | 359 | 470 |
| 3. Derangement and passion | 0.59 | 2.6 | 1.08 | 1.6 | 1.9 | 1.6 | 0.55 |
| 4. Physical suffering | 120 | 115 | 119 | 74 | 89 | 77.3 | 17.7 |
| 5. Passion | 25 | 60 | 33 | 50 | 68 | 54 | 124 |
| 6. Vice | 143 | 58 | 122 | 160 | 27 | 131 | 94 |
| 7. Grief for another | 13.7 | 18.8 | 14.9 | — | — | — | — |
| 8. Discord in family | 117 | 117 | 116 | 24.3 | 38 | 26.5 | 106 |
| 9. Unhappiness due to financial conditions | 145 | 59 | 124 | 157 | 43 | 132 | 109 |
| 10. Dissatisfaction with one's situation | 11.7 | 9.8 | 11.3 | — | — | — | 2.2 |
| 11. Remorse and shame | 2.5 | 21.4 | 7.1 | — | — | — | 5 |
| 12. Fear of punishment | 78 | 36 | 68 | 149 | 133 | 147 | 36 |
| 13. Suicide after murder | 9 | 2.2 | 7.4 | — | — | — | — |

*The motives of suicide are, as is evident, predominately immoral; the more honorable and just motives pale by comparison with the number of dishonorable ones.* Unrequited love, pain and anguish over another, especially over the loss of a relative, and remorse and shame are seldom listed, whereas vice, love of money, and dishonorable motives in general are the most active. The following case, for example, belongs to the curiosities of suicide statistics: a father kills himself to provide for his children with insurance.

The situation appears in an even worse light if one considers that suicide is, in almost all cases, the tragic end of a long chain of mistakes and moral defects, and that even where the motives appears honorable, the act is still an escape from the despair en-

---

Oettingen has published the following table:

| Causes | % Male | % Female |
|---|---|---|
| Mental illness (including political and religious fantasies) | 29.1 | 46.8 |
| Physical suffering | 11.4 | 11.3 |
| Disrupted financial conditions | 14.9 | 6.4 |
| Vice (drunkenness, gambling, dissipation, etc.) | 14 | 5 |
| Family quarrels | 9.6 | 10.1 |
| Fear of punishment (including remorse, shame, pangs of conscience) | 10.3 | 8.2 |
| Weariness with life | 5.9 | 4.1 |
| Passion (anger, despair, jealousy, ambition, unfortunate love) | 2.9 | 5.9 |
| General dissatisfaction with one's situation | 0.9 | 0.8 |
| Grief for another (loss of relatives) | 1.0 | 1.4 |

Brierre de Boismont found these causes among the 4595 cases recorded by him:

| Causes | No. of Suicides |
|---|---|
| Mental illness (*folie, délire aigu*) | 707 |
| Drunkenness | 530 |
| Illness | 405 |
| Domestic sorrows | 361 |
| Sorrow in general, other circumstances | 311 |
| Love | 306 |

gendered by one's own guilt. Almost every suicide, as we see from the efficacy of its causes,[61] has been prepared long in advance; for this reason one must view suicide as the termination of a long development and recognize that suicides, with few exceptions, are immoral.

This sounds severe and requires some explanation. "Immoral" means many things because there are many kinds of immorality. The suicide, on the whole, can be better than many who remain alive; he also can be as bad or worse than the living. By his act, however, he demonstrates a moral weakness, a lack of moral principle which can be evaluated correctly only if one considers that the determining causes in the great majority of cases are so minute and trivial that we can hardly comprehend how such petty

| | |
|---|---|
| Poverty | 282 |
| Loss of money, greediness | 277 |
| Weariness with life | 237 |
| Character (weak, overexcited, sad, or hypochondriac) | 145 |
| Pangs of conscience, fear of scandal or of prosecution | 134 |
| Bad conduct | 121 |
| Laziness | 56 |
| Jealousy | 54 |
| Gambling | 44 |
| Unemployment | 43 |
| Pride, arrogance | 26 |
| Various political motives | 38 |
| Unknown motives | 518 |
| | 4595 cases |

Finally, the official report for Italy in 1874:

| Causes | % Male | % Female |
|---|---|---|
| Poverty, loss of wealth ............ | 28 | 11.5 |
| Weariness with life, domestic misfortune ............ | 13.2 | 7.3 |
| Unrequited love, jealousy ......... | 4.8 | 6.8 |
| Fear of punishment, scandal ...... | 5.8 | 5.2 |
| Drunkenness .................... | 1.8 | — |
| Physical illness .................. | 26.7 | 40.4 |
| Mental illness ................... | 19.7 | 28.8 |

61　　Cf. chap. 4, no. 1.

causes can have a result of such magnitude. For it is a fact that the great majority of men bear similar, identical and, even far worse misfortunes, uprightly, and for every man whose life becomes intolerable, there are thousands who endure and triumph over the same misfortune. The special immorality of suicides therefore rests on their characteristic hopelessness and despair, on their lack of trust, on their belief that the destiny of man be improved, and on their lack of energy to work willingly for the betterment of their destiny.

Accordingly, this may clarify what is meant by the immorality of suicides. First, the statistical evidence concerning motives shows us that most suicides lead a life that is immoral in many respects; they are given to drunkenness and every kind of debauchery. Immoral conduct then creates a disposition to suicide. Secondly, the suicide reveals the highest degree of that typical lack of principle, and, mistaking the true mission of life, shrinks from and casts aside the labor and work of man for the sake of others.

4. Naturally, much may be said in detail about the various immoral causes and motives, but I will confine myself to the most important ones.

A. Most suicides are committed in an emotional or passionate state, or in a mood whose make-up eliminates clear deliberation. The story is told of a young man who, as the result of a quarrel, suddenly fastened on the idea of suicide; he ran to a store to buy a gun; the dealer gave him too high a price; a violent argument occurred between buyer and seller, and finally the hot-head forgot why he wished to purchase the weapon. A scholar decided to throw himself into the Thames, but on the way was attacked by thieves and forgot his purpose. A woman decided to throw herself into the sea; on the way, by chance, a vessel of cold water—the anecdote takes place in winter—was poured on her head and her desire for suicide was cured forever.

The sudden seizures of the suicide impulse are like the violent cries of some children who eventually do not know why they are crying; like the child, the overwrought man does not really know why he wants to kill himself. If they have the undeserved good luck to fail as a direct result of their great agitation and haste, their intention, their suicidal impulse, disappears just as it appeared. If their suicide attempt miscarries, such people are always glad, as Kant rightly observes, to have their self-inflicted cuts sewn up. The man who in complete desperation throws himself into a well gives those who run up, after the cold bath has restored his senses, the best advice on how to pull him out.

Such cases are very instructive, and along with suicides committed by the mentally ill, offer the best key to a psychological understanding of the suicide's mental state.

Unrequited love has a more destructive effect on the woman than on the man. He, in turn, destroys his life only too often through overweening ambition. In fact, many researchers have already stated that megalomania is one of the greatest evils of our time. Suicide statistics confirm it; it can happen, for example, that a wine-taster kills himself because he does not want to suffer the shame of having erred in a type of wine. Such insignificant things make life bearable or unbearable for man!

B. The rubric "weariness with life" needs some clarification. There are, namely, men who in fact take their lives from boredom: ennui, laziness, idleness, shirking labor. In a few cases, an actual disgust with life appears; this is a morbid condition and frequently develops among ascetics and roués.[62]

C. Alcoholic beverages play an important role. The intoxicated person kills himself easily, whether his intoxication results from habitual or one-time drunkenness; in general any drinking, and not just to excess, is dangerous because of its evil-disposing effects. The intemperate person ruins his health and morality, destroys body and soul, and finally reaches weariness with life, even impressing it on the coming generation like the mark of Cain.[63]

[62]    In the monasteries of the Middle Ages, this illness was given the name *accedia*. Chaucer well describes the condition.

[63]    The morbidity and mortality of drinkers is higher than that of non-drinkers; their average length of life is shorter. According to Oesterlen, 4.59 percent of beer drinkers die annually, 5.99 percent of liquor drinkers, and 6.19 percent of those who drink both.

Children conceived while their parents were intoxicated are often born with a predisposition to mental derangement. This is true not only for the children of drunkards, but also for the children of usually tem-

A frequent thesis is that drunkenness is increasing in all nations and, as Casper, Lunier, David, Brierre de Boismont, and others believe, that the increase of suicide parallels that of alcoholism. But, overlooking the fact that the question of the general increase in drunkenness is difficult to answer, and that many investigators assert the opposite, Sweden serves as an example of a constant increase in suicides with a simultaneous decrease in drunkenness and particularly in suicide as a result of alcoholism. The increase in the tendency to suicide, therefore, does not everywhere depend directly or exclusively on the increase in alcoholism. Where there is much drunkenness, there may also be many suicides; but where there are many suicides, there are not always many drunkards. Suicide and drunkenness, as Baer correctly observes, have a common source in the way in which justified and unjustified demands for a so-called mode of life worthy of men are inherited and pursued in an unhealthy manner by all classes of civilization. The search for gratification, for idleness, for luxury, for a splendid appearance, the frivolous light-heartedness of cynical-materialistic thoughts and actions, the inability and impossibility of carrying on the stern struggle for existence with such an outlook on life— the pseudo-civilization that produces these also produces drunkards and suicides.[64] Drunkenness is thus related to suicide as an effect of one and the same great cause; they are both a partial phenomenon, if I may thus express it. Suicide is the negation of hap-

---

perate parents—children who owe their existence to a harmful hour of drunkenness. Flemming, *Pathologie und Therapie der psychosen*, p. 107. Cf. Magnus Huss, *Über chronische Alkoholkrankheiten oder Alcoholismus chronicus* (German trans., V. C. Busch), 1852. Renaudin (*Annal, med.-psychol.*, 1853, Jänner) substantiated the parallel between the increase in drunkenness and the increase in both mental illness and idiocy. On the other hand, Morel (*Traité des dégénérescences*, etc., 1857) shows that many illnesses favor the appearance and spread of drunkenness, through which it is apparent how drunkenness and the dangers of life stand in an intimate reciprocity.

[64]    Baer, *Der Alcoholismus, seine Verbreitung und seine Wirkung auf den individuellen und socialen Organismus, sowie die Mittel, ihn zu bekämpfen*, 1878, p. 310.

piness; drunkenness, the religion of materialism, is supposed to replace it. If man is what he eats, he believes and hopes according to what he drinks—death.

Despite this relationship, however, drunkenness can be and often is a direct, effective cause of the tendency to suicide.[65]

Not all alcoholic beverages have an equally deleterious effect; liquor is the worst, and the tragedy is that its consumption is everywhere increasing at a frightening rate, especially among the lower classes.

Finally, it must be noted that the effect of drunkenness is not the same under all conditions. In cold regions there is more drinking than in milder climes; thus it is that in England, Germany, and especially Russia, alcoholism is a stronger cause of the suicide tendency than in the southern areas. The male sex is more affected by this vice than the female. The poor usually yield to the use of raw liquor, and many professions are especially favorable to the development of drunkenness: singers, musicians, and such. Many poets and men of genius are easy preys of drink, and it is known that in this century even a crowned ruler died of *delerium tremens*. These and similar variations obviously modify the suicide frequency, insofar as they are also modifications of a strong cause of suicide.

D. Where Bacchus lights a fire, Venus waits to tend the furnace. *Sexual immorality,* because of its destructive effect on the physical and mental welfare of the individual and of whole peoples, is especially alarming; considering the acknowledged licentiousness of our time, it is one of the strongest indirect causes of the modern suicide tendency.[66]

Statisticians inform us of the increase of *illegitimate births, obscene crimes,* especially *rape* (among the cultivated classes!), and finally of *prostitution*; in short—the sexual life of modern society is base and immoral. The appaling indirect affect of the last-mentioned dark evil on the spread of the suicide tendency is to be

---

[65]    According to Browne Reid (*The Temperance Cyclopaedia*, p. 217) drunkenness is the most powerful cause of suicide, followed by domestic troubles, cares of life, physical pain, and mental illness.
[66]    The unfavorable effect of onanism should be especially stressed.

especially borne in mind.[67] Prostitution and its handmaid, syphilis, sap the strength of civilized peoples; the debility of mind and body makes it more difficult to bear psychical and physical illness, and for this reason it spurs the tendency to suicide.[68] Public and secret prostitution increases today in all areas and, what is most terrible, this despicable profession is a stage of transition, because, as Parent-Duchatelet has shown, prostitutes return to society as soon as possible and then as wives and mothers infect the chastity and morality of nations. The increase in suicide, as Haushofer says, thus forms the sinister counterpart to this great collective guilt of society.

E. A characteristic phenomenon is *suicide after murder and manslaughter*, as a result of remorse and pangs of conscience over a rash act.

But murder can also be carried out as the result of a previously conceived suicidal impulse.

Thoughts of suicide are often the primary emotions and murder follows; thus, for example, fathers kill their children so that they may more easily be able to take their lives.

Again, men who are about to commit the horrible deed kill those who disturb them at the crucial moment.

Murder as an act of revenge is relatively seldom committed before suicide. Considering that insults, maltreatment, etc., are effective causes of suicide, it might be thought that many people would first take their revenge and then kill themselves. But it is not in keeping with the nature of suicide to view the individual ego as the cause of weariness with life, as if it were a kind of self-accusation and confession of complicity in the great collective guilt of society.

F. As a curiosity we mention that attempts at suicide are also made out of speculation. The newspapers reportedly print news of swindlers jumping into the water to arouse sympathy and receive gifts: one such subject has repeated his comic act in many cities,

---

[67] Prostitutes very seldom take their lives.

[68] Syphilis breeds many diseases that are closely related to mental illness and the tendency to suicide: scrofula, tuberculosis, English disease, gout, neuralgia, rheumatism.

supporting himself by attempted suicide until he was finally forbidden to practice his trade.

5. The motivation of suicide is, as one can easily imagine, different in different circumstances. Thus the varied seasons—to recall only the most important influence—allow different maxima of the same form of suicide to appear; city and rural areas, certain sexes and ages, and the different kinds of occupations and economic conditions all have their own peculiar motivations.

On the whole, different motives operate in different nations, or the same ones in unequal strengths, but it is significant that *in spite of larger or smaller deviations, the same motives appear in all countries and among all peoples, and, as the statistical evidence demonstrates, also have a relatively equal strength.* This fact shows that *the general, diffused tendency to suicide can be traced to one or more universally effective causes* whose definition is the problem of our next investigation.[69]

6. It remains only to compare *the moral education of suicides with the intellectual education,* and to interpret the unity of the two. We know that the tendency to suicide is caused by half-educa-

---

69    Unknown causes and motives indicate only that it was not ascertained which of the various motives was operative. These are not completely new causes and motives or those which have been overlooked, but ones which were not substantiated because those responsible for ascertaining causes must often spare the feelings of the relatives in a tragic situation. The true cause is frequently hidden, and a false one given, usually mental illness, melancholy, or something similar. The following would be classified as "unknown" causes and motives: In many areas, the superstition is widespread that one who hangs himself hears wonderful music, angels singing, and sees a radiant paradise. I know of one case where a young peasant desired this pleasure and wanted to hang "for a little while." The luckless youth paid for his curiosity with death.

Similarly, cases are reported where someone wanted only to attempt suicide, in order to study the effects of hanging. Bacon tells us of his friend who wanted to hang for a short while to observe in himself the symptoms of strangulation. He would have paid for his curiosity with his life had his acquaintance not chanced to find him at the critical moment and rescued him.

(Both these cases are really "self-manslaughter," but would appear to be suicides if we did not know the motives of the deceased).

tion. If we now discover that it is also caused by lack of moral principle—as we shall briefly term it—beyond and in addition to intellectual half-education, then the social mass phenomenon of suicide shows us modern society in its true light. Civilized society is weary of life, but its weariness springs from its defective intellectual and moral education: intelligence and morality have not been either well or uniformly cultivated and perfected. We are too wise to be good, too bad to be completely wise. Our outlook on life and the world is not harmonious, neither good nor beautiful enough to sustain us or to let us enjoy life. To state it briefly and frankly: half-intellectual and half-moral education is the great cause of the modern weariness with life: this "half-" gives us a false standard of earthly happiness and satisfaction; it makes bitter the fruits of our progress in all fields of practical life, and year in, year out, claims an untold sacrifice of suicide.

7. *Religious education.* The morality of man, his whole labor and striving, preserves in religion that essential inspiration which stamps man with the mark of the divine. It is not our problem to investigate what religion is and how it appears among men; it is sufficient for us to know that it exists and that, like the invisible fragrance of the flower, it invests man with his true value. Remove the fragrance of the flower and it will delight your eye, but you will no longer find it so delicate; remove religious feeling from man and you have made of him a creature which you respect and perhaps even admire, but one which you cannot love with a full heart.

Religion—I am thinking especially of monotheistic religion—gives man comfort in all situations of life through theism and the belief in immortality, hope in the face of adversity, and the stimulus for the love of mankind. The religious man is therefore joyful in all the circumstances of life; his faith, his conviction, and his assurance bind him not only to heaven, but also to earth, to life.

The living practice of religion, the subjective feeling, naturally leads to an inner union of like-minded men and expresses itself in the life of the church. Thus arises religious organization, which permeates the entire life of society. All agree that humanity needs a spiritual guide to the true, the good, and the beautiful, but this guide can only possess that power which is able to fill the innermost depths of the human soul, and that is religion. Thus, the power of religion is so great and is visible in all the works and ways of men. This spiritual power over the people, however, is wielded by the church (public religious opinion and, in particular, the clergy), the religious organization of society.

If the practice of religion disappears, the power of the church disappears, along with comfort, hope, and joy in life. Individual spirits may well be able, as they believe, to live the true, the good, and the beautiful without any religion, yet that is really mere deception. For example, if Mill wishes to found a religion of humanity without theism and belief in immortality, he still wants it to be a religion; and the only thing we would have to investigate is whether religious feeling is even possible without these two doctrines, as often stated. Mill wants no Christianity, but he wants a religion— surely he himself lacked most a genuine and warm religious feeling. Those familiar with Mill's works, especially his ethical and sociological writings, will have noted his deficiency. Comte, who founded a religion of humanity, has deep religious feeling and is certainly Christian, but he seeks to unite this religious feeling not with God, but with men. A man like Mill, who seeks to surpass positive religion in goodness with his philosophy, will naturally provide for himself, to a certain degree, that which any of the better religions could have afforded him. But the great mass of people have no substitute at all if they give up their religion. But how many spirits like Mill are there? I know very few, and yet I know many philosophers and educated people. One often hears the opinion that religion is for the masses only, not for us—the educated. The educated! Of the thousands who say that, there is hardly one among them who even approaches the education of Mill; rather, these are the men of this half-education whose worth we have described previously.

*In fact, the modern half-education and lack of moral principle appear as irreligiosity; and thus we finally conclude that the modern tendency to suicide has its true cause in the irreligiosity of our time.* The above exposition of the meaning of religion for the life of humanity makes this understandable. A harmonious religious world-view makes life tolerable under all circumstances, even the life of a Job; irreligiosity makes it unbearable with the first blow.

Many objections can be raised to our conclusion. For example, a German cultural historian does not consider irreligiosity as the cause of the modern suicide tendency because many men, brought to religious frenzy, take their lives—on account of religion! It is not to be believed. Religious feeling, if it is misguided, naturally leads to mental illness, like every other misguided feeling. If men become insane from joy, is joy therefore an evil? And if such an unfortunate person takes his life in his madness, has he taken it from joy?

Block the French statistician and national economist, has given more thought to the problem. He believes that the connection between religion and the suicide tendency is not certain for the following reasons: variations in religion occur along with variations in education and wealth; religion is very poorly taught and thus has little effect; a large number of suicides are committed by the mentally ill; many motives are unknown, and many are falsified.

I answer: Variation in religion coincides, to be sure, with the variation in education and wealth; but what follows from this? Only that one may not make religion the sole cause of the tendency to suicide without qualification. But to the extent that religion, considered along with all other causes, plays a significant or the most significant role in the life of mankind, its effect is stronger and more visible than the other simultaneous causes. Concerning education in particular, we know that a higher degree of education is directly favorable to the development of the suicide tendency; and it is quite evident to all that in our day it is the educated people who are not spiritual and even less religious. The connection between these two phenomena will be treated in following sections; but this much is now evident, that a man without religion and morality—and we have found that for the most part the tendency to suicide also rests upon immorality—cannot endure the labors of life like the religious-moral man. As matters stand, life can only be sustained by labor, indeed, only through hard labor. The relationship between wealth and suicide tendency has already been indicated. To be sure, religion is poorly practiced ("taught" is not the right word; religion cannot simply be taught, but must be lived), but in this respect the defect itself is, as has been indicated, favorable to the development of the suicide tendency. The suicides of the mentally ill do not contradict our assertion if it cannot be shown that their mental illness arises in a way unrelated to religion. We shall examine the matter in detail. Unknown and false motives do not mean motives of such a peculiar nature that they would throw a completely different light on the nature of the suicide tendency.

To examine other objections is not worth the effort, because, I am convinced, this whole exposition gives evidence for the truth of my assertion; the objections are also very superficial. I might add that all the researchers who have closely analyzed the phenomenon of suicide and who have sought to get to the root of the problem, have recognized irreligiosity as the true cause of the modern suicide tendency, including Casper, Blanc, Lisle, Winslow, Brierre de Boismont, Wagner, Morselli, Oesterlen, Hausner, and most other statisticians and physicians.[70]

8. The question now arises as to which religions and confessions are most favorable to the development of this morbid tendency.

An accurate answer may only be given in relation to the European religions and confessions because data concerning the religions of other continents are meager. Primitive religions are inimical to suicide; Buddhism, whose teaching of Nirvana favors to a high degree the ascetic flight from life, strongly favors suicide. Mohammedism, like the Pentateuch and Christianity, does not promote the suicide tendency.

Among the Christian confessions, the Greek Church (united

---

[70]   Wagner's researches are especially interesting and instructive. This conscientious investigator was forced to admit the influence of religion, especially of confession. The statistical data convinced him that *religion and confession belong with those factors which most clearly manifest their influence on the suicide frequency* (*Die Gesetzmässigkeit in den scheinbar willkürlichen menschlichen Handlungen,* 1864), pp. 180, 277.

and not united) is most inimicable to suicide; the Catholic Church follows, and the Protestant Churches are the most favorable to suicide.

According to Morselli, there appear the following average number of suicides per one million inhabitants:

Greek (united and not united) ................... 40
Catholic ....................................... 58
Mixed (Catholics, Protestants, and other sects) .... 96
Protestants .................................... 190

Per one million inhabitants, Legoyt counts:

Protestants .................................... 102.7
Catholics ...................................... 62.3
Remaining Christians ........................... 36.2
Jews ........................................... 48.4

In Austria per one million inhabitants:

Jews ........................................... 30
Greeks ......................................... 99
Catholics ...................................... 100
Protestants .................................... 123

*It is an established fact that suicide occurs more frequently among Protestants than Catholics; the Greek Church shows the fewest number of cases.*

The following tables of Morselli may serve as confirming evidence for the statement.

| Area | Suicides per Million | Inhabitants per Thousand | |
|---|---|---|---|
| | | Catholic | Protestant |
| A. Catholic nations[71] | | | |
| Spain | 17 | 999 | — |
| Portugal | 13 | 999 | — |
| Italy | 32 | 995 | 2 |
| Belgium | 68 | 996 | 4 |
| Corsica | 28 | 999 | — |
| Luxemburg | 35 | 995 | 5 |

[71]    By Catholic or Protestant countries, we indicate here those which have less than one-tenth of their population belonging to other sects. "Mixed" refers to those which have five-tenths of one or the other.

| Area | Suicides per Million | Inhabitants per Thousand | |
| --- | --- | --- | --- |
| | | Catholic | Protestant |
| France | 150 | 982 | 16 |
| (a)  Dép. Seine | 400 | 998 | 2 |
| (b)  Dép. Nord | 110 | 996 | 4 |
| (c)  Dép. Pas de Calais | 147 | 992 | 8 |
| (d)  Dép. Seine et Marne | 383 | 992 | 8 |
| (e)  Dép. Seine et Oise | 288 | 991 | 9 |
| (f)  Dép. Aisne | 298 | 990 | 10 |
| Swiss cantons[72] | 65 | 984 | 15 |
| Austria | 72 | 919 | 41 |
| B.  Areas with mixed religions and Catholic majorities | | | |
| District of Münster | 40 | 898 | 94 |
| District of Oppeln | 53 | 888 | 92 |
| Dép. Doubs | 114 | 886 | 114 |
| Dép. Ardêche | 85 | 884 | 116 |
| Dép. Drôme | 162 | 882 | 118 |
| Dép. Duc Sèvres | 111 | 880 | 120 |
| Brabant (North) | 6 | 879 | 116 |
| Alsace (Upper) | 143 | 855 | 116 |
| District of Cologne | 57 | 816 | 140 |
| Dep. Lozère | 55 | 844 | 156 |
| District of Trier | 53 | 836 | 153 |
| Ireland | 14 | 767 | 234 |
| Bavaria | 72 | 713 | 275 |
| Swiss Cantons | 172 | 700 | 294 |
| District of Posen | 73 | 672 | 283 |
| District of Freiburg | 74 | 653 | 332 |
| District of Coblenz | 74 | 652 | 329 |
| Baden | 157 | 648 | 331 |
| Dép. Gard | 115 | 643 | 357 |
| Alsace (Lower) | 130 | 642 | 322 |
| Danubean Principalities | 180 | 635 | 358 |
| District of Karlsruhe | 105 | 613 | 370 |
| District of Düsseldorf | 81 | 593 | 394 |

[72]   Swiss cantons which are Catholic: Tessin, Uri, Unterwalden (above and below the forest), Appenzell (inner section), Wallis, Schwyz, Luzern, Zug. Mixed, with Catholic majorities: Solothurn, Freiburg, St. Gallen, Geneva. With Protestant majorities: Aargau, Graubündten, Thurgau, Basel, Glarus, Bern, Neufchatel. Protestant: Schaffhausen, Waadt, Zürich, Appenzell (outer section).

| Area | Suicide per Million | Inhabitants per Thousand | |
|---|---|---|---|
| | | Catholic | Protestant |
| District of Osnabrück | 74 | 554 | 442 |
| District of Bromberg | 65 | 545 | 409 |
| District of Marienwerder | 71 | 485 | 482 |
| **C.  Areas with mixed religions and Protestant majorities** | | | |
| District of Mannheim | 73 | 480 | 482 |
| District of Danzig | 95 | 470 | 499 |
| District of Arnsberg | 86 | 430 | 559 |
| District of Breslau | 191 | 406 | 574 |
| District of Wiesbaden | 147 | 385 | 583 |
| District of Minden | 66 | 390 | 596 |
| Netherlands | 35 | 367 | 613 |
| Province of Gelderland | 34 | 368 | 620 |
| Province of Utrecht | 41 | 370 | 621 |
| Kingdom of Prussia | 138 | 331 | 651 |
| Province of Holland (North) | 43 | 278 | 663 |
| Province of Overyssel | 25 | 297 | 687 |
| Württemberg | 162 | 304 | 687 |
| Jaxt Region | 120 | 301 | 687 |
| Hessia-Nassau | 158 | 263 | 708 |
| Black Forest Region | 150 | 259 | 736 |
| Province of Zeland | 41 | 259 | 736 |
| Province of Holland (South) | 35 | 246 | 738 |
| Swiss cantons | 239 | 260 | 738 |
| District of Erfurt | 197 | 251 | 741 |
| Oldenburg | 198 | 228 | 764 |
| District of Königsberg | 153 | 200 | 786 |
| District of Cassel | 167 | 166 | 806 |
| District of Leignitz | 252 | 158 | 830 |
| District of Hildesheim | 155 | 150 | 842 |
| Hanover | 153 | 119 | 874 |
| **D.  Protestant areas** | | | |
| Region of Neckar | 190 | 81 | 907 |
| Province of Frisia | 55 | 82 | 908 |
| Province of Gröningen | 97 | 70 | 908 |
| Swiss Cantons | 279 | 68 | 922 |
| Province of Drenthe | 63 | 52 | 923 |
| District of Berlin-Potsdam | 195 | 25 | 940 |
| England | 70 | 53 | 946 |
| District of Aurick | 120 | 22 | 959 |
| District of Hanover | 153 | 29 | 960 |

| Area | Suicides per Million | Inhabitants per Thousand | |
|------|---------------------|----------|------------|
| | | Catholic | Protestant |
| Waldeck | (62) | 21 | 962 |
| District of Magdeburg | 231 | 29 | 962 |
| District of Köslin | 83 | 16 | 965 |
| District of Stettin | 144 | 6 | 970 |
| District of Frankfort | 191 | 16 | 972 |
| District of Gumbinnen | 89 | 12 | 976 |
| Kingdom of Saxony | 311 | 21 | 976 |
| Saxe-Meiningen | 264 | 6 | 983 |
| District of Lüneberg | 190 | 10 | 986 |
| Schleswig-Holstein | 228 | 6 | 988 |
| District of Stade | 163 | 6 | 989 |
| District of Merseburg | 238 | 7 | 990 |
| District of Stralsund | 197 | 5 | 991 |
| Mecklenburg | 167 | 2 | 992 |
| Hamburg | 301 | 2 | 992 |
| Saxe-Altenburg | 303 | 1 | 998 |
| Lauenberg | 156 | — | 999 |
| Denmark | 258 | — | 999 |
| Sweden | 81 | — | 1000 |
| Norway | 75 | — | 1000 |

Concerning the effect of the different Protestant churches, we have few reliable inductions. In 1858–59, there were per one million inhabitants in Austria:

| Area | Catholic | Lutherans | Reformed | Greek United | Others | Unitarians | Jews |
|------|----------|-----------|----------|--------------|--------|------------|------|
| Bohemia | 69 | 162 | 114 | — | — | — | 81 |
| Moravia | 67 | 58 | 72 | — | — | — | 12 |
| Galicia | 45 | 18 | — | 47 | — | — | 10 |
| Bukowina | 80 | — | — | — | 34 | — | — |
| Hungary | 41 | 60 | 74 | 14 | 15 | — | 30 |
| Translyvania | 130 | 90 | 83 | 29 | 24 | 94 | — |
| Military Border | 28 | 32 | — | 91 | 22 | — | — |

Wagner concludes from these tables with some justification that the Reformed churches are more favorable to the development of the suicide tendency than the Lutheran. He infers this from the figures for Hungary (where there were, in 1870, 887,063 Lutherans and 1,720,920 Reformed); however, in Transylvania and Bohemia, where there is also a greater number of Reformed, the evidence is just the opposite, while Moravia would certainly confirm his view.[73]

We will do better to confine ourselves to our main tables, and there we see clearly *that suicide appears with a significantly lower frequency in Reformed countries than in Lutheran ones.* The suicide tendency is significantly lower in England, Scotland, and the Netherlands than in the purely Lutheran Saxony, Denmark, and Prussia. The relatively higher frequency in Switzerland still does not reach the height of the Saxon countries. We may justifiably conclude therefore that *the Reformed Churches promote the tendency to suicide less than the Lutheran.*

We possess for other churches only the meager data cited above for the Unitarians; detailed estimates for individual churches in Scotland, America, etc., are entirely lacking.

9. We should now compare specific suicide data with the religious situation of urban and rural populations, occupation, etc., and especially with nationality and country, but we have not yet completely examined the nature of the suicide tendency, and must temporarily defer this investigation until we have first acquainted ourselves with the correct relation between the suicide tendency and psychosis and the increase in both.

But this much is already clear, that religion and confession in themselves, or some roll on which a man's name is entered, do not prevent or favor the tendency to suicide; that depends much more on religiosity and spirituality themselves. It must be noted: not every religious and confessional organization of society has the same kind of disposing effect, but the quality of religious and spiritual feeling, the religious-moral state of individuals and whole peoples, has a determining effect. If it is therefore said that Catholicism is less favorable to the suicide tendency than Protestantism, this can mean, on the one hand, that the Catholic belief is less disposing; on the other hand, that the Catholics are more religious or spiritual than Protestants. Of course, this would certainly not be

[73]   In Transylvania in 1870 there were 209,080 Lutherans, 296,460 Reformed, 53,539 Unitarians; in Bohemia at the end of 1869, 46,415 Lutherans, 59,706 Reformed; in Moravia, 20,355 Lutherans, 36,880 Reformed.

valid for all Catholics, because in Catholic France and Austria significantly more suicides are committed than in Protestant England. The question is, as Wagner says, not so much, perhaps not at all, the dogmatic differences of individual religions, as the degree to which each of them at present is really an object of inner faith for the mass of its adherents.

The investigations of Chapter 5 will clearly show us, however, how the suicide frequency is to be comprehended as an index of religious life.

## Section 3. The Suicide Tendency Examined from the Psychological Point of View: Suicide and Psychosis

1. Mental illness interests us not only as a strongly effective cause of suicide—a third of all cases are to be traced back to mental illness—but also as a contemporary social evil, which, as might be expected from the outset, stands in close relation to the present suicide tendency.

Public opinion today explains almost every suicide through the mental illness of the victim, obviously sensing the inner relationship of the suicide tendency to psychosis. Healthy common sense finds it inconceivable that a man can take his own life.[74] People also fear a judgment of public opinion, which still always brands suicide as an immoral act despite its frequency, although on the whole the condemnation of this unholy act is rather mild, even lax.[75]

In the literature, Esquirol has stated the view that every suicide is committed in an irresponsible state. That this is not so is shown by the simple fact that many people who at the last critical

---

74     In Iceland, a man who had previously tried to take his life would be acquitted of a crime against the person, because he would be considered irresponsible and not to be punished. The North American Indians consider suicide to be the result of a mental disorder; therefore, whether they consider it an heroic or evil deed, they pity the victim.

75     Relatives fear above all the suspicion that they bear any guilt for the calamity.

moment are prevented from carrying out their intention evidence sound judgment after their rescue. But that their rescue itself could remove the mental illness is not acceptable from a psychological point of view. Given the required funds to recoup his losses, a ruined businessman who wishes to take his life would certainly desist if he were mentally healthy, but, if he were mentally ill, even money could not rescue him. Many, but not all, suicides are committed in an irresponsible state.

The ideas about psychosis that prevail in cultivated and even scholarly circles are usually deficient and inadequate. This is the reason that even statisticians, if they are not psychiatrists and psychologists, follow unscientific principles of classification in their recording of suicides. For example, Wagner's classification is defective; mental disturbances are placed next to mental illness along with the passions; brain fever serves as a single class, etc. This leaves us then with the task of clarifying the entire matter.

PART 1: It is uncommonly difficult to draw a sharp distinction between the normal and abnormal inner life. Heretofore, neither the psychologists nor the statisticians have succeeded in constructing the average man, that type according to which nature seems to form the individual. Nevertheless, the psychologist, the statistician, the sociologist, the doctor, the lawyer, the teacher, in short, all of us, operate with some conception of the average, normal man.[76] It is very difficult even for the most able psychiatrist to diagnose the first symptoms of mental illness; in practice, there are often certain definite and conclusive symptoms, but it is not easy to describe these symptoms accurately, primarily because so much would have to be said.

Mental illness usually develops very slowly and also does not show such acute effects as physical illness. It is often discovered only after it has reached an advanced stage, and frequently the symptoms of the illness are considered to be the causes themselves; "reasonable" people can certainly be ill, and the "ill" rea-

---

[76] Concerning the average man, see Quetelet, *Physique Sociale*, and Morpurgo, loc. cit., p. 47 ff.

sonable. Anomalies of mood, will, and thought, and the basic sensory and motor disturbances are considered as the elementary derangements. One's self-perception and state of mind are disturbed; the mood becomes irritable or apathetic. Thought becomes illogical, proceeds slowly or too rapidly causing a greater or lesser confusion to appear. Memory is often weakened and hallucinations appear. The will either becomes very weak or too strong and intense. Violent impulses often arise, especially to muscular activity which can become totally irresistible in many cases. Often this is disturbed, as we see in estatic states with their cataleptic stiffness. A general feeling of illness appears, often becoming very intensive, and finally a gradual change of self-consciousness follows. Loss of perception is accompanied by ecstacies, hallucinations, and illusions.

All these symptoms can be present and still not constitute a true psychosis. The sick state rests essentially on the fact that certain nervous conditions, states of mind, feelings, emotions, passions, judgments, and directions of will emerge from the inside out, through the illness of an organ of the mind, while in the healthy state all these symptoms are created by external forces. The mentally ill person is the greatest egoist; his egoism, of course, is not of an ethical, but of a pathological nature. In health, harmony exists between the individual and his environment; in sickness, it is disrupted. His psychological states assume an abnormal intensity and duration, and by this differentiate themselves from healthy, normal states. No one notices it, for example, when a person is sad, but he is noticed if he is sad for a very long period, if his state is not proportional to the external stimulus, and if a trivial cause has an unexpectedly strong effect.

The classification of psychoses—insofar as it is at all possible —is most accurate when the psychological viewpoint is used to perceive the anomalies of the inner life.

Considered from this viewpoint, psychical life offers two fundamental states within which the psychical anomalies also occur. On the one side we have a depression of the morbid mental states, and on the other side their exaltation. The different forms of these two basic groupings appear as different stages of a prolonged process of illness, which steadily increases and ends with the total destruction of inner life. This process can be altered and disturbed by intervening psychical and pathological events; nevertheless, it is definitely perceivable in every illness: after the elementary disturbances, the state of depression usually appears and is then transformed into the state of euphoria until complete mental breakdown and imbecility are reached.

Along with this natural process of psychical illness, corresponding physiological and anatomical changes occur in the organism.

The first stages of psychosis are curable, but not the last two secondary disturbances.

When the borders of normal mental life are crossed which, as we have said, is not easy to determine, a psychical condition of depression is exhibited. This is characterized by an enormous feeling of oppression, anxiety, and sadness—"*Seelenschmerz*"; emotions and emotional conditions remain fixed. In the first stage, that of hypochondria, there is seldom any indication of a decrease in intelligence; there is at most a mental monotony, because the sick person concentrates on certain things, usually his feeling of bodily illness, so that the false judgments of the patient almost always relate to his state of health.

Melancholy is an illness of a higher degree especially characterized by an enormous sensitivity and depressing feelings of sorrow that accompany every nervous agitation; in this condition, desire leads to sorrow. Nothing can relieve it; nothing can give peace. Often complete lethargy is exhibited. Self-consciousness is gradually altered by anomalous ideas, hallucinations, and illusions, and is often completely metamorphosed by continuous delirium. Not infrequently there arise false impulses and directions of the will which aim at the destruction of the environment or of one's own person. Painful emotions, insurmountable feelings of anxiety, and finally delusions and mental delerium are, in this state of psychosis, the most frequent and most general causes of suicide.[77]

---

[77]     For example, the sick person hears voices which order him to kill himself.

Among the mentally ill, those suffering from melancholy have the highest suicide frequency.[78] This form of illness expresses itself in manifold ways.[79] One can well analyze melancholy according to the various attitudes of the direction of the will, considered from their motor side; thus the subdivisions of melancholy includes melancholy with lethargy, melancholy with the expression of negative and destructive impulses, and finally melancholy with agitation of the will in transition to delirium.

Exaltation is to psychical depression as being outside oneself contrasts with being inside one self. It reveals itself by an energetic display of strength, excess, unrest, and passion; the sick person is usually in a brighter state of mind. The false thinking and willing arise more independently, without a profound agitation of the spirit, and usually have the character of psychical weakness. The will can no longer be led by the will of others. In delirium, exaltation expresses itself through unconscious, spontaneous, now acute, now chronic displays of strength. As a destructive mania, it often drives the victim to murder, but never to suicide; at most, the maniac accidently suffers harm or meets with an accident. Insanity in this phychiatric sense is recognizable by a complete transformation of self-consciousness; the result is an overevaluation of the self. Actions are done with purpose, through determinations of the will, but ideas are wandering, false—"insane."

[78]    A suicidal monomania is often mentioned. Esquirol has established a special class, monomania, in contrast with mania. Here his classification is incorrect, however, because psychical conditions are not considered. Only external observations are taken into account. Also, it is not at all accurate to say that the sick man has a single, abnormal, fixed idea, but is completely healthy in all other respects. All so-called monomanias are symptoms of a more general course of illness. For investigations on this subject that are very interesting from the psychological point of view, see *Annal. med.-psycho.*, 1853. Cf. Bariod, *Etudes critiques sur les monomanies instinctives. Nonexistence de cette forme de maladie mentale*, 1852.

[79]    Griesinger uses these categories: melancholia religiosa, demoniacal possession, melancholia metamorphosis (with the delusion that one's own personality has been lost), and, finally, homesickness.

The incurable psychological conditions are mental derangement and imbecility.[80]

3. *For the classification of suicides from a psychological point of view,* with respect to the above, we note the following:

Suicide is committed either in a completely healthy or in a completely unhealthy state; it can, however, also be committed in an indefinable condition in which neither state can be determined with certainty. (1) The intention of killing oneself is conceived in a psychotic state; (2) psychosis appears only after the decision and as a result of the decision; (3) finally, a complex of both cases can appear.

The forms of psychosis itself may be presented according to the following schema:

A. Doubtful
B. 1. hypochondria
   2. melancholy
   3. delirium
   4. insanity
   5. mental derangement
   6. imbecility

Because the deed has been committed in some stage of psychosis, does not, from a scientific viewpoint, deny the accountability and responsibility of the actor. In general, that man is considered irresponsible who has been deprived of freedom to act for his own welfare and happiness, who lacks clear ideas and judgments concerning objects and purposes concerning the consequences of his actions, and finally concerning his own self. Public opinion considers every mentally ill person unaccountable and irresponsible, but psychology does not identify psychosis with total lack of freedom and therefore admits a certain degree of responsibility among the mentally ill.

4. The short description of psychosis that we have offered here suffices to interpret the relation of this illness to the suicide tendency and properly to evaluate it. The personal life experience

[80] The phenomena of idiocy and cretinism, also other types complicated by paralysis and epilepsy, are of no importance here.

necessary for it, and the generally known accounts of the evil by Shakespeare and others can be assumed among educated readers.[81]

*Most suicides are commited when the mind is in a definite state of depression.* The man who considers himself so unfortunate that he voluntarily decides to give up life must necessarily experience a great deal of mental anguish and pain. This is also demonstrated by the fact that melancholy is generally the mental illness of suicides. Mortal terror excites the victim to such a degree that the terrible deed in most cases is committed in a state of mind close to one of the psychoses. Goethe says that the mental state in which one is capable of suicide is always a confused, degenerate condition: no truth in the perception of things, no foresight into an often immediate future, no insight into circumstances, an unfortunate focusing of all mental powers on a single black point. Descuret correctly calls suicide a delirium of self-love.

Nonetheless, cases also appear in which the act is committed in cold blood, in which the decision to be or not to be is made as calmly and in so cool a manner as a decision about any other trivial act. Naturally, such cases are not frequent.[82]

81    Maudsley considers this presentation superior to those in psychiatric frames of reference. He is correct insofar as the psychical condition of the will is concerned.

82    The argument often arises as to whether suicide is a brave or cowardly act. To settle the argument, one must first conceive of a completely responsible actor, and understand the conception "courage" completely psychologically, not ethically, somewhat in the sense of the ancient cardinal virtue of bravery. If one thinks that courage is present in all who possess a certain degree of physical strength, who master an inborn energy of will, and who are aware of the situation in which they must be tested, then there is no reason why there should be no courageous suicides and why otherwise stalwart men could not face death bravely. In spite of great mental anguish, the distraught person can face death uprightly and bravely, because even the most courageous perhaps have attacks of fear.

Another question concerns whether it is braver to give up life or to bear patiently the blows of fortune. In the first instance, courage is required only one time; the second requires endurance. The analysis of suicide notes shows that in most cases the last feelings of the unfortunate stem from a very disconsolate and anguished state of mind; in the majority of cases, great mental anguish and fear of death is expressed. Brierre, p. 298 ff.

There are no special indices as to whether a suicide was committed in some degree of mental disturbance, except the facts given by the post-mortem examination. Beyond this the generally standard symptoms of psychoses are valid. Relevant factors are: whether a trivial motive has provided the impulse for the act; whether there was possible excess in the execution and in the choice of means, of place, and of time; and whether previous attempts at suicide have been made. Suicides who are mentally ill seldom write about their last moments. In addition, the victim's whole life should be taken into account because only then can the decision and the act be fully grasped psychologically.

PART 2: 5. Having investigated psychosis from a psychological standpoint, let us now seek to discover the social significance of the malady. We therefore investigate the causes of psychoses in the same order in which we have studied the causes of the tendency to suicide.

(1) The influences of nature, both terrestrial and cosmic, are only disposing causes to the appearance and spread of psychosis, and what we said about them in our investigation of their effect on the appearance of the suicide tendency also hold true here.

It is to be noted in particular that the unusual effect of climate, meteorological conditions, etc., attacks the organism and thus dispose to psychosis. With respect to the seasons, most people fall ill in summer (May to August).[83]

Early morning is dangerous for the person suffering from melancholy, according to Maudsley; if he awakens too early to renewed suffering, then suicide is very often attempted.

Among cosmic influences, moonlight has a disquieting effect on the sick person.

---

[83]   Because suicide develops gradually, it is impossible to control this estimate accurately, although heat definitely has an unfavorable effect. Naturally, one may not draw hasty conclusions about the time of day at which the sick person expresses his intent. Esquirol has asserted that delirium develops often in summer, seldom in winter; the relationship between the seasons and other forms of illness is unknown. Cf. Jacobi, *Die Hauptformen der Seelenstörung*, 1844, I, p. 568.

(2) Cities are more favorable to the development of mental illness than rural areas.

(3) Mental illness increases from puberty on.[84] Zeller establishes from 20 to 30 years of age for men and from 30 to 40 for women as the period of most frequent mental illness; the fading beauty of women and the appearance of their climacteric years with their disappearing hopes for happiness are said to be effective causes; therefore, women over 40 years have a high rate of suicide.[85]

No special change in susceptibility to illness seems to appear in old age. Were one to include the many cases of senile inbecility, then old age would indeed prove to be a very unfavorable condition.

On the whole, the different age levels have different forms of mental illness, just as they have different temperaments. Imbecility is frequently found in childhood and old age—in youth, mania; in maturity, melancholy; and among the aged, mental derangement.

(4) Bodily constitution, especially the state of health, has a disposing and determinate effect on the appearance of psychosis. The following harmful effects on the central nervous system with their direct and indirect influences are to be especially emphasized: (1) injury to the head (effect of excessive heat or cold, internal malformation of the brain cavity, etc.); (2) narcotic intoxication, paralysis, convulsions, (epilepsy); (3) inflammation of the brain and typhus; (4) loss of blood, physical exhaustion (through hunger, thirst, intemperance, exertion, age); (5) abdominal distension and plethora (caused by gluttony, sedentary way of life, decrepitude, pregnancy, puberty, failure of menstruation, etc.); (6) fever; (7) organic heart and lung disease; (8) tapeworm and similar afflictions; (9) results of sexual incontinence; (10) other illnesses, especially gout, rheumatism, etc.

Concerning bodily constitution in general, the so-called "ner-

84    Esquirol claims that in cases of mental illness, the first menstruation is always associated with the tendency to suicide.
85    *Journal für Psychiatrie*, I, 1, p. 18.

vous constitution" is especially favorable to the development of psychosis.

The psychical disposition of individual temperaments are of great significance.

Those temperaments characterized as exalted, eccentric, sad, hypochondriac and melancholic, sentimental, indecisive and timorous, fearful and cowardly are more susceptible to illness than others because all these states in and of themselves are related to psychosis, and because the determining psychical causes, which we will treat below, are also closely related to all these dispositions.[86]

(5) Heredity provides a very effective individual predisposition to psychosis.

No doubt psychosis, like many physical illnesses, can be and is hereditary. But the effect of heredity should not be overemphasized.[87] The researches and statistical analyses are usually too superficial. The mentally ill child need not have inherited the malady because his parents are or were mentally ill. Investigators look for heredity much too much and therefore find it everywhere. It should be precisely stated whether both parents, or one of them, had the same form of psychosis as the child; the period in which the psychosis developed in the parents and in the children must be examined, whether the parents—one or both—were ill at or before the conception of the child, whether a previous psychosis could still have an effect on the conception in question. Further investigation should be made as to whether any physical defect was inherited which, under favorable circumstances, would lead

[86]   A person of sanguine temperament has little inclination to suicide, like the phlegmatic person. The choleric temperament, endowed with a vivid imagination, often suppresses the emotional impulse to violent deeds. The so-called melancholy temperament, which shows in its name the corresponding form of mental illness, is especially conducive to the development of the suicide tendency.

[87]   Moreau traces nine-tenths of all cases back to heredity, but this is a decided exaggeration. Maudsley says that certainly one-fourth, perhaps one-half, and possibly three-fourths of mental illnesses are inherited. Schlager admits only 4 per cent, considering heredity effective only in those cases in which one of the parents was mentally ill before or at the time of conception, *Zeitschr. der k. k. Gesellsch. d. Aerzte in Wien*, 1860, nos. 34, 35.

to psychosis not only in the parents, but also in the child. When all these and many other precautionary measures have been methodically applied, it should be asked how upbringing, physical infection, imitation, and all the remaining conditions together operate on the child, and whether the psychosis must not develop naturally, without heredity. One should especially investigate the earliest years of life in which a fragile nervous system can sustain lasting disturbances.

In many cases that are alleged to be hereditary, children can be affected through fear of their inheritance; this applies especially to the fear of having inherited the suicide tendency.[88]

The inheritance of the suicide tendency in particular occurs when the disposition to a form of psychosis or the psychosis itself leads to suicide in the child as well as in his parents. The children can also inherit psychical dispositions which lead to mental illness and to suicide under certain conditions. But there is no inheritance of the idea of suicide or the suicide tendency in the sense that an idea, a judgment, or any emotion and tendency (love, will) could be inherited as a result of which one would be compelled, as it were, to take his life.

Only dispositions are inherited, but it is impossible accurately to represent one's forebears. Obviously, psychical inheritance occurs indirectly in a physiological, morphological, and pathological way, but how we are to conceive of this no one yet perceives.[89]

---

[88]    Cf. Maudsley, *Die Zurechnungsfähigkeit der Geisteskranken* (intern. Biblioth.), p. 177; Falret, p. 355.

[89]    The inherited evil appears in the most variable forms in different generations. Morel, for example, gives the following picture of successive degeneration:

Generation I    shows: moral depravity, intemperateness in drink.
Generation II   shows: drunkenness, maniacal assaults, general paralysis.
Generation III  shows: hypochondria, melancholy, *taedium vitae*, murderous impulses.
Generation IV   shows: imbecility, idiocy, extinction of the family.

If it be asserted that heredity operates in the psychological sphere, reason dictates that this must mean the inheritance of that psychical ac-

(6) Sex. More men than women are usually found in public asylums, since it is easier to nurse women than more unruly men in a private home.[90] On the whole, however, women appear more susceptible to mental illness than men.

---

tivity which we know as inward perception, because we have no control over unconscious activity—supposing there is such a thing. Therefore, only conscious psychological phenomena of one of the three basic classes of such activity must be inherited, or combinations of these.

The inheritance of ideas can only mean that besides the ideas that I have gotten through experience and retain in memory, I have also inherited ideas in my consciousness. But inner perception is aware of absolutely no difference between inherited and acquired ideas. If there are such ideas, we should remember that we already had them as children, and that, in the course of our experience, other ideas were added to these. Certainly we could enter the world with ideas, but because there is no difference between both kinds of ideas, how is one to know that any are transmitted? It is asserted that the primary psychological activities inherited are those in which our ancestors were involved most frequently. Every man has intense images of color. Do those born blind have images of color? Even though sight is lacking, the brain, the organ of images, is sound. There should exist images of colors, then, if the principle of heredity is to be understood in this way. Or should one say that inherited ideas, in contrast to those which are acquired, are superior ideas? But images (representations) possess differences only of intensity, not of quality. For this reason, judgments could not be inherited, because ideas which serve as a basis for judgment are not inherited. Therefore, in like manner, no resolutions or applications of will or temperament can be inherited. Does it appear that we inherit premises from which we draw conclusions only from experience? Or do we inherit conclusions for which we lack premises? Can one have an inherited anger without knowing why he is angry? Can one hope, without knowing for what? And so forth.

This simplified examination should satisfy the psychologists and demonstrate that there is no inheritance of psychological activity, but only of dispositions. Psychologically, heredity explains nothing but only impedes explanation. This is true because instead of explaining the appearance of psychological phenomena, the proponents of hereditary causes are left with the problem of explaining heredity itself. Only with the solution of this and a knowledge of our long post-primeval origins can the phenomenon in question be studied from this point of view.

[90] Attempts are frequently made to derive the greater mental morbidity of women from their nature, but menstrual disturbances, the ills and discomforts of childbirth, and similar things hardly match the dangers

The number of suicides committed by the mentally ill is about equal for both sexes, yet here, too, the feminine sex seems to lead.

(7) No time of life is completely safe from psychical illness, yet many age levels are more favorable to it than others.

Even in childhood almost all forms appear, albeit rather seldom, particularly the states of mental imbecility down to the deepest idiocy. Maniacal states (delirium) appear less frequently, melancholy only in very isolated instances, though this particular form is significant for the development of the suicide tendency. Children who commit suicide usually show certain anomalies, such as cruelty to animals.[91]

Suicide in childhood is most unnatural, and usually indicates the inheritance of psychotic dispositions.

From the onset of puberty, mental illness increases in frequency; the years of full mental and physical maturity are most dangerous, approximately from 25 to 45.[92]

No special change in susceptibility to illness appears to come with old age.[93]

*The different age levels show corresponding forms of mental illness, just as they show different temperaments.* Imbecility frequently occurs in childhood and old age; mania appears in youth; melancholy, the mental illness of suicide, appears in more mature years; among the aged there is frequent mental derangement.

---

to which a man is exposed. Drunkenness and immorality in general are greater among men, and must therefore lead to mental illness more often. The male sex certainly shows more severe forms of the evil than the female, and so there are more men than women in asylums. Female insanity has a lower mortality, as the mortality of women in general is lower than that of men.

In Germany, for example, men have a somewhat smaller share of insanity than women. Mayr, *Die Gesetzmässigkeit im Gesellschaftsleben*, p. 209.

91      Forbes Winslow, *Obscure Diseases of the Brain*, 1859, p. 186.

92      Zeller gives 20–30 for the male sex, 30–40 for the female. The climacteric years of women are also said to have an unfavorable effect, and some have claimed an unfavorable climacteric period for men from 50–60.

93      We do not include senile imbecility here.

(8) The unmarried are more susceptible to mental illness than the married.[94] *Married women show a higher frequency than married men*; the fact is explained by their early marriage and by bad treatment of women on the part of men. In any case, domestic cares are one of the most active causes of psychosis.

Widows show a higher frequency than widowers; the divorced are in the most unfavorable situation.[95]

Previous statements concerning illegitimate children are also valid here.

(9) Psychosis can easily develop during imprisonment. Many prisoners are hardly responsible in themselves; added to this, then, are pangs of conscience, a yearning for relatives and freedom, cares and sorrows, obsessions, bad living conditions, restricted movement, etc. Isolation appears to be most dangerous; women and uneducated persons especially find isolation difficult to endure.[96]

(10) Occupation and class differences promote psychosis in different ways. Ferrus states that those trades which demand the least bodily expenditure of energy have the highest frequency; other authors come to the opposite conclusion.

There are fewer mentally ill among the upper classes than the lower.

---

[94]   It should be noticed that the number of unmarried is generally greater than that of the married. Single persons who have become mentally ill usually do not marry.

[95]   Among the unmarried in Bavaria there were 11.10 mentally ill per 10,000, among the married only 5.94, among the widowed 16.3, and among the separated 63.62. Mayr, loc. cit., p. 210.

According to the most recent data from England, the men predominate strongly from 20–40 years, the women from 40–60, over 60 the men again. For every married person there are 2.83 single, 1.5 widowed. Chapman, "Einfluss von Alter, Geschlecht, Ehe auf die Disposition zur Geistesstörung," in the *Centralbl. f. Nervenkrankh.*, 1879, p. 26. (The data refer to admissions into asylums).

[96]   In the work of Delbrück, the point is stressed that psychoses appear more among criminals with passionate motives than among those who commit crimes against property, especially in cases of murder and manslaughter, then rape and arson. Cf. *Zeitschr. für Psychiatrie*, 1854, pp. 57 and 375.

(11) There is greater susceptibility to mental illness in a dense population, with its severe and stormy competition, than in a less concentrated one; therefore the city has more mentally ill than the rural areas.

(12) The Caucausian race shows the strongest disposition, while of the remaining races psychosis almost never appears among the primitives.

(13) According to Hausner, the Germanic peoples have the highest number of mentally ill, the Romance peoples the next highest, and the Slavs least of all.

There are the following number of mentally ill per 10,000 inhabitants (according to Haushofer):

| | | | |
|---|---|---|---|
| Norway | 34 | Ireland | 15 |
| Denmark | 28 | France | 13 |
| Iceland | 26 | Bavaria | 11 |
| Saxony | 26 | Belgium | 10 |
| Elbe Duchies | 25 | Sweden | 10 |
| Hanover | 17 | England | 9 |
| United States | 15 | Scotland | 9 |

In Austria, there is one ill person for every 1200 inhabitants; in Hungary, one for every 1170, or about 8.0 and 8.7 per 10,000 inhabitants.

On the average there is one sick person for 772 inhabitants in civilized states, one for 478 inhabitants in the productive population (from 20 to 60 years); but the estimates are not precise.[97]

The rates of suicide as a result of mental illness are unequal among different peoples. Of every 1000 suicides, according to Block, the following number were mentally ill:

| | |
|---|---|
| France | 340 |
| Prussia | 333 |
| Saxony | 337 |
| Belgium | 350 |
| Italy | 330 |

[97] According to Brigham, for example, there are supposed to be three times as many mentally ill in the United States as in England. Pierquin, however, states that there are 1:783 in England; Hitsche gives 1:500 for Wales alone. Tuke states 1:300 for England and Wales, including idiots!

(14) In free states under certain circumstances it is easier for mental illness to develop than in authoritarian states.

(15) Political crises of all sorts—revolutions, agitations, and war—decisively increase mental illness; their consequences are most favorable.[98]

Arndts has observed that the nervous tensions which develop during wars are only gradually lost over a prolonged period of time.

(16) Military personnel, especially officers, suffer from psychosis more than civilians.[99]

(17) Poverty strongly disposes to psychosis, but the disorganization of financial conditions appears to be more often a cause of suicide than of mental illness.

Merchants in cities and provinces, including the Jews, frequently become insane.

Nothing can be determined at present as to the influence of the dominant economic methods of production. Investigations indicate that agricultural areas in England have more mentally ill than industrial districts, while the opposite is true in Belgium.[100]

(18) On the whole, psychical causes are the most frequent and the most effective causes of mental illness. Seldom is the brain directly and strongly irritated as, for example, by fright; psychosis most frequently appears in indirect ways from psychical causes. They at first influence certain deviations from normal organic processes, which result in illness of the brain as a secondary effect.[101]

---

[98]  Laborde, *Les hommes et les actes d'insurrection de Paris devant la psychologie morbide*, 1872; Schwab, *Allg. Zeitschr. f. Psychiatrie*, 1880, p. 279.

[99]  Frohlich, "Über Psychosen beim Militär," *Allg. Zeitschr. für Psychiatrie*, 1879, p. 303. According to Bertillon, illness appears among officers four times as often as among troops.

[100]  A note on the effect of strikes is interesting. It has been observed that the strikes in the coal and iron industries in Glamorganshire in England diminished the outbreak of mental illness and the commission of crimes. This favorable result was probably induced by the turning of attention to new goals and by the greater moderation in drinking. See *British Med. Journ.*, 1873, October.

[101]  Griesinger, p. 168.

The psychical causes of psychosis obviously must lie in social life and social activity as it is conditioned by the contemporary outlook on life.[102] But the social institutions of the present are surely bad if mental illness is so frequent and continues to increase.[103]

Let us listen to the judgment of a doctor.

Everywhere—says Guislain—where breeding, the arts and sciences, and the religious concepts of Europe are at a minimum, mental illness appears less and less frequently, and finally disappears altogether.[104]

Comparing the original and persistent customs of the Arabs and Indians with our life filled with excitement, movement, and ferment—we have the solution to our problem.

What fills our thoughts? Plans, innovations, reforms. What is it for which we Europeans strive? For movement, excitement. What do we experience? Agitations, illusions, and deceptions.[105]

In our densely populated cities in particular, thousands of dif-

---

[102]   The most frequent psychological causes are: fright, anxiety, horror, sorrow, joy, indecision, anger, vexation, hate, jealousy, pangs of love, ambition, pride, religious despair and visions, homesickness, sentimentality, etc.

[103]   Several investigators refuse to admit the continuous increase of mental illness, but statistical data prove this beyond all doubt. The number of insane asylums and their inmates is certainly increasing. In England, the number of insane is said to have multiplied ninefold within twenty years (Bucknill et Tuke, *Psychol. med.*, p. 32). Even admitting that more attention has been paid to the mentally ill in recent years, that now more poor people are being treated than previously, and that in hospitals the length of life of the patients has increased, a constant increase nevertheless must be granted.

At a session of the Verein deutscher Irrenärzte, Dr. Hasse substantiated the frightening increase in psychosis.

[104]   Guislain considers the peoples of Asia, Africa, and the unsettled Americas, where psychosis very seldom appears.

[105]   In this respect, I must note that purely intellectual activity, overexertion itself, leads to psychosis in the most infrequent cases. Those which are cited are not caused so often by mental labor as they are by other accompanying circumstances: emotional states, excesses, use of means to produce insomnia, etc. Substantial mental labors are part of our time, but this labor is for the most part unsystematic and in this, in my opinion, lie its dangers and excitements.

ferent forces seek to assert themselves, while immutable customs predominate among Asiatic populations. We find these incubators of mental derangement among peoples who throw off the yoke of authority, among peoples who form associations, seek to make their own laws, and have a literary calling, in nations where an incessant impulse drives men to flee the sphere circumscribed by their birth. The representative man in our civilization lives in awareness of his environment. The exaltation of his spirit demands all his thoughts; he wants to grow, wants especially to grow in the eyes of those who observe him. He feels the need to leave his present state and strive for a higher rank. He never considers his mission finished but believes himself always to be on the way, and he looks everywhere for more desirable positions. When the emotions of the masses are nourished by ideas of emancipation, all the passions are released; hopes produce delusions; the family is destroyed in that which is most dear to it, its most beautiful feelings. Revolts ensue; kings are knocked from their thrones; thousands of men fall by the wayside, thousands are killed.

The result of this is that the greater the excitement which dominates men, the more their minds are affected; the more their feelings and passions are stimulated, the more they exceed their bounds. The peoples of European and North American civilization are practically in a continuous state of intoxication: drunk with ever-new impressions. This is not the case among peoples who approach more closely to the natural state, who remain far removed from the activity which we call "the world." We do not possess statistical tables of mental illness for another time of greater social peace, but I am convinced that the number of mentally ill was once much lower than it is today. The number of mentally ill is also higher in the countries where greater freedom is the rule than where there are more restrictions. The Turkish, Russian, and Italian governments show a singular contrast, with respect to what has been said above, to the English, French, Belgium, and North American governments.[106]

The origin of mental derangement must not be sought solely in violent passions.

[106] Guislain's *Leçons orales sur les Phrénopathies* appeared in 1852.

Primitive peoples have even stronger passions than the civilized nations, but they are much less disposed to mental illnesses. Their vengeance is abominable, their cruelty fearful, but their delicate feelings are covert; they do not cry and seldom laugh. The peculiar character of these peoples is the paucity of their choices, the uniformity of their customs and their habits, the immutability of their social structure, much more limited needs, habits of abstinence—an instinctive life, a crude life which has taught them to bear hardships, to steel themselves against pain, to defy danger, to endure torture, to meet death with courage and peace of soul. Among them we find much more resignation, less unrest, less anxiety and fear. They possess more self-control and express few of their inner feelings. They have the strength to hide pain, to contain their wrath, and can nurse a grudge for years. The primitives consider the intellectual haughtiness, the rhetorical gestures, the characteristic cheerfulness of European peoples as signs of insanity.

But we develop within us a delicacy of feeling that is unknown to the barbarians. European civilization desires a rise on the thermometer of delicate passions. It is obvious that they go beyond the sphere of the moral, beyond the feelings which come from the heart. It cannot be doubted that the words love, delicacy, friendship have another meaning for us than for the Asiatic, the African, the American. Our whole aim is to indulge our great sensitivity. How often do our eyes fill with tears without reason; how often is our heart burdened with sorrows.

One should not think that primitive men are less genuine or less passionate in their love for their wives than those in nations which are under the influence of European civilization. Nor should one think that among the peoples which bear the name "wild" or "barbarian" there is less inward love of children and parents for each other. Women, although they submit to a coarse and active life, inspire respect and they often become the object of an actual cult. Children love their parents with the love which we call veneration. Likewise, the place of age among the American Indians is next to that of their tutelary god. Among the primitive peoples, there exists a love of family that is *not* second to ours. Yet the largest number of mental abberations appear in the European family.

In what way does the family of the modern world differ from the family in the ancient world? Among primitive peoples, conjugal, maternal, and child-like love is naturally simple; it is free of a large number of cares and troubles known to us. In our society, the family can maintain itself only by the greatest sacrifice, by which it satisfies a great number of needs. The roof under which the European family lives, the bed in which its members rest, the clothes which each wears and which serve to protect the easily affected body, and the food with which each one is nourished can be acquired only by the most arduous and sustained exertions. For us, the love of wife, husband, children—the love of family—is not the most sacred or the purest; it is often an ideal, an affectation which springs from the mind, but not from the heart, and it is impressed on the heart by reading, through music, by the enjoyments of the dinner table, by alcoholic beverages, by tricks of coquetry, by intemperance, by a handful of gold. The man of our civilization is exposed to stimulations unknown to the child of nature. The feelings which are implanted by love of one's fellow man have assumed a point of development among the white race for which one will look in vain among the barbaric peoples.

Here too lies a source of aberrant behavior. Mental illness, in this respect, is the illness of humanity, of brotherhood; it especially attacks those who are free.

From this we can draw the conclusion that what we call European customs, social factors, and progress presuppose conditions that many men can realize only with the destruction of mental health. But no single cause is grounded in this diffusion of civilization; rather many causes are present in it: a large number of influences that simultaneously increase the number of individuals susceptible to mental disturbances.

We are led to indict a system that has been valued by the peoples of Europe for more than half a century. For eighty years, one has not stopped saying: "Give man more freedom!" The goal of this position has been described as the emancipation of the human race. We have all believed in a happy result. But this long experiment has reached its end, and what does it reveal? The poorhouses are full, the jails crowded with thieves and murderers, the insane asylums overflow; half the nations take arms against the other half, and a professional army is created which attempts to hold all parties to the struggle in check; egocentrism develops, an extraordinary development of feeding one's personality; family bonds are shattered or weakened.

Great dangers for the mind lie in the contemporary social upbringing, in which many evils are present: very ambitious men, such as those classes who leave their natural station, that class especially which exploits an economic depression wrought by overproduction, in other words those engaged in commerce and industry.[107] Social interests have always created mental derangements, but they have increased to the degree that provocations and mental excitations have become more numerous and more intensive. For this reason, there are today a higher number of mentally ill than in the Middle Ages, a lower number in Russia than in England and France, and for this reason also the incidence of mental illness among the Turks and Arabs is very limited.

To this extent, we must—disregarding several trifles—consider Guislain to be completely correct. That which we call civilization, enlightenment, cultivation, and progress brings into being widespread psychosis; it is the modern *"Sturm und Drang"* which creates a morbid emotionalism in society. Civilized man finds himself in the pathological state of a general nervousness which is called forth by modern social institutions and nourished by them, and which leads on the one hand to psychosis, on the other to suicide.

PART 3 : 6. *Both the tendency to suicide and psychosis spring from exactly the same causes,* and we must therefore conclude, with respect to their nature as contemporary social mass phenomena, that both phenomena are really partial phenomena, two different aspects of one and the same social process.[108] This relationship is important for us—more important than the fact that psychosis is an effective cause of the suicide tendency, and we must therefore investigate it more closely.

107    Megalomania is increasing everywhere in our day; Haushofer bemoans undisciplined freedom.
108    Joy itself (without psychosis) does not directly bring about suicide, while it does cause many mental illnesses.

We have found that in the final analysis the modern suicide tendency can be traced back to irreligiosity, and the question now arises *how the general agitation which becomes visible in the generally widespread psychosis of the day is related to this irreligiosity. Is it also the result of irreligiosity?*

Modern irreligiosity of the masses corresponds, as we have seen, to the rise of education, that is, half-education, and is also closely related to immorality. We must look then for the answer to our question in these three facets of one and the same thing.

An *intellectual enlightenment and education* which is orderly and in harmony with all other developments cannot cause agitation and psychosis. But a disorderly exertion of the brain, precisely because it is disorderly, easily becomes overexertion, and agitates to the degree that it is also one-sided and inharmonious accomplishment. As soon as the balance between understanding and spirit is upset, spiritual vigor and endurance vanish. Alienation, agitation, and mental illness are the results. *But our intellectual education in fact has this defect,* and it is therefore the cause of the generally widespread nervousness and psychosis.[109]

With respect to the moral factors of society, it must be noted that psychosis, just as suicide, is conditioned by imprudent and immoral conditions: immoral family relationships, drunkenness and sexual sins are the most frequent direct causes of mental illness, while the sins and errors of fathers have an indirect effect on the children through heredity.[110] Only a very few cases are caused

---

[109] In this respect, Dr. Hasse has also drawn a scathing, but correct, critique of our public school affairs.

[110] According to a compilation by Esquirol, of 1,266 cases the following were caused by:

| | |
|---|---:|
| Inherited predisposition | 337 |
| Domestic sorrows | 278 |
| Intemperance of all kinds | 146 |
| Misuse of spirits | 134 |
| Disrupted financial conditions | 49 |
| Fright | 35 |
| Excess mental exertion | 16 |
| Excess joy | 2 |

by honorable causes—and one could almost say, motives—as is true of the tendency to suicide.

Finally, irreligiosity is not a positive, but only a negative cause of psychosis. Since one religion and church no longer guide man, society has in feverish haste repeatedly sought newer and newer things, and so it is that psychosis is quite widespread in the most enlightened countries. *In any case, the psychosis produced by unsystematic, excessive effort is most prevalent in civilized countries.* The matter must be understood in this way, for as it is easy to perceive, psychosis in uncivilized, unprogressive regions can be caused by ignorance and physical degeneration, as a result of poverty and other conditions. It would be quite possible therefore that in earlier times, in the Middle Ages, psychosis was not exactly uncommon, but arose from quite different causes, while the modern nervousness and mental illness are conditioned by completely different causes. *It is not only a matter of the number of ill, but also the causes and forms of the illness.*

The official statistics, insofar as one may trust them, in fact agree with our deductions.

Psychosis appears more intensively among Protestants than among the Catholics and Greeks.[111]

Melancholia—the psychosis of suicide—and delirium are the dominant forms of the illness among Protestants; among Catholics, insanity and imbecility are most prevalent, and among Jews, insanity in particular.

Here, religion and confession have a disposing and determining effect, just as on the suicide tendency.[112] In the latter respect, according to what has been said, irreligiosity is negative

---

[111]     Hausner calculates one sick person:

      among Protestants ............ per   491
      among Catholics .............. per 1088
      among Greeks ................ per 1795

    Cf. Burrow, *loc. cit.*, p. 185; cf. Kolb, *Statistik*, p. 213.

[112]     Hausner is of the opinion that critical, brooding, and morbid Protestantism disposes more easily to psychosis, because of its nature, than the other two rigidly dogmatic religions.

and unfavorable, religiosity favorable. But religiosity is unfavorable when, as in America, lively religious feeling is sometimes led astray. It must also be remarked that religious psychosis—according to Greisinger a main form of melancholy!—appears more frequently among Protestants than among Catholics. (I do not believe I must prove that this unfavorable effect of a false religiosity does not contradict our explanation of the relation between psychosis and irreligiosity.)

7. If it is asked whether, among all conditions, suicide frequently appears where psychosis is intensive, the answer should be that the parallelism is everywhere decisive, as is obvious from the above exposition. Thus, for example, mental illness is very intensive in America, suicide is low; the relationship is reversed in China. But suicide generally will also be frequent where agitation and psychosis are intensive, and thus the statistical estimates concerning both phenomena generally agree.

But the psychological relationship between the two—in the foregoing paragraphs we investigated it etiologically—is the following.

Psychosis develops from the same causes, under certain conditions, and terminates in suicide, so that this is a resultant of a longer process of development; a third of all suicides are of this kind. Or suicide (and attempted suicide) is committed in the beginning of psychosis, so that this, if life has not been ended, would naturally develop further; suicide appears as a correlative phenomenon of the same process, and, as Winslow says, often as the first clear sign of psychosis.

But both phenomena can also arise in such a way that the same causes evoke suicide in one person, psychosis in another.

It is to be remembered, with respect to suicide which is committed in the absence of psychosis, that most suicides are probably committed in a state of mind that borders on the abnormal, and that a minimum number of suicides are committed by individuals with a clear, healthy, and unclouded mind. Therefore, the modern suicide tendency appears to be thoroughly morbid and unhealthy; it is, along with psychosis, the tragic manifestation of the general agitation and nervousness conditioned by modern civilization.

PART 4: 8. Only a few words remain to be said concerning the diffusion of the morbid suicide tendency.

The great mass of suicides in all civilized countries are to be explained by the conditions in which men find themselves; this means that the same causes are effective everywhere. But also, as with all social mass phenomena, a second principle is active which contributes much to the diffusion and intensity of the malady: imitation and contagion.

Imitation as a psychological principle is rather widely recognized.[113] From birth man learns to act by imitation; he forms and strengthens his will by imitation, and if the process is strictly considered, he does nothing but imitate. A trivial example, to which little thought has been given, is the mode of moral striving toward ideals.

Imitation is especially active among children and primitives, and in general among less educated, more dependent, and weak characters. Under certain conditions, imitation can have such a rapid effect that it actually becomes a form of psychical contagion. It is known that fear, horror, grief, and similar states have a contagious effect. But mental illness, especially melancholy—and this is important for us—is also contagious, and it is therefore apparent that a morbid tendency, morbid ideas, feelings, and strivings can spread unconsciously, one might say, in a society. History provides many examples of the same endemic or epidemic more or less morbid mental currents.

The suicide tendency is similarly contagious and many cases, especially those which are distinguished by some unusual characteristic, can be directly traced to imitation.[114]

---

113   We can cite the morbid search for martyrdom among early Christians during the crusades, seizing all of Europe with religious delusions, infecting children and moving them to foolish undertakings; the Flagellants, Bianchi of Italy, the Pastaureaux of France, and other phenomena are to be explained in part as psychical and psychotic contagion.

114   Goethe relates that the suicide of Kaiser Otto induced an imitation of it in him.

In the age of humanism, many suicides imitated the suicides of ancient philosophers.

*Certain ideas of actions are very quickly transformed into the action itself,* and this happens so fast that the will cannot intervene, either in a favorable or unfavorable sense. If, for example, we stand next to a precipice and look down, the idea of jumping brings with it an act of will—and often the deed itself. In fact, a case is reported in which a young husband surrendered to an overpowering impulse and threw himself into a ravine.[115]

A somewhat different type is the sickness commonly called St. Vitus Dance, which entirely manifests the character of psychosis and frequently ends in suicide.[116]

*The more monstrous the idea, the stronger is its effect.* Only thus are we able, for example, to explain many murders and monstrous deeds, and what is of most relevance here, many suicides.

---

In Versailles, at the time of the revolution, 1300 men killed themselves in a single day!

A man hanged himself in the Hotel des Invalides after a lengthy period during which no suicides were committed; in the following fourteen days five others hanged themselves.

[115] I have observed in myself that quite often when I stand close to the tracks on which a locomotive is roaring towards me the impulse to cross the tracks arises.

The peculiar attraction of still water, which Homer in his *Sirens* and Goethe in the *Fischer* have described, should also be noted. (Goethe's *Fischer* is not completely true to nature. He has the water roaring and foaming, whereas it must be placid if it is to be seductive; this is obviously a hysteron-proteron; the poet has the ascension of the virgins of the water and the roaring of the water, which was placid at first, produce the same wish.)

[116] Just such a compulsive dancing mania appeared epidemically along the Rhine and in the Netherlands during the fourteenth century. Those attacked by it showed an extraordinary preference for water and often threw themselves into the Rhine. During the fifteenth century, Tarantism was predominate in Italy; afflicted persons were completely apathetic; music alone made them dance wildly. When they had reached a fever-pitch of excitement, they threw themselves en masse into the waves of the sea; we even have songs from this period in which this manner of death was glorified. Cf. Hecker, *Die Grossen Volkskrankheiten des Mittelalters, histor.-pathol. Untersuch.*, edited by Hirsch, 1865. (In an earlier age, the same dancing mania occurred in Madagascar, in Abyssinia, and among the Negroes of the West Coast of Africa. Cf. Globus, *X Jahrg.*)

The appalling idea seizes the mind and its manifestation follows almost mechanically,[117] often against one's better judgment. Byron says that no one can take a shaving razor in his hand without thinking of a quick death. In fact, the case of a man is reported who is very religious and moral but who cannot shave alone because totally overpowering thoughts of suicide come over him.[118]

Cases of suicide of a very peculiar sort, for example, throwing oneself from cathedral domes and the like, quickly find an imitator.

The conception of modern society as excessively agitated makes us recall that fantasy is constantly stimulated in the theater and by the many newspaper reports of suicides, murders, and accidents, and nurtured by the most monstrous acts. This makes it easy to understand that, on the one hand, many suicides are to be traced solely to the force of this psychological law, on the other hand, that in any case it expedites the act. It follows, however, that the suicide frequency resulting from this law must be higher and will continue to rise the greater the overall frequency already is; a lower frequency lessens the effectiveness of this law.

Thus, the high suicide tendency of the present appears, if we consider it psychologically, as a modern illness of the mind, and its diffusion is analogous to the phenomena of earlier centuries in which delusions were widely spread: *the suicide tendency of the present rests upon the delusions of civilization.*

117     A man has related to me how he once seized on the idea of suicide because of a triviality; from that moment on he fought against this terrible temptation, and ultimately he wanted to carry out the deed in order to free himself from the idea.

118     The assertion is made that the more recent custom of owning a revolver may increase the suicide frequency.

# 3

# THE KINDS AND
# FORMS OF SUICIDE

1. WE SHALL TREAT briefly the kinds and forms of suicide in this chapter only as a supplement to the preceding. This special investigation is of interest not solely because of the importance of its object, but because it contributes to an understanding of the suicide tendency.

2. Obviously, every suicide strives to take leave of life in the quickest way possible; he avoids unnecessary pain, seeks rather to make death as painless as possible, and spares himself great effort because his life energy has been broken.

3. Present suicide statistics indicate that hanging is used most frequently; drowning forms one-third to one-fifth of all suicides. Shooting is high, while slashing and stabbing is less frequent; next to jumping from high places and asphyxiation by charcoal fumes, poison is used. Isolated bizarre kinds of suicide appear, as for example, burning oneself, starvation, self-burial, freezing and suicide by different forms of detonation. Being run over, especially by locomotives, shows a high frequency.

4. The choice of means is determined by the situation in which the person finds himself. Usually the suicide chooses what is at hand, because in the excitement of the moment he makes no extensive search for different means. For example, in regions where there are bodies of water, drowning appears more frequently than in a desert; that is self-evident. Therefore, in south and west Europe drowning appears more often than in the north, and in the

cities more often than in the provinces, because cities mostly lie on rivers and other waters.[119]

The seasons have an effect in that more drownings occur in summer than in winter, but not to the same degree that death is sought in general, because the rope is used proportionately most frequently.

Terrain determines, for example, the choice of throwing oneself into an abyss, etc.

Men hang themselves more often than women, who prefer drowning. Shooting is used almost exclusively by men. Women also prefer charcoal fumes, jumping from windows, and poison.

Hanging occurs most frequently among youths and the aged.

With the development of physical strength and courage, the choice of means also changes: the boy hangs himself, the girl leaps into the water, the youth and man of strength shoot themselves, the mature woman hangs herself or throws herself into the water, the aged hang themselves.

Bodily constitution, certain conditions of debility, often dictate the choice of a more passive type of suicide, for example, being run over, etc.

Nationality has a noticeable effect on the choice of means.

The French and Romantic peoples, in general, often shoot themselves; the Scandinavians, Germans, and Slavs frequently hang themselves. The Parisians—men—choose drowning more often than shooting. In Italy, men shoot themselves most frequently; women drown themselves; but hanging is less frequent than in all other lands.

In Austria since 1861, cyanide has often been used; in Vienna especially poisoning has increased. (Glatter, *die Volksbewegung Wiens*, 1865–69). Before 1840 the rope was used most often. (Springer, *Statistik der osterr. Kaiserstaaten*, 1840, p. 80).

Yugoslavs shoot themselves more often than the northern Slavs because they are a people under arms; also their hot temperaments

119    Because most suicides wish to die as comfortably as possible, the cold waters in the north of Europe are not popular as a means of committing suicide.

lead to this choice of firearms, as it does with the French and Italians.

Occupation determines the choice of means in that it often supplies means with which one can commit suicide; the chemist poisons himself; the soldier shoots himself; the miner throws himself into the coal mine, etc.[120]

In the Austrian Army almost three-fourths of the suicides are committed by shooting.

The influence of the remaining conditions (citizenship, confession, etc.) cannot, at this time, be substantiated.

5. *The motive of suicide is closely related to the choice of means* through a more or less conscious association of ideas. As the soldier condemned to death is "pardoned" from the rope to die by shooting, one can likewise distinguish vulgar and noble types of suicide. The rope is generally considered as a vulgar means.

The person who is unlucky in love seldom hangs himself; many suicides, therefore, have a certain touch of the romantic, especially those from unrequited love, suppressed feelings of freedom, and similar motives. Such kinds especially appear in youth, because the older a man is, the more suicide loses its romantic character.[121]

The cultivated Romans seldom hanged or drowned themselves, but they drank poison, stabbed themselves, or starved themselves.[122]

6. In the excitement of emotion and passion, one grasps the best means available without looking around; the mentally ill are often discovered with the most bizarre means.

In psychosis, attempts which miscarry are very frequently repeated.

That morbid condition of mind is peculiar in which men experi-

---

[120]    Seamstresses and tailors often asphyxiate themselves in charcoal fumes.

[121]    Casper believes that hanging indicates a calmness in sorrow; the suicide locks himself in his closet, giving up his life by the quiet means of the rope. Those who shoot or drown themselves indicate ostentatiousness; the former type of death appears more frequently among the French, who even in their last moments wish to place themselves *en scéne.*, p. 80.

[122]    Tschirner (*Leben und Ende merkwürdiger Selbstmörder,* p. 7) is of the opinion that, compared with the Romans, our suicides are vulgar.

ence a sensual pleasure in pain and therefore mutilate themselves in a monstrous way; such men usually mutilate their genitalia. The question here concerns dying more than it does death; while the usual suicide, who wants to die, seizes means which are certain and as painless as possible, this type chooses the most monstrous tortures and forsakes the attempt if he cannot kill himself in this peculiar manner.[123]

7. Certain types of suicide show an impulse toward healing.

Thus, for example, the opening of a vein evidences an attempt to quiet hot and restless blood; the feverishly excited person has the drive to cool himself; another again wants to drink something and therefore seizes poison; finally, a third abstains from food and drink.

One may deduce from the choice of means the state of health or mind of the unfortunate.

8. Besides direct, active types of suicide, there are also indirect, passive types. One who is weary with life often wishes he were dead, but does not have the courage to take his own life; therefore, he accuses himself before a court of having committed a crime which is punishable by death; many even commit such crimes to die.

9. So-called *double suicide* often appears among lovers; either each of them kill themselves, or the man first kills his loved one and then himself.

10. Statistics substantiate an increase of hangings.[124]

From the increase in hangings, Oettingen infers an increase in weariness with life, in drunkenness, and in dissolute living—for those infected with these vices almost always use the rope.

In general, a change in the means of suicide can appear through the change in many individual and social conditions.[125]

---

[123]    The Christian martyrs often showed such a desire for death. Similar conditions can be observed with soldiers in battle, who are often seized by a great desire for dying and death.

[124]    This type of suicide allows the surest substantiation of suicide, while remaining types may often be mistaken for accidents.

[125]    Casper (p. 84) mentions that poisoning by sulfuric acid often appeared in his age because this acid had been introduced by the use of lighters and English blacking.

In any case, the kinds of suicide have become more complex through time and, to a certain degree, more ingenious. But hanging can hardly be displaced as long as there are suicides.[126]

11. Finally, it must be noted that suicide among the Chinese, Japanese, and Turks has been a privileged death penalty.[127]

[126]    This kind of death is most frequent for more than one reason: rope is always available everywhere. It is cheap, rather certain, and painless, and does not evoke horrifying fantasies of the condition of the body after death. Finally, the fact that hanging has almost become the general customary death penalty also contributes to this.

[127]    Diez, *Der Selbstmord*, 1838, p. 76.

# 4

# TOWARD A HISTORY
# OF THE TENDENCY TO SUICIDE

1. SURVEYING THE VARIOUS causes of suicide, it will be seen that most are disposing causes, few are determinate causes; considering further that the determining causes are for the most part petty or trivial, the conclusion is reached that the decision to give up life is not determined by sudden disturbances of society and of the individual, but that almost always *a longer psychical or physical process must be assumed*. The mass phenomenon of suicide manifests itself in this way as *an historical process,* as *a collective guilt* of society, and our problem then is to discover regularity in the movement of this process.

2. Our history of the suicide tendency is based on the following sources:

First. In general historical works we find several incidental but insufficient estimates of suicide; the material is more complete in the special histories of the suicide tendency and the works which are concerned with suicide.[128]

For the nineteenth century and the end of the eighteenth, we possess reliable statistical estimates which irrefutably confirm the increase in the present suicide tendency.

Second. Should the historical sources themselves be declared

---

[128]    Buonafede, *Istoria critica e filosofica del suicido,* 1761 (1st ed.) ; in the French ed.: Armellino and Guérin, *Hist. crit. et philos. du suicide,* 1841; Szafkowski, *De la mort violent chez les peuples de l'antiquité.* Numerous estimates are found in Lisle and Brierre de Boismont.

inadequate, this still does not make a history of the suicide tendency impossible. We will use in our investigation the one and only method that should be applied in investigating the historical connection of causes and effects in social life, and which must, if it is rightly applied, yield a correct result. The next chapter will show, however, whether we have chosen the right path in our sociological research.[129]

3. With the above-stated expedients, the following may be said with certainty regarding the history of the suicide tendency in Europe.

Suicide is not generally discovered among primitive peoples and the uncivilized nations, and we also find that suicide was the exception among the early Greeks; a morbid suicide tendency arose only after the Peloponnesian War, reaching its greatest intensity at the time when Greece belonged to Rome. There also was no suicide among Romans in the early period of the Republic; only in the time of the emperors did it develop and spread over the entire empire, as far as it was civilized. One can say that as early as the first century before Christ, and even more in the first and second centuries after Christ, the entire ancient world had yielded to a pessimistic outlook on the world; as a result of this, weariness with life and suicide were common in that magnificent period of transition. Greece, Rome, Egypt, and the Orient were gripped by woe, unrest, and weariness with life.

With the propagation of Christianity, the suicide tendency disappeared, and the Catholic Middle Ages had no knowledge of it. The isolated cases which are reported are not the result of a generally widespread morbid tendency but are to be explained by several unfavorable outlooks, institutions, and social conditions of the time. Suicide very seldom appeared among women; and we have actually read of only one case that occurred in the course of many centuries in which a Spaniard is said to have killed herself

---

[129]    Because I cannot venture into a broad methodological discussion, I shall indicate only that I mean the method of Comte, Tocqueville, and Mill.

because she feared that she would not be able to control her passion during the absence of her husband. This report may be exaggerated, but it is in any case the expression of the fact that in the Middle Ages suicide appeared very infrequently and only in isolated cases.[130]

Suicide became more frequent during the Renaissance and Reformation; a morbid suicide tendency can be traced as early as the eighteenth century, and in our century this tendency is very common and very widespread. *For the past hundred years, it can be demonstrated with compelling evidence that suicide is regularly*

---

130     The extent to which suicide appeared unnatural and immoral to Catholics may be seen from the following very characteristic teaching of Mariana, the well-known Spanish historian. Although he allowed the murder of tyrants, his conscience forbade him to consider the suicide by poison of the tyrant himself. In and of itself, he saw that much could be said for this means, yet it is too cruel to compel man to give up his life himself, because nature decidedly forbids suicide to every being. *De rege et reg. inst.* I, chap. 7.

The celibacy of the priests brought to many cloisters a peculiar melancholic illness, already mentioned as *acedia* or *accidia*, the result of the unreasonable weakening of body and mind—by asceticism, fasting, prayer —in which many took their lives. It is comprehensible that superstitious ideas and physical and psychological abstinence must lead to insanity. Such Christian penitents act like their Indian brothers and, therefore, by the mortification of the flesh, are easily led to suicide. This is true because the ascetic is really nothing but a moral suicide, showing what man can, but should not, do. There was, for example, a "holy man" who lived for 50 years in a cave like a wild man; another spent all of 30 years on top of a 60-foot high column and kneeled 1,240 times a day in constant prayer! Despite this, the cloisters have prevented more suicides than they have caused, as Lecky says, being places of refuge for the helpless and the troubled in general.

The morbid desire for martyrdom broke out as an epidemic; therefore, the Church has rightly viewed only certain cases as martyrdom and proscribes the others, with Augustine.

The hapless witches often committed suicide to escape torture. In general, the deed was committed only in cases of most extreme need— hunger, pestilence, and persecution—and then when immorality broke in somewhere. Cf. Lecky, *Sittengeschichte Europas* (German trans. by Jolowicz, 1870), II, p. 34 ff.

*increasing in all the states of Europe, and that the morbid tendency
progressively gains in intensity.*

4. The following statistical tables prove the constant increase
of suicides in all nations and cities. This increase, as it appears in
these tables, may be explained in no other way than that suicide is
in fact becoming more and more frequent.[131] *In the course of this
century, the suicide tendency has at least tripled in most civilized
nations;* the increase in population proceeds significantly more
slowly.[132]

[131]    For the objections to this assertion and its negation, cf. Wagner,
p. 116.

[132]    The following table illustrates the growth of population:

| States | Four-Year Observation | Annual Increase in Percent | Doubling Period |
|---|---|---|---|
| United States of America | 1850–60 | 2.98 | 23 |
| Norway | 1855–60 | 1.71 | 41 |
| Russia | 1850–56 | 1.45 | 48 |
| Kingdom of Saxony | 1855–61 | 1.45 | 48 |
| Scotland | 1855–62 | 1.36 | 51 |
| Prussia | 1858–64 | 1.38 | 51 |
| England and Wales | 1861–63 | 1.31 | 53 |
| Sweden | 1855–60 | 1.23 | 56 |
| Denmark | 1845–60 | 1.01 | 68 |
| Württemberg | 1858–61 | 0.97 | 72 |
| Spain | 1857–60 | 0.95 | 73 |
| Belgium | 1856–60 | 0.90 | 77 |
| Mecklenburg-Schwerin | 1856–61 | 0.89 | 78 |
| Portugal | 1858–61 | 0.87 | 80 |
| Greece | 1862–64 | 0.81 | 86 |
| Italy | 1863–68 | 0.72 | 96 |
| Hanover | 1849–58 | 0.72 | 97 |
| Baden | 1861–64 | 0.71 | 101 |
| Bavaria | 1855–61 | 0.64 | 109 |
| Switzerland | 1850–60 | 0.61 | 114 |
| Netherlands | 1850–59 | 0.56 | 124 |
| France | 1861–64 | 0.42 | 165 |
| Austria | 1855–58 | 0.32 | 217 |
| Cisliethania | 1857–69 | 1.004 | — |
| Transliethania | 1857–69 | 0.921 | — |

| Period | France | Belgium | Austria[a] | Italy | Spain | Portugal | Kingdom of Saxony | Prussia | Bavaria | Denmark | Sweden | Norway | England and Wales | Scotland | Ireland |
|---|---|---|---|---|---|---|---|---|---|---|---|---|---|---|---|
| 1776} 1780} | — | — | — | — | — | — | — | — | — | — | 191 | — | — | — | — |
| 1780} 1785} | — | — | — | — | — | — | — | — | — | — | 232 | — | — | — | — |
| 1786} 1790} | — | — | — | — | — | — | — | — | — | — | 248 | — | — | — | — |
| 1791} 1795} | — | — | — | — | — | — | — | — | — | — | 281 | — | — | — | — |
| 1796} 1800} | — | — | — | — | — | — | — | — | — | — | 286 | — | — | — | — |
| 1801} 1805} | — | — | — | — | — | — | — | — | — | — | 383 | — | — | — | — |
| 1806} 1810} | — | — | — | — | — | — | — | — | — | — | 399 | — | — | — | — |
| 1811} 1815} | — | — | — | — | — | — | — | — | — | — | 437 | — | — | — | — |
| 1816} 1817} 1818} 1819} 1820} | — | — | — | — | — | — | — | — | — | — | 122 (average) | — | — | — | — |

[a] In its present-day dimensions (1881).

| Period | France | Belgium | Austria[a] | Italy | Spain | Portugal | Kingdom of Saxony | Prussia | Bavaria | Denmark | Sweden | Norway | England and Wales | Scotland | Ireland |
|---|---|---|---|---|---|---|---|---|---|---|---|---|---|---|---|
| 1821 | — | — | — | — | — | — | — | — | — | — | — | — | — | — | — |
| 1822 | — | — | — | — | — | — | — | — | — | — | — | — | — | — | — |
| 1823 | — | — | — | — | — | — | — | — | — | — | 151 | — | — | — | — |
| 1824 | — | — | — | — | — | — | — | — | — | — | — | — | — | — | — |
| 1825 | — | — | — | — | — | — | — | — | — | — | — | — | — | — | — |
| 1826 | — | — | — | — | — | — | — | — | — | — | — | — | — | — | — |
| 1827 | — | — | — | — | — | — | — | — | — | — | — | — | — | — | — |
| 1828 | 1739 | — | — | — | — | — | — | — | — | — | 177 | — | — | — | — |
| 1829 | (Ave.) | — | — | — | — | — | — | — | — | — | — | — | — | — | — |
| 1830 | — | — | — | — | — | — | — | — | — | — | — | — | — | — | — |
| 1831 | — | — | 626 | — | — | — | — | — | — | — | — | — | — | — | — |
| 1832 | — | — | (average) | — | — | — | — | — | — | — | — | — | — | — | — |
| 1833 | 2319 | — | — | — | — | — | — | — | — | — | — | — | — | — | — |
| 1834 | (Ave.) | — | — | — | — | — | — | — | — | — | 164 | — | — | — | — |
| 1835 | — | — | — | — | — | — | — | — | — | — | — | — | — | — | — |
| 1836 | 2340 | — | — | — | — | — | 214 | 1436 | — | 241 | — | 104 | — | — | — |
| 1837 | 2443 | — | — | — | — | — | 264 | 1502 | — | 269 | 214 | 124 | — | — | — |
| 1838 | 2586 | — | 774 | — | — | — | 261 | 1453 | — | 292 | — | 163 | — | — | — |
| 1839 | 2747 | — | (average) | — | — | — | 246 | 1474 | — | 297 | — | 140 | — | — | — |
| 1840 | 2752 | — | — | — | — | — | 336 | 1480 | — | 261 | — | 135 | — | — | — |
| 1841 | 2814 | — | — | — | — | — | 290 | 1630 | — | 337 | 201 | 148 | — | — | — |
| 1842 | 2866 | — | — | — | — | — | 318 | 1598 | — | 317 | 206 | 144 | — | — | — |
| 1843 | 3020 | — | 774 | — | — | — | 420 | 1720 | — | 301 | 200 | 123 | — | — | — |
| 1844 | 2973 | — | (average) | — | — | — | 335 | 1575 | 244 | 285 | 225 | 121 | — | — | — |
| 1845 | 3082 | — | — | — | — | — | 338 | 1700 | 250 | 290 | 227 | 152 | — | — | — |

| Period | France | Belgium | Austria[a] | Italy | Spain | Portugal | Kingdom of Saxony | Prussia[b] | Bavaria | Denmark | Sweden | Norway | England and Wales | Scotland | Ireland |
|---|---|---|---|---|---|---|---|---|---|---|---|---|---|---|---|
| 1846 | 3102 | — | — | — | — | — | — | 1767 | 220 | 376 | 222 | 146 | — | — | — |
| 1847 | 3647 | — | — | — | — | — | 377 | 1852 | 217 | 345 | 227 | 139 | — | — | — |
| 1848 | 3301 | — | — | — | — | — | 398 | 1649 | 215 | 305 | 244 | 140 | — | — | — |
| 1849 | 3583 | — | — | — | — | — | 328 | 1527 | 189 | 337 | 225 | 149 | — | — | — |
| 1850 | 3596 | — | 843 | — | — | 30 | 390 | 1736 | 250 | 340 | 228 | 174 | — | — | — |
| 1851 | 3598 | 165 | (average) | — | — | 29 | 402 | 1809 | 260 | 401 | 235 | 172 | — | — | — |
| 1852 | 3676 | 150 | — | — | — | — | 530 | 2073 | 226 | 426 | 337 | 174 | — | — | — |
| 1853 | 3415 | 161 | — | — | — | 48 | 431 | 1942 | 263 | 419 | 261 | 137 | — | — | — |
| 1854 | 3700 | 189 | — | — | — | 27 | 547 | 2198 | 318 | 363 | 228 | 146 | — | — | — |
| 1855 | 3810 | 166 | — | — | — | — | 568 | 2351 | 307 | 399 | 204 | 146 | 1314 | — | — |
| 1856 | 4189 | 216 | — | — | — | — | 550 | 2377 | 318 | 426 | 193 | 129 | 1349 | — | — |
| 1857 | 3967 | 190 | 1086 | — | — | — | 485 | 2038 | 286 | 427 | 212 | 169 | 1275 | — | — |
| 1858 | 3903 | 194 | (average) | — | — | — | 491 | 2126 | 329 | 457 | 215 | 155 | 1248 | — | — |
| 1859 | 3899 | 243 | — | — | — | — | 507 | 2146 | 387 | 451 | 196 | 145 | 1365 | — | — |
| 1860 | 4050 | 222 | — | — | — | — | 548 | 2105 | 339 | 468 | 238 | 127 | — | — | — |
| 1861 | 4454 | 226 | — | — | 248 | — | 643 | 2185 | — | — | 288 | 145 | 1347 | — | — |
| 1862 | — | 214 | 1086 | — | 211 | — | 557 | 2112 | — | — | 294 | 147 | 1317 | — | — |
| 1863 | — | 207 | (average) | — | — | — | 643 | 2374 | — | — | 284 | 138 | 1315 | — | — |
| 1864 | 4946 | 188 | — | 709 | — | — | 545 | 2203 | — | 411 | 312 | 129 | 1340 | — | 77 |
| 1865 | — | 267 | — | 728 | — | — | 629 | 2361 | — | 451 | 330 | 144 | 1392 | — | 67 |
| 1866 | 5119 | — | 1265 | 588 | — | — | 704 | 2485 | 410 | 443 | 309 | 121 | 1329 | — | 83 |
| 1867 | 5011 | — | 1407 | 753 | — | — | 752 | 3625[b] | 471 | 469 | 371 | 131 | 1316 | — | 87 |
| 1868 | 5547 | — | 1556 | 784 | — | — | 800 | 3658 | 453 | 498 | 366 | 130 | 1508 | — | — |
| 1869 | 5114 | — | 1375 | 633 | — | — | 710 | 3544 | 425 | 462 | 356 | 131 | 1588 | 119 | 100 |

[b] Prussia enlarged its political boundaries in 1866.

| Period | France | Belgium | Austria[a] | Italy | Spain | Portugal | Kingdom of Saxony | Prussia | Bavaria | Denmark | Sweden | Norway | England and Wales | Scotland | Ireland |
|---|---|---|---|---|---|---|---|---|---|---|---|---|---|---|---|
| 1870 | 4157 | 338 | 1510 | 788 | — | — | 657 | 3270 | 452 | 486 | 369 | 148 | 1554 | 133 | 80 |
| 1871 | 4490 | 367 | 1560 | 836 | — | — | 653 | 3135 | 418 | 505 | 321 | 128 | 1495 | 116 | 112 |
| 1872 | 5275 | 356 | 1677 | 890 | — | — | 687 | 3467 | 405 | 464 | 309 | 132 | 1514 | 106 | 102 |
| 1873 | 5525 | 377 | 1863 | 975 | — | — | 723 | 3345 | 447 | 439 | 337 | 126 | 1518 | 120 | 86 |
| 1874 | 5617 | 374 | 2151 | 1015 | — | — | 723 | 3490 | 450 | 439 | 394 | — | 1592 | 109 | 99 |
| 1875 | 5472 | 336 | 2217 | 922 | — | — | 745 | 3278 | 459 | 394 | 376 | — | 1601 | 123 | 75 |
| 1876 | 5804 | 439 | 2438 | 1024 | — | — | 981 | — | 522 | 506 | 409 | — | 1770 | 144 | 111 |
| 1877 | — | 470 | 2648 | 1139 | — | — | 1114 | — | 650 | — | 430 | — | 1699 | 179 | 90 |
| 1878 | — | — | 2578 | — | — | — | — | — | — | — | — | — | — | 180 | 93 |
| 1879 | — | — | 2515 | — | — | — | — | — | — | — | — | — | — | — | 90 |

| Period | Paris* | Vienna | Berlin | Hamburg | London | Stockholm | Edinburgh | Glasgow | Dublin | Petersburg | New York |
|---|---|---|---|---|---|---|---|---|---|---|---|
| 1690–1699 | — | — | — | — | 236 | — | — | — | — | — | — |
| 1700–1709 | — | — | — | — | 278 | — | — | — | — | — | — |
| 1710–1719 | — | — | — | — | 300 | — | — | — | — | — | — |
| 1720–1729 | — | — | — | — | 478 | — | — | — | — | — | — |
| 1730–1739 | — | — | — | — | 501 | — | — | — | — | — | — |

* In Paris in 1783 there were 150; 1793 to 1804, an average of 207 cases annually.

| Period | Paris* | Vienna | Berlin | Hamburg | London | Stock-holm | Edin-burgh | Glasgow | Dublin | Peters-burg | New York |
|---|---|---|---|---|---|---|---|---|---|---|---|
| 1740 } 1749 } | — | — | — | — | 422 | — | — | — | — | — | — |
| 1750 } 1751 } 1759 } | — | — | — | — | 363 | 23 | — | — | — | — | — |
| 1760 } 1761 } 1769 } | — | — | — | — | 351 | (22) | — | — | — | — | — |
| 1770 } 1771 } 1779 } | — | — | — | — | 339 | 16 | — | — | — | — | — |
| 1780 1781 | — | — | — | — | 224 | — | — | — | — | — | — |
| 1788 } 1789 } 1790 } 1791 } 1797 } | — | — | 35 | — | 274 | 46 | — | — | — | — | — |
| 1799 } 1800 } 1801 } 1804 } 1806 } 1808 } | — | — | 60 | — | 347 | 46 | — | — | — | — | — |
| 1809 1810 1811 | — | — | — | — | — | 61 | — | — | — | — | — |

| Period | Paris* | Vienna | Berlin | Hamburg | London | Stock-holm | Edin-burgh | Glasgow | Dublin | Peters-burg | New York |
|---|---|---|---|---|---|---|---|---|---|---|---|
| 1813 | — | — | — | — | 363 | | | | | | |
| 1815 | — | — | — | — | | 109 | — | — | — | — | — |
| 1817 | — | — | — | — | — | | | | | | |
| 1818 | — | — | 360 | — | — | | | | | | |
| 1819 | — | — | — | — | — | | | | | | |
| 1820 | — | — | — | — | — | | | | | | |
| 1821 | — | — | — | — | — | | | | | | |
| 1822 | — | — | — | 59 | — | 171 | — | — | — | — | — |
| 1823 | — | — | — | — | — | | | | | | |
| 1824 | — | — | — | — | 42 | | | | | | |
| 1825 | — | — | — | — | — | 171 | — | — | — | — | — |
| 1826 | — | — | — | — | — | | | | | | |
| 1827 | 261 | — | — | — | — | | | | | | |
| 1828 | 279 | — | — | — | 41 | | | | | | |
| 1829 | 307 | 45 | — | — | 35 | | | | | | |
| 1830 | 269 | — | — | — | 25 | | | | | | |
| 1831 | 359 | — | — | — | 48 | — | — | — | — | 22 | — |
| 1832 | 369 | — | — | — | 52 | | | | | | |
| 1833 | 325 | — | — | — | — | | | | | | |
| 1834 | 360 | — | — | — | — | | | | | | |
| 1835 | 393 | — | — | — | — | 158 | — | — | — | — | — |
| 1836 | 415 | — | — | — | — | | | | | | |
| 1837 | 433 | — | — | — | — | | | | | | |
| 1838 | 483 | — | — | — | — | | | | | | |
| 1839 | 486 | — | — | — | — | | | | | | |
| 1840 | 511 | — | — | — | — | | | | | | |

| Period | Paris* | Vienna | Berlin | Hamburg | London | Stockholm | Edinburgh | Glasgow | Dublin | Petersburg | New York |
|---|---|---|---|---|---|---|---|---|---|---|---|
| 1841 | 501 | — | — | — | — | | | | | | |
| 1842 | 516 | — | — | — | — | | | | | | |
| 1843 | 551 | — | — | — | — | | | | | | |
| 1844 | 541 | — | — | — | — | | | | | | |
| 1845 | 534 | — | — | — | — | 152 | — | — | — | — | — |
| 1846 | 526 | — | — | — | — | | | | | | |
| 1847 | 698 | — | — | — | — | | | | | | |
| 1848 | 481 | — | — | — | — | | | | | | |
| 1849 | 609 | — | — | — | — | | | | | | |
| 1850 | 612 | — | — | — | — | | | | | | |
| 1851 | 603 | — | — | — | — | | | | | | |
| 1852 | 593 | — | — | — | — | | | | | | |
| 1853 | 606 | — | — | — | — | | | | | | |
| 1854 | 642 | 67 | — | — | — | | | | | | |
| 1855 | 648 | 82 | — | — | — | 211 | — | — | — | — | — |
| 1856 | 710 | 66 | — | — | — | | | | | | |
| 1857 | 675 | 62 | — | — | — | | | | | | |
| 1858 | — | 83 | — | — | — | | | | | | |
| 1859 | — | 70 | — | — | — | | | | | | |
| 1860 | — | 65 | — | — | — | | | | | | |
| 1861 | — | 68 | — | — | — | — | — | — | — | — | — |
| 1862 | — | 71 | — | — | — | — | — | — | — | — | — |
| 1863 | — | 93 | — | — | — | 469 | — | — | — | — | 100 (average) |
| 1864 | — | 104 | — | — | — | — | — | — | — | 57 | |
| 1865 | — | 110 | — | — | — | — | — | — | — | 59 | |
| 1866 | — | 98 | — | — | — | — | — | — | — | 61 | — |

| Period | Paris* | Vienna | Berlin | Hamburg | London | Stockholm | Edinburgh | Glasgow | Dublin | Petersburg | New York |
|---|---|---|---|---|---|---|---|---|---|---|---|
| 1867 | 700 | 109 | — | — | ⎫ | — | — | — | — | 78 | — |
| 1868 | — | 144 | — | — | ⎬ | 469 | — | 15 | — | 89 | — |
| 1869 | — | 107 | — | — | ⎭ | — | 12 | 11 | 11 | 102 | — |
| 1870 | — | 99 | — | — |  | — | 14 | — | 10 | 125 | — |
| 1871 | — | 132 | 188 | — | — | — | 7 | 15 | 13 | 152 | — |
| 1872 | — | 141 | 200 | — | — | — | 14 | 18 | 11 | 167 | — |
| 1873 | — | 152 | — | 104 | — | — | 6 | 13 | 7 | 141 | — |
| 1874 | — | 214 | 255 | 89 | — | — | 11 | 14 | 13 | — | — |
| 1875 | — | 205 | — | 100 | — | — | 9 | 15 | 13 | — | — |
| 1876 | — | 210 | — | 125 | — | — | 11 | 11 | 8 | — | — |
| 1877 | — | 198 | — | 150 | 240 | — | 12 | 22 | 11 | — | 150 |
| 1878 | — | 193 | — | — | — | — | 22 | 14 | 6 | — | 148 |
| 1879 | — | 297 | — | — | — | — | — | — | 4 | — | 142 |
| 1880 | — | 307 (133) | — | — | — | — | — | — | — | — | — |

133   The last two estimates are based upon the Vienna police district.

Accurate estimates concerning attempted suicide are lacking for understandable reasons; examining the meager data before us, we conclude that they are at least equal to one-third of the actual suicides.[134]

5. The increase in suicide is not uniform and of equal intensity among all peoples and under all conditions.

Wagner observes that in countries where general circumstances are analogous, the increase is similar, more precisely in middle Europe (Germany, France, Belgium); similarly, the German countries of kindred race—Austria, Prussia, Bavaria, Saxony—show a great similarity in the rate of increase. The Scandinavian countries also show a similar increase.

Considering males and females separately, many differences appear.

In Austria and Italy, the increase is uniform; among men it has been, in most recent times, relatively greater in Norway, England, Bavaria, Sweden, Württemberg, Belgium, Switzerland, and greater among women in Denmark, Baden, Saxony, and Prussia. In 1839–58, Blanc found a greater increase among women in France.

The greater increase of the suicide tendency among women is to be traced back to the modern movement of so-called "emancipation," and may be strongest where the emancipation movement is greatest among men and women.

The situation is understandable: when the female sex seeks to be emancipated from its previous social position to compete with the male sex, the generally operative social factors must then attack women more than men, who, because of their previous position in life, have grown more resistant to dangers than women who have been protected from them. Moreover, emancipation, like every movement, brings aberrations and abuses with it which even more adversely affect women.[135]

---

134    According to Boismont, statistical estimates in general represent only a half of the suicides actually committed or attempted.

135    Women committed a large share of the suicides in Vienna from 1868 to 1878: 26 percent more than in the Austrian empire; in Paris, from 1874 to 1878, suicides among women rose 23.3 percent and in Berlin, from 1869 to 1876, they rose 25 percent. Nervousness among women, especially

A sad sign of the times is the increase in suicide among children.

Finally, it must be noted that in Austria suicide is increasing in the metropolitan areas more than in the surrounding rural areas. Conditions favorable to suicide have frequently appeared in the rural areas only in more recent times and therefore, have a stronger effect than in the city, where the populace has grown more accustomed to them through time. What is valid for Vienna naturally holds also for other cities, especially the larger cities.

6. *Psychosis probably was also frequent in previous eras of great suicide tendency.* Thus we know that contemporary primitive peoples and uncivilized nations seldom are mentally ill, while civilized peoples are agitated and strongly psychotic. What is valid today also holds true for the past, and, because the suicide tendency today is also connected with a general nervousness, the earlier suicide tendency probably also arose together with the same phenomenon. In fact, the declining pagan peoples were very much agitated, as the history and literature of that time informs us. In the Middle Ages there were probably few mentally ill and no generally widespread nervousness; only in the present era does mental illness and its corresponding psychosis generally increase. The present rise suggests a contrary decrease in the Middle Ages.[136]

7. Our investigation shows: *in all times and among all peoples isolated suicides appear, but as a social mass phenomenon it appears periodically.* The morbid suicide tendency was especially strong at the time of the fall of the ancient cultural peoples— Greeks, Romans, Egyptians. The Christian Middle Ages did not

---

among the better classes as a result of increased intellectual pretensions, is seriously increasing; among the poorer classes, here more from somatic causes, nervousness is likewise increasing. From the scientifically authenticated increase of nervousness, one can conclude with great probability that there is a relatively high suicide frequency among women. Cf. Rheinstädter, *Über weibliche Nervösität: ihre Beziehungen zu den Krankheiten der Generationsorgane und ihre allgemeine Behandlung.* (Volkmann's Samml. klin. Vorträge, 188.)

[136]   Calmeil, *Sur la folie depuis la renaissance jusqu'à nos jours,* is unknown to me.

know the morbid tendency at all; on the contrary, it appeared in more recent times, has grown progressively since the Renaissance, and today has reached such an intensity among all civilized nations that it must be seen as the peculiar malady of the present: *it is the "social question" in the proper sense of the word*.

The morbid tendency to suicide is probably always connected with a greater or lesser general nervousness. In any case, the increase in the suicide tendency along with the increase in mental illness is today the saddest and therefore most significant sign of our times.

# 5

# CIVILIZATION AND

# THE TENDENCY TO SUICIDE

## Section 1. The Development of the Modern Suicide Tendency

1. OUR INVESTIGATION has shown that in the final analysis the morbid suicide tendency of the present is caused by the irreligiosity of the masses. Moreover, since we know that the suicide tendency increased in recent times and is increasing, irreligiosity must also have increased and be increasing with it. But if the morbid tendency appears periodically, it appears as an external sign of the periodic irreligiosity of the peoples. The problem that we must solve in this part of our work is then clear: it must be established through a cultural history whether and how the religiosity of peoples changes in certain periods to bring about that strange and harmful pessimistic mass mood in which suicide is practiced as a legitimate escape from every kind of misfortune and dissatisfaction.

That this investigation—in the manner of a philosophy of history—must be as brief as possible is clear from the whole plan of this book, and therefore the reader should not object because a great deal is assumed, much only indicated and outlined: the principles can still be correct nevertheless, and it is these that matter.

2. We proceed on the assumption that we have identified the nature of suicide as a social mass phenomenon of the present day, and interpreted it from a psychological point of view. Accepting this, we conclude that the nature of the suicide tendency has been the same in all times, and that the same fundamental causes have

always generated this morbid tendency. Exceptions can appear, but in and of itself the phenomenon has always been the same: "Men are what men always were."

In order to find the empirical law according to which the morbid suicide tendency periodically develops, we begin with the following consideration. Considering the variable degrees of the suicide tendency among extant peoples, we find two extremes: *the primitive peoples show no suicide tendency at all; the civilized peoples, on the other hand, show a very intensive one.* If one were to compare a particular Negro tribe of the African interior which has not yet been touched by European influences with the North Germans and the Danes, he would have the two extremes factually defined: in the latter a large suicide tendency, in the former none. Between these two extremes the remaining peoples may be classified according to a statistical measure, so that we can in this way "represent" in the proper sense of the word the development of the suicide tendency. With this classification, the entire historical sequence can be seen, since the psychical mass mood of the present corresponds perfectly to similar past mass moods. It is the task of the sociologist to provide a proper methodological evaluation of this cross-section as a means to a longitudinal history.

In contradistinction to the irreligiosity of the civilized, one could cite the religiosity of the primitives as the basis for the fact that among the latter the suicide tendency does not appear. This conclusion would be justified, but I do not know whether in this way we would understand the significance of the fact in question. For it could also be said that children in Denmark, Germany, and wherever suicide is frequently committed, do not commit suicide because they in contrast to adults are religious. But the primitive is like a child, unfinished, lacking every higher striving; lazy and indolent, he is intent only on his immediate material gratification; his world-view is the simplest imaginable: lost in a sensual outlook, he has not yet reflected on life and its value, and is satisfied with everything. Therefore the morbid suicide tendency cannot develop in him at all. The primitive is interested only in the external world; what is inside him is and remains invisible; he lives entirely in vision, hearing, etc. This objectivity of the primitive (and children) itself explains to us why he does not commit suicide. In order to wish for death, a man must have recognized what is inside him, must have observed not only the external world, but also his internal world. Whoever loves death is psychically ill and deranged and relates everything to himself. The man of nature is objective, the civilized man subjective. Thus we find murder, manslaughter, and war to be the order of the day among primitives; everything which excites the primitive he relates to the external world, and thus never arrives at the point of relating anything uncomfortable to his own ego. The educated, on the other hand, relates much or everything to himself, is in himself where the primitive is outside himself and is thus more likely to commit suicide rather than murder. Thus, also, is explained the fact that *everywhere that murder frequently occurs, suicide is infrequent and vice versa*; thus, for example, Italy on the one side and Germany on the other.[137]

Religion does not have that practical significance for the primitive which it has for us; this is attained only when a man puts aside primitive and childish things, when he recognizes his inner life and reflects upon the value of life. Then he no longer lives blindly for the day alone, but orders his actions in accordance with a cultivated world-view. Religion then exercises an elevating and proverbial influence on him; then does he first decide for or against life according to ethical principles. Religion does not really prevent suicide in the man of nature, but his nature itself prevents it, his natural instinct for self-preservation; among the civilized, on the other hand, their ethico-religious world-view bestows on life all value or all lack of value. Religion impedes their suicide.

What has been said is not contradicted by the exceptional appearance of suicide among primitive peoples, but confirmed by it. We are informed, for example, that the primitives who take most readily to the use of European liquor commit suicide more frequently than other tribes; the American Indians also frequently committed suicide—in addition to abortion—to escape the un-

---

137    Hausner, *Vergl. Statistik v. Europa*, I., p. 178. Cf. Morselli, p. 246.

usual torture and severe treatment of the Spaniards. Boudin assures us that the Negro in America very frequently commits suicide for the same reason. The ancient inhabitants of Spain killed themselves in droves when the Romans conquered their country and disarmed the people. *All such cases are to be explained by the primitive people concerned becoming acquainted with a higher civilization.* It is a well-known law that sudden, abrupt contact with a higher culture ruins and destroys the less developed peoples. Suicide is then only a special phenomenon in the general decline and it is not committed by pure primitives, but by those who are corrupted (see no. 10).

Suicide appears among many primitive peoples as a result of certain social, political, and national-economic views. Thus, for example, the ancient Celts and Scandinavians killed themselves because they considered natural death shameful and only death by choice honorable; aging men threw themselves from cliffs, and Valerius Maximus tells us that birthdays were celebrated with wine, funerals with jubilation and singing. Today, the same custom predominates among the Battas of Sumatra, whose aged must kill themselves. The old, ill, and infirm often must kill themselves out of regard for the means of subsistence; if they do not do it themselves, they are killed.

When we speak of the state of nature, we mean the true state of nature which is little in evidence today but which must be interpreted sociologically on the basis of the excellent work of Waitz, Tylor, and others, if order and method are to be brought into the chaos of studies concerning the "state of nature." Contemporary primitives have evolved in many ways from this ancient condition and have developed in their own way; what has been said is valid therefore only to the degree to which the level of primitivism—and a certain degree of development does not exclude this—has not been superseded. In the proper sense of the state of nature, we say that there should be no tension, no psychosis, no pessimism, and therefore, also, no morbid suicide tendency among primitive peoples. The cases which do occur among them are really self-slaughters and not suicide, and the known cases of suicide do not show any morbid love of death. Among primitive peoples, war is the rule and an exceptional love of peace in one or two tribes is an exception; suicide is also an exception to the rule.[138]

The fact that the man of nature does not know the morbid suicide tendency, as compared with the civilized man, explains the periodic appearance of the morbid suicide tendency. Recognizing that all contemporary civilized peoples gradually developed from the state of nature, and that the morbid tendency to suicide is absent among primitive peoples but is present among the civilized to a high degree, it thus follows that *the morbid suicide tendency gradually increases among all peoples who have progressed in their development; the social mass phenomenon of suicide is the fruit of progress, of education, of civilization.*[139]

If one shows therefore where and when civilization is greater among a people, or among different classes of a people, one can thus determine with approximate certainty the intensity of the suicide tendency. For example: the educated Germans should show a higher suicide frequency today than the less educated Spaniards;

[138]   The causes and motives of suicides among primitives are as follows: depression in illness, conditions of debility, hard labor, emotions of anger and revenge; the primitive kills himself because he has been insulted and then blood-revenge is to fall upon the head of the person insulting him; unrequited love and jealousy, fear of illness (disfiguration through smallpox), fear of mockery and scandal, sorrow over the loss of a loved one. The primitive frequently accedes to eccentric ideas and thus becomes the sacrifice of an unbridled imagination; but in this instance the situation is that of self-slaughter and not of suicide. Primitives who have yielded to the vice of drunkenness commit suicide with relative frequency, and those who have come in contact with Europeans commit suicide most frequently. Cf. Darwin, *The Descent of Man*, p. 117; *Novara-Reise*, II, p. 309; Wuttke, *Geschichte des Heidentums*, I, p. 189; II, p. 133; Waitz, *Anthropologie*, II, p. 210, VI, p. 117; Grimm, *Deutsche Rechtsaltertümer*, p. 486; Peschel, *Zeitalter der Entdeckungen*, p. 548; *Völkerkunde*, p. 154.

[139]   As a precaution, I must remark that I use the words civilization, education, and progress in their usual sense, that is, they refer to the collective condition of the "first" European nations, in contrast to the peoples and tribes of the remaining continents. However, it should not be said that this civilization (education, progress) is good in all and every respect; the conception should not be understood in the pithy sense nor as expressing praise or blame.

accordingly, the suicide tendency is generally greater today than in the Middle Ages, and, finally, the same law is also valid for the development of the Roman, Greek, and other cultures; the Romans of the Republic certainly did not have the high suicide tendency they had at the time of the emperors. The same law likewise holds for various educated classes of one and the same population; rural inhabitants, for example, show a lower suicide frequency than urbanites, and so on.

The statistics and history of suicide completely verify our law. *But one should guard against thinking at the same time of a natural law:* this is the situation, but it does not always hold under all conditions.[140] The English, for example, who are at least as civilized as the Germans and French, show a lower suicide frequency in spite of their education. Half-education, not education, is the proper cause of the suicide tendency, for it manifests itself in irreligiosity and in the lack of a unified world-view. For this reason, one may not say that want of education hinders the suicide tendency; Spaniards, Italians, and other peoples show a low suicide frequency, not because they are uneducated, but because they are at the same time religious and spiritual. Spain and Scotland both have a small suicide frequency despite differences in their education; both countries are very religious, overlooking for the present the quality of their respective religions.

Finally, it must still be noted that the state of nature sketched above should not be confused with the conception of uneducated (applied to Christian peoples). When it is said that the Spanish and Portuguese are uneducated or uncivilized, it does not mean that they live in a state of nature; this condition may be approached here and there in a few districts, but, on the whole, all Christian nations have gone beyond the state of nature. Therefore, religion has for them the great significance we have ascribed to it because their entire social and private life is no longer guided by instincts but by ethical norms which become the more necessary the more involved and complicated the collective condition of the civilized world becomes.

[140]     Concerning the difference between natural law and empirical law which is important for sociology, see the logical writings of Mill or Bain.

3. In order to understand modern civilization, one must know the Greek, Roman, and Mosaic-Oriental culture that rests at the base of our culture; the secondary influences of the ancient Orient can remain unmentioned here because of their slight significance.

We begin with the Greek.

In the state of nature and the related so-called Heroic Age, the Greek people, as mirrored in the poems of Homer, had a healthy lust for life and a naïve serenity which every energetic and industrious nation partly achieves. Happy and satisfied with their situation, sentimentality and a pessimistic evaluation of life were strange to them, and suicide appears only as an exception.

This objective state lasted until about the sixth century B.C. We see this clearly in the development of poetry and philosophy. Subjectivity awoke in the sixth century, forcing itself freely into political reorganization and contemporary lyric poetry. The philosophy of the period, however, is still completely objective and simple: the thinkers are still interested in the external world, although the poets are already intoxicated with their feelings. When drama reached its heights in the following century—a culmination of poetry and the dominance of the people's vital energies—Socrates brought philosophy from heaven down to earth; the Greek people then worked at the conscious shaping of life.

At about this time, however, the struggle of philosophy with folk religion began, and Socrates was not its only victim.[141] The missionary activity of these men and their students greatly shook the already shaky edifice of polytheism; the uneducated themselves became philosophical, so that even as cynics the dregs of the people became interested in the teachings of Socrates.

The beginning of the Greek people's decline is already mirrored in Plato. The disastrous Peloponnesian War and the Macedonian invasion following it, with all its tragic results in the political sphere, are only the external signs of an inner spiritual

---

[141] Concerning the great influence of religion on the collective life of the Greeks, cf. Schomann, *Griech. Altertum*, II, p. 121 ff.; concerning the decline of the folk religion at the time of Alexander, cf. Becker-Marquardt, *Handbuch d. röm. Altertum*, IV, p. 64; concerning the serious decline during the second century of Christianity, *ibid*. III, p. 345.

disintegration of the people. In Plato's writings we can clearly see this disintegration: folk religion was no longer able to satisfy or guide the people, and this great thinker therefore wished to make his philosophy into a religion. The whole life of this great and noble man is understood and valued only when seen in this light.

The power of Greek thought reached its culmination in Aristotle. Social life was already so disintegrated and corrupt, inasmuch as the people were particularly in need of ethical leadership, that from then on no Greek of theoretical significance appeared. The Epicurean and Stoic schools were exclusively concerned with the practical question of life, and, although basically different in principle, both nevertheless sought to answer the same questions: how to find and to bestow peace and satisfaction in an age of despair? But what peace did these educated religions give to the human spirit? One leads directly, the other indirectly, to suicide —a dogma of belief in Stoicism!

No wonder that after such an intellectual decline in philosophy a disintegrating skepticism was spread abroad. But instability and insecurity only became greater; incapable of independent thought, men grasped at eclecticism, and finally were completely swallowed up in the Oriental and mystically oriented religions, as were also the Romans and the Egyptians.

That is, in short, the course of development of Greek culture, and the ethical outlook on life of the heathen Greeks corresponds to it. They always treated morality naturalistically; Plato himself, among the most idealistic of all Greek thinkers, lacked a true moral sanction for ethical law, which he so frequently confused with natural law. Ethics became at most a permanent part of politics. Certainly individual virtues were practiced and certain striking characteristics were developed, but no individual or social emphasis is given to a perfectly educated moral character, and men lacked the unifying and elevating bond of love. Thus the political disunity in great things and small; thus such a small people was unable to unify itself with its own power; thus the relatively swift dissolution of the Greek states and tribes. Intellectual education was unable to rescue the people; morality soon disappeared and was replaced by widespread licentiousness; finally, the best despaired of life and taught the people to die with dignity and decorum, even though they were not able to live with dignity and decorum.

This development of the life of the Greeks corresponds to the development of their suicide tendency. Until about the time of the Persian War, suicide seldom appeared among the Greeks, who were famous for their joyful outlook on life; from then on we find cases of suicide depicted more frequently in their literature until, finally, such a pessimistic outlook arose that suicide was commended and prized as a unique and excellent end. How unstable the enlightened Greeks were is best shown by the high number of suicides found among their most significant philosophers and great men.[142]

4. What is valid for the development of Greek culture is also true for the development of the Roman, but we can study more carefully the decline of the ancient folk religion among the Romans and the effect of this process on the life of the people.

Being pious and God-fearing in all things, the Romans were able to extend their dominance over the entire world as a result of their inner and outer moral strength and power. Polybius, the historian and theoretician of the *orbis terrarum*, clearly perceived that the fear of God made the Romans so powerful, more powerful than the other nations, but at the end of the Republic this religiosity had disappeared among the leading educated classes (Mommsen, vol. II, p. 179).

Acquaintance with Greek philosophy estranged the people from folk religion without, however, offering them that assurance which is afforded by a religious world-view.[143] The philosophical

---

[142]   It is extraordinary that so many outstanding men of antiquity committed suicide: Empedocles—Aristotle and Pythagoras are also believed to have taken their own lives—Speusippus, Diogenes, Perigrinus, Hegesias, Stilpo, Zeno, Cleanthes, Arcesilaus, Carneades, Aristarchus, Eratosthenes, Erasistratus, Demosthenes, Isocrates, Themistocles, Cleomenes; surely Charondas, Lycurgus, Codrus, and many others. Among the Romans: Lucretius, Atticus, (Seneca), Silius Italicus, Petronius, Lucan, Scipio, Cato, Brutus, Cassius, Marc Anthony, Otho, perhaps Marcus Aurelius, and many others.

[143]   Horace, C. I., 34. Cf. Becker-Marquardt, *Handbuch d. röm. Altertum*, 1856, IV, p. 63. Becker correctly remarks that Greek philosophy, with

systems that found sympathy among the Romans were not of a sort to guarantee full satisfaction and peace: the pantheism of the Stoics, the self-contradictory and unstable religion of suicide, cultivated an honorable character, but the large majority of the educated found their faith in the Epicurean system. At the same time, the characteristic intellectual trend is found in the Skeptic school, and later, the morbid mind delighted in the fraudulent teachings of Oriental mysticism. The Romans were unable to create anything of their own in this area; not that they lacked the talent, but for the quite natural and simple reason that they found developed elsewhere that which they sought and which could be had without toil. Thus, Roman civilization was a continuation of the Greek; the Romans created nothing new, outside of jurisprudence, but only sought to assimilate and broaden what had been perfected; Roman culture thus bears the characteristics of a certain incompleteness, clearly illustrated in the eclectic method not only of the philosophers, but of the educated in general.

Roman religion was gradually modified by the Greek enlightenment.

Already during the Republic the Roman state religion had mixed with the Greek and in this way assimilated many new elements; with the extension of Roman domination, new cults were continually absorbed, until finally, in the second century, a mixing of almost all the religions of the world had taken place.[144]

This characteristic process is usually seen as a sign of the religious decline of the Romans. The original Roman religion must certainly have lost much of its purity and solidity; without doubt the educated classes, especially the philosophers, were also to blame, because they interpreted the different cults only as different

---

which the Romans were acquainted, was thoroughly irreligious. Lucretius quite openly preached a hatred for the folk religion; *De rerum natura*, I, 62–101, V., 1194 ff. Becker compares the first century of the Empire with our eighteenth century; the state of mind and tendency inimical to religion dominated in both; III, p. 430. Cf. Denis, *Histoire des théories et des idées morales dans l'antiquité*, II, p. 28 ff., p. 41 ff. Gibbon, *The History of the Decline and Fall of the Roman Empire*, chap. XV.

[144]    Arnobius, *Adv. gent.*, VI, 7: civitas onmium numinum cultrix.

forms of one and the same veneration of God, to which they were related. Through the mixing of the most diverse cults and ceremonies, religion became mere formalism; it may be thought that a coarse superstition and spiritual delusion had to appear as a consequence—since the faithful, and those lacking faith, were dragged from one altar to another. But one must also consider this mixing process from another perspective.

It lay in the principle of polytheism willingly to assimilate strange cults and repeatedly to introduce or to create new ceremonies and religious usages, until finally the emperor was considered an apotheosis. No harm was done to the conception of divinity if newer and newer divinities were taken in with their cults; while only the best and soundest minds logically moved toward monotheism, the people consistently adhered to this development of the polytheistic system. While only a few understood and upheld the unity of the divine, others multiplied divinities and approached unity in this way, because as divinities multiplied, the demands for unity and harmony had to assume more and more violent forms. The tolerance granted to all religions indicates this, for this tolerance was nothing more than the striving for union and unity. The religion of the Romans, the state religion, had undoubtedly been a guide, but its only real consequence was that the Emperor was called Pontifex Maximus; yet this event demonstrates the existence of a deeply felt need for religion—although also a foolish religiosity.[145]

All great minds of the Augustan Age felt the force of religious disorganization and knew that society, in spite of its political greatness, was sick internally. Reading the poets of the time, looking into the works of contemporary historians, and probing the writings of the philosophers—one finds only insecurity, sadness, laments, unrest, boredom, skepticism, indifference, and weariness with life.[146]

Horace is full of laments; in Propertius, Lucian, in short in all the poets, is reflected unrest and weariness with life of the time.

145   Cf. Hausrath, *Neutestamentl. Zeitgesch.*, II, p. 42.
146   Cf. Hausrath, *loc. cit.*, III, p. 481 ff.

Livy relates this in the foreword to his history and Tacitus is in agreement, sad and serious through and through. Seneca (*de. tranqu. an.* II, 13) pronounces his judgment on the period in the memorable words: "weariness, dissatisfaction with one's self, and a wallowing around to no purpose abides."

This general dissatisfaction and unrest corresponds to the private and public morality of the time.[147]

No wonder that in a period of such intellectual and moral anarchy, the people were distraught and sounded a tragic and pessimistic note. It remained for the greatest Roman investigator of nature to write a hymn—to suicide. Pliny taught that suicide is evidence of human perfection: the greatest consolation for the imperfect nature of man remains the fact that not even God can do everything, because he cannot take his life if he should want to; on the other hand, God has bestowed this great benefit on man in his troublesome earthly life.[148]

Naturally, the better minds sought to combat this state of hopelessness. Seneca, who as a Stoic, considered suicide allowable and who finally committed it himself, preached against the general "passion for suicide."[149] There was intense interest in a new revitalization of religious life.

Augustus and many men around him endeavored to achieve a religious and moral reorganization. The emperor constructed and reestablished the temple, introduced new cults, and actively took part himself in all ceremonies; he had become Pontifex Maximus.[150]

Virgil, friend of Augustus, created an epic in which he strove

---

[147] Cf. Friedländer, *Darstellungen aus der Sittengeschichte Roms*; Becker, Gallus; Lecky, *Sittengeschichte Europas*.

[148] *Hist. nat.*, II, p. 5; cf. II, p. 63; VII, p. 54. When Becker (III, p. 490) and, agreeing with him, Friedländer (III, p. 490) emphasize that the number of atheists and unbelievers in general was a small minority in contrast to the mass of believers, the malady does not decrease because of such a limitation, but rather increases. Cf. p. 168, n. 2.

[149] Cf. *Epist.* 24.

[150] Livy calls him: "Augustus Caesar the founder and restorer of all the temples."

to reawaken the remembrance of the old religiosity and strength of morals.[151]

Horace censured the crimes of his time with acid words. Livy bemoans and condemns the general unbelief (X., 40); Tacitus wrote his *Germania* with the same view, and Juvenal criticizes the instability of his contemporaries even more harshly than does Horace.

These and similar efforts succeeded in establishing respect for religion and in producing a purer religiosity and morality, so that, in the time of the Antonines, Rome witnessed a short renaissance.[152]

Marcus Aurelius was deeply religious, even superstitious.[153]

This reaction encountered the despised and persecuted Christian religion, which was appointed by Providence to rescue and save the declining and corrupted paganism of the Rome world empire.

5. The pagan Roman world had experienced, despite its culture, complete dissolution at the time of the birth of Christ, and was weary of life to the depth of its soul. Philosophy and culture could not free or rescue man; the remnants of a renewed formalism and ritualism could not still the hunger of the soul. Mosaic theism, with its law and ceremonial, also could not take hold of man's des-

[151]    Concerning the *Aeneid* as a religious epic, cf. Boissier, *La Religion romaine d'Auguste aux Antonins*, I, p. 259 ff.
[152]    Becker-Marquardt, *loc. cit.*, pt. III, p. 430, 434; Friedländer, *loc. cit.*, III, p. 430. One may compare Cicero and Marcus Aurelius in this respect. Although Cicero studied philosophy eagerly and perceived and fought the defects of the Epicurean doctrine and many other systems, he remained unstable in his own life; philosophy educated his head, but not his heart. Though demanding in theory that the truly reasonable man live according to the exalted teachings of philosophy, he had no honorable and exalted impulse as he watched his beloved daughter die and saw his fatherland decline. His letters show us an indifferent, unstable, opportunistic politician, no true philosopher. It is also he who, although in theory he forbade suicide, admired the freely chosen death of Cato. And this undeserved admiration is required reading in our schools to the present day. Hume has already remarked upon the instability of Cicero; *Essays* II, p. 352, (ed. Green Grose).
[153]    Cf. Boissier, *loc. cit.*, Foreword.

tiny and rescue him; the Jews themselves were weak and in need of deliverance.

In this time of general longing for a savior and deliverer, Jesus appeared,[154] the Messiah, and His life and His teachings did rescue mankind. The longing was stilled; life received its true value; despair vanished. Men no longer required suicide as their singular means of salvation in this earthly life.

How this renewal and rejuvenation came to be is contained in the nature of Christ's teachings and their influence on the world.[155]

The basic tenet of the Christian teaching is its exalted and pure monotheism, the belief not only in a just and holy, but also in a loving God, the Creator and Ruler of the universe and of man, His child. Such a faith gives man support in all situations and vicissitudes of life, fills him with hope, bestows confidence upon him, and blesses him with strength. Thus all monotheistic religions are inimical to the appearance and extension of the suicide tendency: Christianity, Judaism, Mohammedanism. (Pantheistic Buddhism encourages suicide, and it is not without meaning that Stoicism, the philosophy of suicide, was pantheistic.)

From the belief in God the Father it follows, as has already been indicated, that Christ entrusted His entire life to the guidance of an all-knowing and infinitely good Providence; all that God ordained for Him He accepted in humble submission, considering this earthly life as a necessary preparation for eternal life after death. The belief in an omniscient, omnipotent, infinitely good God and the conviction that man has an immortal soul never allow the good Christian to despair, but they make him love and value life in all circumstances.

The belief in a loving father defines as a consequence the relationship of man to man: all are brothers from one and the same father.

Christ gave love a new birth, a boundless love which should

154    Concerning this general longing of the world of the time, cf. Hausrath, *Neutestamentl. Zeitgeschichte.*
155    Here an endless number of excellent works could be cited; I refer only to those few, but living, words of Bishop von Ely: *Christi Lehre und Einfluss auf die Welt.* From the English by J. de la Roi.

itself extend to one's enemies. In possession of this love, Christ knew how to order His life to be pleasing to God under all circumstances; love is the bond which unites Him not only with heaven, but also with earth. Who could despair of life if he had only a particle of this love which Paul describes in the unsurpassed hymn to the love of a Christian? There is a soothing balm for the sufferings of a Job in this holy love.

This exalted system of theism, united with the belief in immortality and the morality of love, has a living foundation and cornerstone in the mediation of the Son of God, in Jesus Christ. With faith in Him, all that is abstract, inaccessible and incomprehensible in his religion vanishes for the Christian, because Christ, the Son of Man, becomes for him the object of faith, of hope, of love, of devotion, of self-sacrifice, of veneration, of worship. The life of Christ in its consistent accomplishment of His own teaching gives for life not a dry, but a living lesson, which the faithful are able to live in and with Christ. Can there be a better, more elevated, more godlike life than Christ's? Rousseau answers, "If Socrates lived and died like a philosopher, then Christ lived and died like a God."

The entire life of Christ is truth; the Son of God taught sublime simplicity, and demonstrated perfect purity and holiness in the proper sense of the word. Nothing external clings to Him and His life, no formalism, no ritualism; all came from within Him; all is true, beautiful, and good. He restricted himself only to the Old Testament in His teaching, avoided all artifice, rhetoric, and unnecessary erudition, but nevertheless instilled a new life into His whole system. His teachings and commandments He gave without any illusions, clearly, precisely, authoritatively; He, the mildest, most gentle, most humble, is forceful, energetic, powerful. He, the Son of God, was born in a despised town in poverty, and yet angels and the entire world served Him: His kingdom is not of this world. He, the Man of God, finally suffered the most ignominious death for his conviction. Can there be a better example of how we should live?

Christianity created a new moral world by the sanctification of the relation of man to God; it raised perfect selflessness to a fundamental ethical principle, created a new principle of life in which every believer could participate. Christianity was a new reality which placed the Christian infinitely above the heathen with respect to ethics; an unphilosophical Christian is better prepared than a philosophical pagan.[156]

Christianity became the true teaching for life; the Gospels teach the love of life and not death. Thus, this new message rescued and saved the dying pagan world; Christianity nipped in the bud the morbid suicide tendency of ancient polytheism and returned life to man.[157]

[156]   When Renan now points to Marcus Aurelius and stresses the ethical greatness of this philosopher who did not believe in immortality, praising him as the glory of human nature, the Christian remembers the following. When his wife died, he did not want to enter into a second marriage for the sake of his children, but he lived with a mistress. When he persecuted the Christians, he is said to have mocked the victims. Could a halfway good Christ do that? The Inquisitors, involved in the delusion that only their particular form of Christianity was correct, ordained the sufferings of their sacrifices with shaking hands, broken voices, and tears in their eyes—says a Protestant author. Cf. Lecky's correct judgment, *loc. cit.*, I, p. 231.

[157]   The question of the conversion of the ancient world has received scant attention by theologians and historians. The former explain it very simply as a miracle; the latter, in opposition to miracle, seek to use externals (preparation by the ancients and so on). Both are inadequate. Certainly one must take into account the times, but, despite all natural development, the personal effect of an ethical genius, as was Christ, must be valued. Men like Paul, Augustine, and others were at least as wise as the moderns who scorn religion, and certainly did not accept the new teaching without mature reflection. Many writers look for the efficacious force of Christianity not so much in the whole of its teachings as they do in single elements of the teachings.

Lecky believes that Christian theologians suppressed the suicide tendency by treating death as a punishment for sins. This teaching certainly contributed to the decrease, but this would have remained ineffective if the Christian evaluation of life and the harmonious world-view had not made life tolerable.

Lecky is also of the opinion that the priests, through the introduction of interment to replace cremation, had in their power an effective means for impressing on people the horror of death by concentrating their fantasies on the horror of decomposition. The same objection is to be raised

6. It is not our problem to show how this conversion was gradually accomplished; we only have to observe its result for society.

In the beginning the simple preaching of the Gospel introduced Christianity to the pagans; after some time a well-organized church arose and this supported and spread the teaching of the Gospel. This organization of the Christian community was the natural result of the inner spiritual life, although not every organization is good or turns out according to the mind of its founder.

Among the many churches of the first century, several claimed certain privileges of authority, but it was the Bishop of Rome who gradually won the greatest recognition, and next to him several bishops in the Orient, especially at Constantinople. As soon as Christianity was made the state religion, the spiritual principle blended with the worldly and political, and, in the degree to which the Roman dominion lost power, the church achieved strength and recognition. The church took over the Roman and Byzantine world empire, and in the West the Roman Papacy arose, while in the East the Byzantine Caesar-Papacy attained dominion; the old antagonism between East and West was introduced into the church, and ancient Rome, which stood higher in the eyes of the world than modern Rome, finally came out of the struggle as the victor in every respect.

---

against this, and, in addition, interment was also not infrequent in antiquity.

It is not the fear of punishment after death which suppressed the suicide tendency. The teaching of immortality offers a positive support for life, a joy in life; the more negative influence of fear of future punishment, which need not necessarily be combined with the teaching of immortality, was naturally very influential among many and was also able to sway many from intentions of suicide, as seen, for example, among the American Indians. The wretched people killed themselves to escape their white tormentors, but as the Spaniards convinced them that they would also lose the opportunity of eternal life through suicide, they abstained from the deed through fear. *But the circumstance was not so much the suppression of a suicide tendency already present as it was the evocation of a mental state such that the thought of suicide did not appear at all.* Therefore, the fear of not being buried and other such punishments which were stipulated for suicides also had little effect.

The Roman hierarchy, with the Pope at its apex, in the course of several centuries formed a tightly organized whole, an organism with austere discipline and order whose fearful completion we can study in the Order of Jesuits. Through this organization, the church succeeded in dominating the people and leading them according to its will.

Thus the belief in authority developed the singular and respectful obedience of the Middle Ages, and with time, arrested all human thought and will. Not only in the religious but also in the political and all related areas, its authority was final; the spirit of tutelage arose which Buckle has described so excellently and which we can still find among Catholic peoples.

The influence of the church of the Middle Ages was of great advantage to mankind. The people were perfectly satisfied for a long time; men felt happy; because religion inspired all aspects of life, the masses accustomed themselves to spiritual guidance, and they had in their unified world-view a fixed support for the tragic vicissitudes of life in the Middle Ages. Special stress must be made of the fact that life at that time, compared with the advances of our century, was difficult in every respect; nevertheless, Catholicism succeeded in shaping the morals and the entire outlook on life in such a way that the morbid suicide tendency could not appear. Catholicism makes its adherents patient and obedient; it bestows on man a somewhat peculiar gentleness and mildness and offers, in its teachings and numerous rituals and ceremonies, so much confidence and hope that it does not allow pessimism to appear.

Perhaps one would object that Catholicism in the Middle Ages found an entering wedge mostly among primitive and powerless peoples, and therefore, according to the foregoing, not the belief but the primitive state of nature brought forth this favorable effect. To the contrary, it must be remembered that up to the present day the Catholic peoples in general have shown a lower suicide tendency than the Protestant, that this favorable effect of Catholicism is therefore still to be found. But overlooking this, the Catholic Church, as it displaced the Western Roman Empire, first satisfied the educated Romans themselves. After conversion, the primitive peoples were soon brought to a high level of education by the church, and the favorable effect did not fail to appear, so that we may accurately assert with Comte that Catholicism was most inimical to the rise and spread of the morbid suicide tendency.[158]

Obviously, the effect of Catholicism ceases wherever it loses or has lost its power over the people, as, for example, in France and Austria, in which countries the suicide tendency is very high.

The Greek Church is identical in principle with the Roman, but the principle of authority has grown in it into a kind of mental slavery. The Oriental church is silent, fearfully silent; there is no preaching, no explanation of holy writ in it, only a silent brooding, a loss of the self in religious feelings. Everything depends on stability; there is no yielding to progress; thus, even art must follow ancient rules and norms.

It is natural that such a religion should totally satisfy the people it dominates. The faithful masses find a total peace of soul, the peace of spiritual death; there is no dissatisfaction, no pessimism, no suicide. But the awakening from this sleep is terrible, especially when the sleeper is rudely awakened; he then has nothing to which he can cling—observe the nihilism in Russia today.[159]

[158]    Comte, *Philosophia positive*, V, p. 308. Several authors have attempted to trace the favorable effect of Catholicism back to several special teachings and institutions of the Catholic Church. Osiander believes the faithful Catholic seldom commits suicide because he could not then partake of extreme unction, but that the Protestant favors suicide because he believes in the remission of all sins, including this last one. Arnold looks for the correct explanation in the indulgence; the forgiveness of sins is easily obtained through the indulgence and, therefore, the Catholic is less inclined to delusions and melancholy. *Beobachtungen über die Natur, Art, Ursachen, Verhütungen des Wahnsinns und der Tollheit*, 1784, p. 23. Tissot considers the monasteries especially favorable, Brierre de Boismont the monasteries and confession, Wagner confession, and so on. All these opinions are correct because the teachings and institutions cited make up the greatest part of Catholicism. Still it is not these things alone which bring about the favorable effect, but rather the whole of Catholicism, what we have called, with Buckle, the spirit of tutelage. In order to explain why Catholicism does not promote the morbid suicide tendency, one must keep the whole in view and not individual parts. Concerning the spiritual power of Catholicism, cf. Channing, *Letter on Catholicism*.

[159]    For a detailed exposition see chap. 5, pt. 2, no. 18.

7. The unified world-view of the Middle Ages bestowed peace and happiness as long as it satisfied men; there was no suicide tendency. Human society was ordered in accordance with the unified world-view; every individual has his fixed place in the complex system. But this ordering and systematization of society in the Middle Ages was, for the most part, only external and authoritative. A unified world-view consistently carried out in the life of individuals and of society can arise in two ways. One is through some authority, more or less external, the Pope, the infallibility of one individual; but the unified world-view can also develop externally from the inner life, as an organic process of the unfettered conviction and certainty of all: Protestantism, free investigation (in the Bible), infallibility of all. A unified world-view can be more or less false, but as there is only one truth, there can justly be only one consistent world-view. Catholicism, with the Pope at the apex, ordered society in this sense, certainly with the best purpose. But lasting and true union and unity can only come to be in the second way we have mentioned. Mankind obviously strives to attain a spontaneous, freely chosen, and conscious union without external authority; although external authority may always aid us, fundamentally we desire to achieve union only through freedom.

Of these two methods of directing a society, the former belongs to Catholicism, the latter, to Protestantism; the first is easier, the latter, more difficult: therefore, the power of unified Catholicism and its superiority when contrasted with splintered Protestantism.

Protestantism developed immanently from Catholicism. Protestantism was actually always with Catholicism, but only by the Reformation did Protestantism become a generally recognized principle accepted by many.

The human mind of necessity had to arrive at Protestantism, in the course of time, as the only true outlook. Learning thus broke through into the area designated as sacred and continued to build on the traditional structure of the Greek and Roman Church. The Catholic Church had to lead to humanism because it had preserved the Latin language and its treasures and had prepared an understanding of them. But humanism was pagan in its nature and was, for the most part, a natural opponent of the church and Christianity; fortunately, it was restricted to only a few at the time of the initial sudden awakening. The fall of Constantinople (1453) certainly gave it new nourishment, but because the Greek language still had to be acquired in the West, the effect of Greek literature on the mass of people of the time was slight; today, we feel its proper effect.

Advancements in science, discoveries of strange parts of the world, and the new humanistic movement were strongly encouraged by the discovery of the art of printing, so that the new way of thinking could not be suppressed any longer despite many and persistent attempts to do this.

This intellectual movement was paralleled by the movement in the religio-ethical sphere; it was the real impelling power of the time. The organization of the church of the Middle Ages had led in time to secular activities, and thus *a general striving for an ecclesiastical reformation naturally arose.* Here and there magnificent attempts were made, as for example in Bohemia, but on the whole the fullness of time had not yet come; not until the sixteenth century was the time congenial to the spirit of a reformer like Luther.

Beginning in the fourteenth century, the Papacy had to relinquish its power step by step. Boniface VIII (1294–1303) was the first to almost lose his total authority; soon afterward, the captivity in Avignon demonstrated the weakness of the Papacy, and the Reformation finally completed the great work of spiritual liberation. But the weakness of the Papacy indicated the fragility of Catholicism.

8. We have already specified the method of Protestantism; we must now seek to disclose *its nature and significance for the religious life of mankind.*

We are often told that Protestantism is synonymous with freedom of conscience, tolerance, and similar things; that is true only to a limited degree, to wit, if we mean by it ideal Protestantism. But of the actually extant Protestant churches, many were and are intolerant and without freedom of conscience, just as is and was the case with Catholicism in different places and particular times. True Protestantism, as an historical principle opposed to the historical principle of Catholicism, proceeds from religio-ethical individualism. The Bible—Christ—and not a Pope is the infallible leader of Christians. From this point of view, the true Christian can only be evangelical. But the principle of free inquiry obviously follows from this. Progress and the possibility of perfection are also recognized by this principle, because men cannot perceive the truth all at once but only in the course of time. Evangelical Christianity recognizes no priests and therefore has no hierarchy; its one head, its one leader, is Christ; the evangelical church is bound to no external limitation. Forms and rituals do not make a man a Christian, but a Christian life, the Christian spirit does. Protestantism, thus conceived and realized, develops the character of every individual in that it makes man independent in every respect; it gives everyone true freedom, makes everyone independent and yet binds all in one beautiful whole. This ideal has been reached only approximately in the numerous Protestant sects. Freedom of inquiry can lead to religious despair; the immature individual is in need of the powerful spiritual leadership of the church; the disoriented individual finds it more difficult to maintain faith because he must do without human-priestly mediation. There are also no rituals and ceremonies to which the man who is in want of true religious feeling can cling. Independence of character is frequently achieved at the cost of love for one's fellow men; therefore, Protestants often show a certain insensitivity along with their great fervor, and this also chills the heart when it appears as ethical rigor.

The faithful Protestant is perfectly happy as an evangelical Christian, and he is satisfied with his life; the false, unperfected Protestant, on the other hand, is not happy: without an ethical guide, without any spiritual control, he surrenders himself, gives in to despair, and is not able to find the desired peace for his soul. Thus it happens that extant Protestantism, compared with extant Catholicism, is more amenable to the appearance and spread of the morbid suicide tendency. For this reason many Protestant countries, Denmark, Saxony, and North Germany, show so large a suicide frequency. Certainly the situation is not the same in all Protestant countries; England and America show a lower frequency, lower than Catholic France and Austria. Neither a good Catholic nor a good Protestant will despair of his life, only the bad Catholic, only the bad Protestant; but the bad Protestant despairs sooner than the bad Catholic because he finds himself much more readily in the midst of instability.[160]

9. Since the sixteenth century, not only has Catholicism fought with Protestantism, but generally the believer has clashed with the unbeliever, *and it is this struggle which impresses its character on the modern development of the human spirit.* Because "the real, single and deepest theme of world and human history, to which all remaining themes are subordinate, remains the conflict of unbelief and belief."[161]

The Reformation generally furthered religious life: not only the Protestants, but also the Catholics achieved victories—because both parties sought not only to fight but also to excel. Nevertheless, the numbers of the unfaithful multiplied in all countries, and suicide became more and more frequent. The first period after the Reformation directed general attention to the religious struggle, and, especially during the religious wars, the suicide tendency could not develop. Many cases probably appeared, especially among the humanists, who also emulated their pagan models in this respect.[162] Only since the middle of the eighteenth century has the suicide tendency developed into a social illness, reaching its greatest intensity in our day.[163]

Since the Renaissance, lack of faith, skepticism, and religious indifference has increased in all Christian countries; the positive folk religion—Christianity—daily lost the beneficial influence which it had formerly exercised. Thousands and thousands might

---

[160]  For a further exposition see chap. 5, pt. 2, no. 8.

[161]  Goethe.

[162]  Lecky, *Sittengesch. Europas*, II, p. 43.

[163]  Naturally, it is not accidental that the question of the admissibility of suicide has been treated so frequently since the Renaissance. Not only did the philosophers draw non-Christian ideas from the opinion of the ancients and find themselves thus forced into discussion, but the frequent appearance of suicide also pushed the question into the foreground. Lecky gives a short historical presentation of the more recent views on suicide and an account of the sources, *loc. cit.*

ask with Strauss: Are we still Christians? and answer: No! Do we still have religion? Yes—and no!

This "we" refers to the educated, and those who, correctly or incorrectly, count themselves among them; the (rural) people are still positively faithful, although the educated, to whom their leadership, more than is good, is entrusted, serve them as a model. We wish to believe, and thus, with Strauss, differentiate positive religion from religion in general, but everything in the positive view that we cannot fit into our own views displeases us. Guizot characterizes this religious striving of our day as a negation of the supernatural in the destiny of man and of the universe, an abrogation of the supernatural element in the Christian, as in every religion in general.[164] And we add to this: the educated proclaim this with a zeal which does not fall short of the religious fanaticism of the Middle Ages.[165]

The various ecclesiastical sects, irritated and challenged by the negation of religion which comes in part from the side of science, are now experiencing a great activity. Their effort seldom leads to a reconciliation but to a suppression of thought, just as science labors toward no true reconciliation. The most decisive but also the most unreasonable protest against human knowledge came from Rome, where the Pope in all seriousness declared himself infallible —it was thus that Augustus at one time introduced the cult of the Emperor, because the religious consciousness of the Romans had declined. In fact, science now dominates the mind of the masses, as can be seen in the influence of the press. The popularization of science, carried out in great style, and the corresponding zest for reading by the public show that the need exists which religion and the church are no longer able to fulfill. But science only satisfies

164  *L'église et la société chrétienne en 1861*, p. 13.
165  Such an "atheistic" fanaticism is found in du Bois-Reymond, for example: "Well-acquainted with the boundaries which thus fixed human understanding, he demands nothing more in addition. At this dizzy height of Pyrronism, he disdains the emptiness which yawns about him, filling it with images of his fantasy, and peers fearlessly into the pitiless, ceaseless driving of nature deprived of divinity. . . ." *Darwin versus Galiani*, p. 29.

the mind; it is an insufficient guide for life and death. It is therefore only partially satisfactory, and offers no moral support; it is
not able to lead the masses.

We surrender our intellects to learning, our feelings to a religion and a church in which we no longer believe and which we no
longer trust—that is the single, but atrocious failure of our civilization. *In all our schools, large and small, only the intellect is cultivated.* The school does not concern itself with ethical guidance, but
surrenders this function to positive religion. Thus, modern society is led by two spiritual forces, learning and religion, but because these forces are engaged in a struggle with one another, the
guidance is both insufficient and destructive. For lack of a unified
world-view, no perfect character can be created, only an intellectual and moral chaos. Every war hurts the victor as well as the van-
quished, and the *Kulturkampf* is no exception to this rule.[166]

In such a time spiritual anarchy can produce no widespread,
fundamental culture, only a half-education, a half-culture, and our
civilization is characterized by an incompleteness, with all its terrible implications for head and heart, which is unable to attain unity
and harmony. Fools and clever people, Goethe says, are harmless;
only the half-fools and the half-wise are dangerous.[167]

But intellectual and moral incompleteness increases with the
increase in the extent and advancement of learning, for it is inconceivable that one could obtain fundamental knowledge with ease:
knowledge is won and digested only with difficulty. "The dangers
of half-education, the superficial sipping of each and all to the complete neglect of a basic and serious study of general knowledge, are
greater today to an even greater extent than previously, as the
greater and more extensive grow the demands made on every truly
educated person, and as the more often such attempts to sip everything become fruitless. . . ." The moral influence of this intellec-

---

[166]   Instructive in this respect is the book by J. V. v. Schweizer, *Zeit-
geist und Christentum*, 1861.

[167]   The *National* newspaper excellently characterized how pernicious
is the present time with the words: "The cultivation of the upper ten thousand has once again sunk to the depths. That is all." June 9, 1878.

tual decline and dullness appears most often where individuals rise, in the worst cases, to a complete disdain for all knowledge and every high purpose in life, the result of which is almost always the wildest, most unbridled life and complete depravity.[168]

Along with a deadening indifference, vexing skepticism and disgusting cynicism are spread; men are dissatisfied and unhappy, and, more and more loudly and menacingly raising their voices, they do not shrink back from a revolutionary reorganization of society.

[168]   H. Beckers, *Über das Bedürfniss einer zeitgemässen Regelung der allgemeinen Studien an Deutschlands Hochschulen,* 1862.

It can easily be seen that where formal education is very good, in Germany for example (cf. p. 68), the dangers of half-education are very great. In England and America, men not only learn in school but in travels, on the railroads, in short, through practical life, while in Germany and here in Austria, life offers little in the way of education. Examine, for example, the graduates of our Hochschulen. In the Gymnasium they learn mathematics, Greek and Latin, the literature of their people, and some natural science; at the university they devote themselves to special studies, taking their exams in philosophy, jurisprudence, or some other special branch and then step into life—but they bring nothing for life with them, nothing at all! In "life" they must, above all, have character—but to this end they have been given nothing; they should be prepared to be citizens —but they know nothing of politics, except what the newspapers regurgitate for them; they become husbands and fathers—but they know nothing of bringing up children, the duties of a husband, what family life requires. The dreary picture is too tragic for me to paint it in more detail, and I leave it to those responsible for the education of our youth to reflect upon. However, even well-regulated schools, in which more attention is paid to the discipline of the instructors than of the students, are of no use if they do not satisfy the demands of life, and our schools absolutely do not answer to these demands.

But the disparity between our intellectual and moral education is even more glaring. Men spend twenty years in school learning more and more, but no one is concerned about their feelings and about their will. (Will someone not object that the Gymnasium student attends classes in religion twice a week? Granted that this instruction were as good as it is bad, it is still instruction, but the will needs instruction also. And who says anything ethical to our university students?) That is the incompleteness of which I speak.

Bacon has already said that a half-knowledge leads men away from God.[169] To the degree that incompleteness spreads, it produces atheism, or worse, observable irreligiosity. There are few true atheists, but there are many doubters and men who have rejected the old faith without replacing it with anything new. But irreligiosity among most men, if not among all, leads to dissatisfaction. As things are, man still needs moral support in life and death in addition to knowledge, but only religion can really offer him this. If he loses such support, if it is unscrupulously taken from him, his peace of soul vanishes with it.[170]

When the faith which elevates and unites one to God disappears, then something horrible transpires. The soul, drawn by its own weight into the depths, so to speak, sinks and sinks without stopping, and drags down with it its intelligence which is now torn from its base, clinging now to everything which it meets in its way through the depths, now in painful anxiety, now with a desperation like the laughter of the insane. Constantly tortured by an insatiable compulsion and thirst for life, it soon snatches at anything, vainly seeking to animate it, to find in it inspiration, to deify it; soon empty abstractions persecute it, then flee, the formless shadows of its fantasy. . . . All high

[169]   A little philosophy inclines man's mind to atheism, but depth in philosophy brings man's mind to religion. *De augm. scient.*, I, Col. 5.
[170]   Speaking of the Stoic's unfulfilled peace of mind, Beneke says: ". . . the destinies and imperfections of other men protest against and sympathize with the unending misery under whose burden millions groan and perish every moment, and with the unending foolishness, pleasure seeking, hate and malice by which the divine image in man is disfigured . . . from this point of view reflection therefore points to religion as the sole means of protecting one's self from gloomy despair or intense exasperation; it forms the necessary complement, or rather the necessary apex and completion of the moral world view." *Grundlinien der Sittenlehre*, II, p. 391. Lichtenberg says: "Probably one of the most difficult arts of man is to provide one's self with courage. Those who lack it first find it under the protective arm of one who possesses it, and who can provide help for us when all is lost. Because there is so much suffering in the world to be faced with courage, no one human being can give enough strength to one who is weak; thus religion is excellent. It is really the art of providing oneself with confidence and courage in suffering with thoughts of God, plus the power to labor against it."

abilities and powers weaken and lie as in a deep sleep; all those mysterious powers of the soul which create a spiritual world order in and around us, a realm of morals which forms the nature of the true inward man, die little by little, and, with a pain which tears at his innermost being, man feels this gradual death of his better self. His soul hungers; he has no nourishment for it; where shall he begin? He kills his soul in order to hunger no more, to experience this inner torture no more . . . torn from his bearings he is like a leaking ship without pilot and rudder tossed here and there on the comfortless ocean of this universe.[171]

The social mass phenomenon of suicide is to be explained in the same way as a tragic result of the prevalent irreligiosity of the masses.

*Today, there are two great classes of men: believers and non-believers, Christians and those who are no longer Christians.* The faithful have a moral support, are happy, satisfied, and reconciled to life, but only a very few of the unbelievers are truly happy and satisfied, because only a few can find a support in life comparable to positive religion. "Moral anarchy" satisfies these few; the majority are destroyed by intellectual and moral anarchy.

Our great tensions and the progressively growing number of mentally ill are to be ascribed on the one hand to *this intellectual and moral anarchy*; on the other hand, it is fed by *a pessimistic world-view* which not only finds its eloquent expression in modern poetry and philosophy, but which also makes life really intolerable for thousands and thousands. Surveying the large number of pessimistic poets of recent times—Young, Byron, Shelley, Poe, Grabbe, Hölderlin, Heine, Kleist (who even played with suicide), Lenau, Senancour, Musset, Foscolo, Leopardi, Carducci, Giusti, Lermontov, Pushkin, Gogol—and comparing them with Schopenhauer's pessimistic philosophy, a direct confirmation is thus seen of the tragedy which the data of suicide so tediously repeat: we are weary with life; we have no real joy in life. Our poets sing

[171]   Lamennais, *Discussions critiques et pensées diverses sur la religion et la philosophie.* Cf. the honest confession of Zöllner in his *Abhandlungen*, III, p. 36 ff.

lamentations of death to the multitudes of suicides; the funeral sermon is delivered in the Frankfurt manner.

10. We must now recapitulate the result of the previous investigation and, with as much precision as possible, trace the social mass phenomenon of suicide to a general principle.

Darwin considered suicide a means of growth; in the struggle for existence the mentally ill and degenerate are destroyed. But this explanation is not adequate for the historical phenomenon, because the problem is to show how and why so many now become mentally ill and commit suicide. The struggle for existence— assuming that it were a social principle—does not explain this because generally it explains nothing. For the same reason, Morselli's generalization also is not an explanation.[172] He agrees with Darwin that suicide is an effect of the struggle for existence and of human selection, which proceeds according to the law of the evolution of civilized peoples.

Wagner generalizes in another way, but also incorrectly.[173] Irreligiosity is not the final reason for the tragic phenomenon, but this and all remaining reasons are functions of a certain inborn natural-mental constitution. The latter is perhaps to be traced back to the varieties of the material substratum of human mental activity, to varieties of brain formation and brain substance, which, although on the surface so trivial, are essential for mental processes. Wagner is correct that the final demonstrable processes are physical processes of the brain, but how do these transformations arise? Why do they appear among certain individuals and, at certain times, more readily than among others? There are mental processes which operate continually in the life of society and which frequently have a pathological and physiological influence; mental illness in most cases also develops from certain psychical processes which in time bring about changes in the organism, and a medical doctor, but not a sociologist, may examine these as the final causes of the disease. The tendency to suicide appears as an historical phenomenon and must therefore be traced back, as such, to a

172    P. 478.
173    Pp. 188, 189.

mental process, not a physiological process. Wagner himself does this when he is of the opinion, in agreement with Lisle, that suicide does not appear where religious ideas are still inner objects of belief for the mass of followers, and where the modern tendency to indifference and the complete emancipation of thought has still made little progress.[174] In this respect, the proper cause of suicide is therefore not transformation of the brain substance, but the historical process cited.

*The contemporary social mass phenomenon of suicide results from the collapse of a unified world-view that has consistently given Christianity its value among the masses in all civilized countries.* The struggle of free thought with positive religion leads to the irreligiosity of the masses, signifying intellectual and moral anarchy and—death. The great achievements in learning of recent times forcibly obtrude themselves on men; most individuals become acquainted with higher culture without proper preparation, and it is a known sociological law that a sudden and unprepared acquaintance with a higher culture results in the decline of the less civilized.[175] As the lower races die out when they come in contact with the higher, that is, more civilized, races in civilized society, those strata of the population which higher culture suddenly invades die out. But it is especially in the large cities where this process operates, because the city with its more intellectual culture dominates the rural population as, for example, the white race in America dominates the Indians. *Suicides are the bloody sacrifices of the civilizing process, the sacrifices of the "Kultur-kampf."*

Every people experiences such a struggle in his history, and so

---

[174]    This confusion explains why we count Wagner, nevertheless, among those investigators who see the proper (social) basis of the malady in irreligiosity.

[175]    Gerland, *Über das Aussterben der Naturvölker*, 1868, p. 84 ff. Anyone who has eyes to see can observe this process among us in Vienna, which absorbs so many uneducated elements, especially from the south of Europe, and "civilizes" them. Thus, in 1869–78, the members of the Greek-Oriental Church here in Vienna showed the relatively highest suicide frequency, in contrast to the general rule.

suicide appears periodically. Among all peoples the moment comes when religion has lost its power over the people, and then suicide always appears as a social mass phenomenon. All modern peoples are now at this stage of their development, and the same phenomenon has appeared among them.

It appears that the development of mankind passes through successive stages of belief and unbelief; its previous development at least evidences this law. Of course, the strength of the Christian folk religion has been disappearing for several centuries, and this disappearance provides the general dissatisfaction and weariness with life. Whether Christianity will disappear entirely and a new folk religion take its place, or whether a new form will appear again and perhaps satisfy the people, cannot be answered by our inquiry.

## Section 2. Verification of the General Proposition Obtained. The Religious Condition of Contemporary Civilized Nations.

1. Our investigation has shown that the morbid suicide tendency of the present is conditioned by the generally widespread irreligiosity. Although the previous materials make this sufficiently clear, I wish to verify or at least indicate in detail the general results of statistical investigations and of psychological and historical analysis.

Obviously only the primary individual and social causes of suicide deserve consideration, and the religious condition of civilized peoples especially must be investigated. If the result of this investigation agrees with the data of the suicide statistics presented in Chapter 2, the correctness of our generalization will then be assured beyond doubt.

2. *The urban population* is to a recognized degree not as religious as the rural population and also shows more suicides than the latter. That which we call civilization in general is especially found in the city. Thought and will are more intensive here and

generate that tension in the denser population which is favorable to the development and spread of psychosis and the suicide tendency. But the influx of the rural population and its sudden entrance into the life of the city especially tips the scale. The *Kulturkampf*, with all its tragic results, is at issue especially in the cities.

Suicides among women are significantly lower than among men. This comes from the fact that men must bear the sorrows of life more than women. Mental labor is the work of men, and they therefore fall more often into that state of discord which conquers joy and teaches the love of death. But the greater religiosity of women always protects them from the morbid suicide tendency.

Suicide is committed more frequently in maturity or when man is most in need of religious support, when the full responsibility of life is upon him. But the fact that contemporary youth have lost their joy in life is the most tragic sign of our instability and a serious accusation against the extant methods of education and child-rearing. In the tender years of life the sensitive heart is infected by the pestilential smell of modern negation and only a few achieve a harmonious education.

Immoral marital conditions and all generally immoral conditions eliminate religious sanction as such and facilitate the disposition to suicide: concubinage, separation, etc.

The great suicide tendency among military personnel is a clear demonstration of our interpretation. The philosophy of life, which at present is manifested by the military services, is wanting throughout in either true moral or religious content, and suicide therefore appears more frequently among soldiers than among civilians. It must be especially emphasized that the men in command, particularly the officers, suffer from the morbid tendency and that intellectual education—only this is promoted—without corresponding moral formation cannot solely suffice for sustaining life. The culture required by the military is generally the prototype which we have described as half-education, and we therefore have a direct confirmation of our view in the high suicide frequency among military personnel.

The statistics, especially on the half-education of the suicide,

have been set forth; the data indicate that the motives of suicides
are seldom moral. The reality of modern superficiality is a fact
of whose existence everyone can be easily persuaded.

2. The remaining conditions do not need to be repeated here.
It suffices to remind the reader to remember what was said about
the research concerning the isolated causes and motives of suicide,
and we therefore turn to our main point: the statement of religious
conditions, and we first consider the Catholic peoples.

THE CATHOLIC PEOPLES. The Reformation
called forth the Catholic Counter-Reformation. The gross conflicts
benefited both parties as far as one or the other side was not actually stifled, which rarely happened. The Roman Church inwardly
acquired new footing and new life, was enriched and strengthened
by religious feeling, and it experienced from without and from
within a glorious renaissance. Theology bloomed anew in the
seventeenth century, and in it we have the best measure of the vitality of Catholic belief at that time. The inward religious life produces the true mystic, a holy Teresa, a St. Francis of Sales, a
Silesius. But the power of the church is best represented by the new
order of Jesuits, under whose artful direction and organization
the hierarchical principal of Catholicism was enunciated as the
*ne plus ultra*. The history of this order is the history of its church.

In the eighteenth century, the Catholic peoples began to lose
their faith, especially the masses among whom the church had built
stable spiritual conditions. The Jesuits were driven from all
countries; but this was only the beginning of the strife, for in all
Catholic lands the state and the church must necessarily provide
leadership if the society has not become devout. Protestantism
answered the question concerning the relationship of church and
state in simple terms, since their church had no external organization with which to deal with worldly things; there is no priesthood
and no hierarchy. But the Roman hierarchy cannot surrender their
power as a hierarchy, and so we see in all Catholic countries the
strife of church and state: in Italy, France, Belgium, (Austria).
But the blooming of Catholic disbelief is best seen in the literary

enlightenment of the preceding century, especially in France; the great revolution tore down the old, decaying edifice.

Our century carried on the destruction with apparent smoothness, because it was systematic; characteristic of our time is the decline of the church-state with its persisting effects on all Catholic peoples and sovereigns. But Catholic internal affairs are characterized by the last general Council and by Ultramontanism. The declaration of the infallibility of the Pope, if it follows logically from Catholicism, indicates that it was proclaimed at the present time to positively recognize—in practice it understood this for a long time, yes always—the great danger in which the Roman church has found itself. In his Syllabus the Pope has characterized modern disbelief better than any other writer.*

The reigning churchly outlook asserts itself as so-called Ultramontanism. It is not concerned so much with belief as with the church, with the means not the end. It is a revival of the true papal view of the Middle Ages, an attempt to bring back the society of passive obedience and belief in authority, to awaken again the Catholic spirit of paternalism. The dangers of revolution and the libertarian tendencies in general sparked the need; the reaction was introduced with the help of the Pope: politicians and poets concur on its assertion as the only soul-saving church. This reaction is generally against freedom and is especially directed against Protestantism.[176] With special reference to the latter, the reaction

---

* [Pope Pius IX (1846–78), Syllabus accompanying the encyclical *Quanta Cura* which was issued Dec. 8, 1864.—Trans.]

[176]    De Maistre's point of view is the basis of the Ultramontanist reaction. In his book on the characteristics of the Papacy, he distinguished the Catholic principle of stability from free Protestantism; he clearly perceives that there exists a very great analogy, of brotherliness and mutual dependence, between papal and royal power, and that every revolt against the former is at the same time a revolt against the latter. How this is related to Protestantism is indicated by another index, that the princes are much more short-lived in Protestant countries than in Catholic. That de Maistre defended the Spanish Inquisition to the end of his life is not strange (*Lettres sur l'Inquisition espagnole*), if one remembers his celebrated essays on the executioner in *Les Soirées de St. Petersbourg. Du*

also turns against the inner protest of Catholics; for there are—this must be candidly declared—many Protestants under Catholic domination, Protestants who know freedom only negatively, not as positive (evangelical) Protestantism. The well-bred Catholics in particular are fervid, thoroughgoing Protestants who are truly odious to the Papists and Catholic formalists, but who remain Catholics all the same because conversion is distressing to them and because they do not wish to become positive Protestants or do not wish to be known publicly.

However, this indicates the peculiar character of the Catholic peoples at the present time. The split between the educated and the uneducated is very wide; both parties have nothing in common. The people are still Catholic and ritualistic, the well-bred are peculiar Protestants, but Protestants to whom it has not yet become convenient to be struck from the roll of Catholic parishes. Therefore, we find in all Catholic countries, without exception, a

---

*Pape*, 1819. With special reference to Protestantism see *Oeuvres inédites* 1870: "Réflexions sur le Protestantisme dans ses rapports avec la souveraineté." He says there: "The great enemy of Europe which it is necessary to stifle by all *legal* means, the deadly ulcer which afflicts all sovereignties and which unceasingly undermines them, the issue of pride, the father of anarchy, the universal solvent, is Protestantism.

"What is Protestantism? It is the rebellion of individual reason against general reason. . . . The Kings are the annointed, the priests are magistrates, the priesthood is an order, sovereignty is holy, religion is civil! The two powers are integral; each confers on the other a part of its force, and in spite of the quarrels which have divided these two sisters, they cannot live in separation." The basis of Christian religion: "The fundamental principle of that religion, the universe before the innovators of the sixteenth century, was the infallibility of the instruction from whence resulted blind respect for authority." Protestantism is a religious and political heresy which blindly believes that no ritual is good and which will remain opposed to the Catholic conception of the individual. Therefore, the state can at no time tolerate Protestantism, but will seek with all permissible severity—"all useless severity is criminal and . . . all severity is innocent if it is necessary (*sic!*)." In short: "Protestantism is positively and, in the last analysis, the religion of the rabble. One invokes the word of God, another the rights of man, but it all adds up to the same thing. The two brothers have smashed sovereignty to distribute it to the multitude."— One cannot say anything worse, or anything better about Protestantism.

certain characteristic indifference and skepticism which cannot be suppressed by all the grandiose efforts of the church's hierarchy. Straight through Catholicism every thinker is provoked to skepticism when religious teaching becomes authoritarian, when one is permitted only blind belief with no attendant conviction and no certain knowledge or judgment. The disbeliever thus ridicules or affects witticism, or easily falls into a gross, petty cynicism. The seasoned Protestant is unsophisticated, not convinced by thought, and has little room for wit and ridicule, because learning to him is not as highly valued as with the Catholic; many teachers and institutions of the church are thus provoked to criticism.

The consequences of such a situation cannot fail to appear. Where the church and religion do not join their strength in the exercise of power, there the church probably remains outwardly in the right, but her inner life is foul. In this way half-education rises to a degree which does not permit the sound development of character, and which leads then, in its emptiness and despair where moral strength is needed, to ennui and suicide.

Half-education is greatest where the modern outlook has made the greatest progress: France and Austria. Where learning has made little progress, in Italy, Spain, and Portugal, there is little half-education and therefore few suicides.[177]

3. We will now review particular Catholic countries in succession, beginning with France, which is typical of enlightened Catholic countries.[178]

---

[177]     With the following exposition, compare what was said (chap. 2, no. 4 et seq.) about education in the various countries.

[178]     One must study for its spirit the collected literatures of all peoples to criticize the religious literature of any one people; from regional and area studies one can then estimate: *biblical propagation, Sunday schools, conversion of unbelievers (external and internal missionary work), church attendance, voluntary bequests for spiritual ends, number of communicants, relative number of clerics, growth of the creed, number of mixed marriages, numbers seeking instruction, etc.*

Of those works which deal with this subject, I especially recommend: Funck-Brentano, *La Civilization et les lois*, 1876; Guizot, *L'église et la société chrétienne en 1861*; LePlay, *La Réforme sociale in France, 1874*; Dollinger, *Kirche und Kirchen, Papsttüm und Kirchenstaat*, 1861; Mari-

Descartes, founder of the modern intellectual temper, was the first to show Frenchmen the viewpoint they should adopt toward the church and positive belief: skepticism. And the French have, for the most part, followed his teaching down to the present day. Anyone who has read the *Discourses* knows how deftly the great thinker turns his thesis of methodical skepticism against the ruling church; and his sojourn into Protestant countries clearly indicates that he probably understood the effects of his outlook on the Catholic Church. After Descartes, skepticism, through Bayle, was directed entirely to the overthrow of religious rule. Eighteenth-century enlightenment was no longer satisfied with skepticism, but passed over to negation and total destruction; the more prudent members of this movement—including Voltaire—truly wished for a natural religion with an inclusive theism, but the aroused masses would no longer be restrained and revolution broke out, the bloody protest against the paternalistic system of the Middle Ages.[179] The specter of revolution sobered the French, and the reaction began against all spheres of theoretical thought and practical application. The schools of philosophy attempted a reconciliation of thought and belief. The poets interested themselves in Catholic-Christian ideals and the ruling classes sought to restore the Catholic political system of the Middle Ages. De Maistre's aforementioned book on the Pope presents itself as a model which the French ruling classes followed as far as was possible, until recently. The refined classes were not free believers, but only conformed externally to Catholicism; De Maistre presents—and it is this special characteristic which Comte rightly stressed—only historical and political, not theological arguments for the restitution of the Pope.[180]

---

ano, *Christianesimo, cattolicismo e civiltà*, 1879; the apologists Hettinger and Luthardt; the Church histories of Hagenbach, Kurz, Möhler, Alzog; *Siebente Hauptversammlung der Evangelischen Allianz: Berichte und Reden*, ed., Riggenbach, 1879.

[179]   Concerning the reigning unbelief among the upper classes, among clerics and the people, see Taine, *Die Entstehung des modernen Frankreichs* (German translation by Katscher), 1877, I., p. 298 et seq., 408.

[180]   Comte, loc. cit. IV, p. 28. It is not beside the point to recall that Comte himself was strongly influenced by De Maistre's work on the

Chateaubriand's *Génie du christianisme* (1802) warmly glows with feeling and daydreams for the Papacy, but its result was not effective. The refined classes remained unbelievers despite really superhuman efforts by the Church.

The religious and the credulous defected to Protestantism, as, for example, Lamennais. Auguste Comte's religion of humanity thus numbers important partisans from the refined classes, and Renan's book on Jesus has become, in fact, a popular work.[181] That the French people no longer cling to the church is indicated by their attitude in the contemporary strife of the Catholic hierarchy against the free republican leaders.

But an odd characteristic of our times is *the attitude of modern French society when confronted by Protestantism.*

Protestantism was quickly extirpated in France, not so much by Catholicism, but because it was considered a political party and, as such had to yield to the centralization of the monarchy which had been operative for centuries. A few remnants of Protestantism were tolerated. But at present a strong sympathy for Protestantism

---

Papacy: he arrived at his view of the positive laws of society through the reactionary Catholic movement and the revolutionary ideas which sprang up about him. Cf. loc. cit. IV, p. 138.

How the official introduction of Catholicism reacted against itself is seen in the following situation. In 1801, when General Bonaparte negotiated the Concordat with the Pope, the Papal delegate was required to travel by night so that he would not be seen in Paris, for it was not known whether the celebrating populace would tolerate his presence. When the Cardinal was presented to Napoleon, he had a golden crucifix which he was to present to Napoleon, but this was not risked and the crucifix was carried to Napoleon by other means. Cf. Thiers, *Hist. du consulat et de l'empire*, 1845, III, p. 274, 444. In general, the history of the Concordats which Napoleon concluded with the Papacy is the history of the entire reaction.

[181]    Comte's development, so far as his life and his mental labors are concerned (in terms of the rule established in n. 187), is an example of the conditions of modern civilized nations. He—who saw the half-education of our times, who sought a new world outlook with all the ardor of his soul and originated a new religion and worked out a noble positive philosophy —was mentally ill himself and sought to take his own life. There is something awesome about the human arena in which men fight their battles!

has awakened among Frenchmen and there are many coversions, particularly of esteemed men: Renouvier, Pillon, Sarcy, Reveilland, Juls Fauvre, etc. Many join Protestantism for political reasons, for "religious opportunities," because they do not wish to entrust the freedom of the nation to Clericalism-Catholicism, perceiving that a republic without religion cannot endure.[182] Truly noble is the evangelical work of the English pastor M'All. Going to Belleville, the seat of the Communards, he distributed religious tracts and learned from the workers that the people yearned for a true religion, not a religion of authority. M'All joined the workers and has already preached evangelicalism in twenty-three sections of Paris and is beginning evangelical work in other cities (Lyon, etc.).[183] To what extent the work has succeeded, one cannot yet judge; but I do not believe that the French will become believing Protestants. I see only their perplexity; Catholicism no longer suits them, and they are incapable of replacing it with something better. I fear that the French are still disposed to a hierarchy; the Church has inculcated the spirit of its thought so deeply that even Comte could not free himself from it. No one has criticized or condemned the consistency and learning of Catholicism better than the founder of Positivism, and, yet, on the other hand, no one—with the exception of De Maistre—possesses the Catholic view more than Comte himself. The French people must first have true religious needs; they will then find the true way. Nowhere has a good religion arisen from mere political, economic, or other similar needs. The French will find no peace for their souls so long as they do not become truly religious. The mere wish to believe does not bring deliverance to any group; only the living belief itself permits it to remain vigorous.

The high suicide tendency, which France and especially its major cities show, develops naturally with the religious instability of the French people. The sturdy edifice of Catholicism buried unfortunate and dissatisfied thousands in its ruins.

4. Religious conditions in Belgium are similar to France. This is natural since its literature stems from France and since in Bel-

---

[182]    Cf. no. 18, concerning America.
[183]    The detailed history of the entire movement is given by H. Bonard, *White Fields of France*, 1880.

gium the French spirit also has a strong foothold. French elements rule all areas of intellectual life.

The federation with Protestant Holland (1815) aroused the Belgian clergy to vigorous opposition, the people freely allowing themselves to be led by the Ultramontanists. However, an unresolved war has existed between liberalism and Catholicism since around 1830, with the former in the advantage at present. The refined classes are liberal and inclined to Protestantism for various political and philosophical reasons; Laveleye, Goblet d'Alviella, Frere-Orban converted to Protestantism. The people, in part, still allow themselves to be led by the clerics.[184] Characteristic of the country is the continuance of the "Catholic" university at Louvain and its antithesis, the scientific "liberal" university at Brussels.

5. Austria, as a Catholic country, resembles France despite differences of nationality. The Reformation was suppressed through the largest part of Austria, and the authority and the power of the church was thereby renewed. The constant warfare against the Turks also strengthened the Christian convictions of the people. But, as everywhere, the spirit of the Enlightenment seized Austria; this was confined much more to the external, ecclesiastical life, while the inner spiritual life was neglected.

The reforming Kaiser, Joseph II, dispensed with all systematic thought and deep conviction. It was he who first broke the power of the hierarchy; he wished to wed the ecclesiastical official to the secular official in a bureaucratic organization. He was concerned first of all with the eradication of glaring abuses, and, although he was also the first to give the patent of tolerance to converted Protestants, he was still far removed from true tolerance, for the achievement and inspiration of true religious feeling did not lie in his heart.[185] The entire reign of Joseph breathed religious indifference, and thus it did not reap blessed fruits.

---

[184]  In 1829 there were 280 cloisters; in 1846, 779; in 1846 there were 11,968 living in cloisters; in 1866, 18,098. In 1846 there was an increase in religious processions carried out in the manner of the Middle Ages.

[185]  When university professors were first exempted in 1782 from the obligation of swearing an oath to the Immaculate Conception of Mary, it was a true benefit for the people of that time; but we find this also in the Kaiser's edicts, for example, those concerning burial ceremonies, etc.

Joseph's successor, awakened by the French revolution, struck up a new friendship with the Church; the Jesuits, previously banished, were recalled to the country (1820) and sought to remove the Protestant spirit and the Enlightenment by all possible means. Metternich's regime removed the stamp of indifference; from week to week the masses were held in check, and every movement was nipped in the bud.[186] The revolution of 1848, a somewhat stronger outbreak than had occurred for several centuries in European society, brought many freedoms, but it also prolonged the established authority of Rome (Concordat). Still, the anti-churchly and the anti-religious spirit was not extinguished, and thus our fatherland, as well as France, presents a sad picture of half-education and religious frigidity, in which the noblest spirits themselves cannot come to a harmonious formation of character.[187] All who

---

[186]  "Light-hearted, rationalistic, patronizing the Catholic Church only in consideration of decisions of state, rich in political thoughts, poor in great ideas to save the state, flexible, pliant, but also like steel concerning matters of state, widely overestimated and excessively criticized after his failures, Metternich possessed everything to endear him to the Kaiser, indeed to make him indispensable." Krones, *Handb. d. Gesch. Österr.*, 1879, IV, p. 619. His helper Gentz perhaps may serve even better than Metternich as a type of the Austrian of the period. At first inspired by the French Revolution, then fearing the horrors of the movement, he turned away from the cause of freedom, so that, like most thinkers of that period, he threw out the baby with the dirty water. By birth a Protestant, he served the church out of purely selfish economic motives. He saw in de Maistre's book on the Papacy the quintessence of the art of statecraft and participated in an empty and frivolous court life, never finding true religious conviction. His letter to the Austrian Kaiser is characteristic; like others, he explains his resignation from the Prussian diplomatic service by his opposition to Protestantism. In it he found, after "manifold, extensive investigation," the "root of all contemporary decadence and one of the main causes for the decline of all Europe." (At that time, Vienna was the convening place of Protestant converts: Fr. v. Schlegel, A. H. Müller, and others.)

[187]  A type of this kind is our Austrian poet Lenau, whose life and development exhibit in microcosm the development of modern man, especially the development of his contemporary pathological condition (psychosis and the tendency to suicide). Sociology certainly cannot apply its observations so well to ordinary individuals as it can successfully employ

lay claim to education are irreligious and indifferent; outwardly they observe the religious rites, but lack an inner life. The peculiar skepticism of the French is not found among us. There is, however, a type of indifference which marks us much more than cynicism. National disputes claim all our intellectual and moral energies; but for a truly moral and unified development of life organization, there is no certain foundation; despite the indifference toward heretical beliefs, we are intolerant, especially of Protestants. This intolerance has been a customary practice and points up the superficial indifference which is not a conscious religious life; it is a known fact that indifference and intolerance go hand in hand.[188] If I could summarize in a word the spiritual atmosphere in which

---

them with outstanding thinkers who experience the intellectual labor of all men in their mental struggles. This kind of study is very fruitful, and the practiced reader has already noticed that I have used the analogy of individual development with social development to its fullest extent. I may take this occasion to remark that this method is scientifically justified. Comte has been the first to apply it, with great advantage, even though he has not sufficiently demonstrated its legitimacy. Häckel has sought to establish it as a fundamental biogenetic law with the help of heredity and adaptation. This law, fundamental also for sociology, signifies that the development of every individual is a short and quick repetition of the development of his peculiar species. Comte, loc. cit., III, p. 242 ff., 8 ff., IV, 442 ff.; Häckel, *Generelle Morphologie der Organismen*, 1866, II, p. 110 ff.; *Natürl. Schöpfungsgesch.* 1874, p. 275 ff.

The excellent biography of Lenau by his friend Anastasius Grün has been widely disseminated and read, making it necessary to indicate only the main points. Catholic in his youth, Lenau matured to Protestantism. This did not satisfy him and then he sank into Spinozaism, which also was unable to give him lasting satisfaction. With God and the world disintegrating, he sought forgetfulness in materialism. Illness, melancholy, psychosis, and attempted suicide are the unhappy end of one of the most noble spirits and champions of our Fatherland. There is naturally a correspondence between his greater poems and this developmental process: *Faust, Savanarola, Albigenser, Don Juan*; suicide is glorified in his lyrical poetry.

[188]    Cf. LePlay, loc. cit., I, p. 171. One sees Austrian intolerance, for example, in the obstacles placed by the authorities in the way of the Free Church in Bohemia, of evangelism and every religious movement in general.

we live, I would call it bureaucratic Catholicism or indifference.[189]

That is the general picture. The various kingdoms and nations differ somewhat in particulars.

The Germans lead in intellectual development and enlightenment. The inhabitants of the Alps in Germany, and among these the Tyroleans in particular, are religious and followers of the

[189]     A glance at the Austrian press vindicates this severe judgment. In 1879 there were some 1020 newspapers and journals; of the 300 political papers, only a few more than 70 are Catholic-conservative. All the rest are rationalistic and most definitely anti-religious. Of the Catholic papers, there were in:

| | | | |
|---|---|---|---|
| Vienna | 11 | Bohemia | 4 |
| Remaining Lower Austria | 2 | Moravia | 3 |
| Upper Austria | 3 | Silesia | 2 |
| Salzburg | 1 | Galicia | 14 |
| Styria | 5 | Dalmatia | 2 |
| Carinthia | 2 | Trieste | 3 |
| Carniola | 3 | Hungary | 10 |
| Tyrol, Vorarlberg | 7 | Croatia | 4 |
| Görz | 2 | Slavonia | 1 |

When one considers that Austria is a predominantly Catholic country and ponders the intellectual power of the press exercised in our time, he must truly feel shame: compared with the non-Christian press, intellectual weakness and the indolence of Austrian Catholicism shows itself in the Catholic press. (While the *Vaterland*, the most significant Catholic political paper, has only 4,000 subscribers, the *Neue freie Presse*, a thoroughly anti-Christian paper, already has 30,000.)

The following approximate data concerning Catholic newspapers and journals may serve as a comparison with other Catholic countries (as I collected the data in 1877):

| | |
|---|---|
| Austria | 88 |
| Germany | 260 (140 of these are exclusively political) |
| Belgium | 143 |
| France | 160 |
| Italy | 140 |
| North America (with six million Catholics) | 100 |

The American weekly *Pilot* has about 90,000 subscribers!

Church. The remaining Germans are neither followers nor religious.

Following the Germans in enlightenment are the Czechs. After they were led back to the womb of the Catholic Church through the brutal executions of the Counter-Reformation, the entire national character declined, to be awakened for the first time to national self-consciousness in our century. In a short time, the Czech people accomplished a great deal, but all advances do not indicate a loss of religiosity. The Bohemians are a  peculiar example of religious  half-education. The memory of Hus has advanced to such a degree among the educated segment of the nation that Cardinal Schwarzenburg at the last Council  of God's Worship declared the country was becoming Hussite internally. But this Hussitism appears as an artistic seedling. The rural populace, especially in Moravia, clings to the priests who have become Ultramontanistic toward all the people for some time. Hussitism remains as a liberal trifle with a united voice and is really the index of enlightenment, but it is not a religious tendency as in the past. It is enlightened half-education and instability, conjunctive with critical national consciousness.

The Poles, embracing a national pessimism with partiality, are not much better in their religious outlook than the other two nations. They occasionally like to be known as Catholics. We do not have anything comparable in Austria, for it is a manner of sympathetic demonstration associated much more with the Orthodox Church suppressed by the Russian tribes.

The educated Poles are rootless and divided, externally and internally, by a mimicry of the French. The nobility in particular, which is very numerous, have seldom embraced the unfamiliar without distinguishing befittingly the good from the bad.

The remaining nations within limits are enlightened. They still retain their unified Christian world-outlook, but with it and through it, they enjoy life more than their enlightened companions.[190]

190     With respect to Transylvania, particularly the Magyars, not much can be said. Religion has often been used as a means to political ends; the small educated class is irreligious, half-education is high, but the masses of people, including the Magyars, are religious and attend church.

Only a few remnants of Protestantism, strictly speaking, have remained in Austria. Now it is true that the churchly minority in general are better than the ruling majority, and it is possible that this is true in this case. On the other hand, it must be made clear that the minority is too small and conforms to the prevailing majority spirit and sentiments. Further, the ministerial offices for our Protestants are inadequate. They are widely dispersed, as is often the case where such conditions prevail.[191]

We shall treat as a whole the adherents of the Orthodox Church in a later discussion.

6. If one wishes to understand the spiritual life of Italy, he must remember that it is not only Catholic but also the Papal seat. Anyone who knows the world-historic significance of the Papacy also understands the present position of the young kingdoms.

The Papacy now demands rigidity and torpidity, signifying *non possumus*. Not by teaching, not by Christianity does it approach us as a superior tradition, but as the authority and master of the mind. Religion is a means for the church, and not as it should be, the end. Although the designs of the priest are good, they do not prevent the rise of half-education.

Humanism had prematurely awakened disbelief, but this new direction of thought was accessible only to a few, and disbelief was not widely diffused. Moreover, the Roman hierarchy was not concerned too often with a little belief or disbelief; it was a Pope— Leo X—who had ridiculed the necessity for the legend of Christ. The Church demanded obedience; therefore, Galileo had to retract, Giordano Bruno and others mounted their funeral pyres, and the partisans of the Reformation produced in their wake the tribunals of the Inquisition. This is striking: within limits, the more distant the people are from Rome, the more widespread is Protestantism; the closer to the Chair of Peter, the more limited was the spread of the Reformation.

The church and state in Italy now struggle for control; but disbelief has still made little headway and the authority and the power of the clergy is unbroken. To be sure, the power of the Papacy in

[191] While there is one secular priest in 1143 inhabitants for Austrian Catholics, there is one minister for every 1647 inhabitants among Austrian Protestants.

the Middle Ages has disappeared, for it cannot oppose the unification of Italy and the annexation of the Papal states; but the Italian still clings to his Church. The people are bigoted and superstitious and stand in fear, so to speak, of the Church. What the Italian feels, when face to face with the Church, is like cowardice; skepticism is almost nonexistent. The Italian laughs, is witty, and derides the priesthood and his superiors, but he nevertheless goes at every opportune moment to his Church. In the recent past, the Enlightenment threatened to curse the politically helpless and confused people with the modern state of ennui. The suicide rate quickly rose, particularly in the northern provinces, where the modern outlook and enlightenment had previously gained a strong foothold.

7. Spain had the advantage, as all Romance peoples in general, of being able to assimilate Roman Christianity more easily and quickly than other countries in which the language and liturgy of the Church was unintelligible. The war with the Moors preserved to a great extent a strong Christian conscience, and it is no wonder that, up to the present day, the Papacy is still powerful in this country. Spain introduced the Inquisition and is the real homeland of the Jesuits, who systematically crushed the new direction of thought (Phillip II); understood in this light—that by the poor condition of popular education, through ineffective means of communication, by a natural isolation from the rest of Europe through which contacts with foreigners has been reduced to a minimum—the country still remains in the Middle Ages. Certainly the modern enlightenment can not be kept completely out of Spain, all the more so as it has the French as neighbors. That the ideas of the eighteenth century also found adherents in Spain is indicated sufficiently by the many political storms in the country. Liberalism—the word "liberal" even comes from the Spanish— struggled against Catholicism (Jesuitism, Papalism) for decency, but it was confined to a few. The people are still churchly and Christian, and thus it happens that the modern temper with its sickly pessimism has still made little progress in Spain.[192]

[192]   Superstition is in full bloom. The idolatry of Mary is so widespread that Christ has been displaced. In every religious family the children pray: "I go to bed with God, I awake with God, the Blessed Virgin Mary, and the Holy Ghost."

Portugal is, on the same basis as Spain, still a Christian nation. The institution of liberties (Pomal) have made no deep mark on the people, and the Catholic Middle Ages have not been shaken.[193]

THE PROTESTANT PEOPLES. 8. The first strong attack for church reform under Hus came from a Slavic people. A century later the Germans awoke to split with the teachers of the Middle Ages, and the Reformation became essentially a product of the German spirit.

To understand the religious position of the Protestant peoples of today, we must set forth the general observations of detailed research concerning the development of Protestantism.

We have previously traced the essence of Protestantism to a negative and a positive principle.[194] As a negation of the Papacy, it had no defined meaning. As such, it maintained that it would recognize the Bible as the sole authority in matters of faith for pure evangelical Christianity. Added to this positive principle is freedom of inquiry within the Bible. With this freedom every hierarchic organization of clerics and of the priesthood collapses; the church itself is the spontaneous, given communion of believers. Consequently, Protestantism is religious individualism through and through.

Its essence is indicated to us from this by the values that Protestantism has established for humanity and which it still provides.

It has renewed the religious life from its inception and has purified Christian teachings, not only for individual adherents, but also for its opponents. It purified teaching and it purified life. With respect to the latter, it has been attained only through difficult labors, especially Calvinism, and that by a consistent, practical application of instruction.

The freedom of inquiry within the Bible leads, in itself, to rationalism, for who is permitted to decide the disputed cases? Either reason or authority. Thus the principle of rationalism is inherent

[193]   The spread of other religions in Portugal is always accompanied by strife. The situation is better in Spain, but, since the restoration of the Bourbons, religious tolerance has largely disappeared.
[194]   Chap. 5, pt. 1, no. 7 ff.

in Protestantism, and it therefore depends upon the degree to which revelation remains true; but naturally it cannot be excluded with justice from the often decried "rationalism." Because opinion is divided on many things, man is gradually trained to respect as real only that upon which all Christians agree. From this it is only a step to natural religion, to the view that only that is real in which all men agree. The development of English deism and rationalism sufficiently demonstrates this statement.

The freedom of inquiry leads to sectarian opinions. In the sheer diversity of sectarian opinions, a weakness of Protestantism appears. But it is also its strength. It is the strength of Christianity and of every religion. Only by this means is it possible to liberate the diverse individuals and peoples of Christianity so that they may achieve a world religious view. It is only possible through sectarian developments. That two major sects, the Roman and the Byzantine, considered themselves by their size and organization as the true Christianity did not alter the fact that they were also the only sects then in existence.

The natural development of many sects leads man to tolerance, tolerance of true religious freedom; it is this new virtue that Protestantism has taught civilized peoples through the course of time.[195]

The freedom of biblical criticism, its truth resting on the authority of rationalism, brings knowledge to Protestantism, especially philosophy. Revelation had prospered in opposition to philosophy, and Protestantism was rationalism par excellence. But even there, where the belief in revelation is vital, Protestantism's attitude toward knowledge is not as hostile or absolutely negative as is that of Catholicism. Protestant peoples recognize the limits of knowledge more readily than Catholics. But Christianity is also almost never found in many Protestant countries, if one will not accept the name for the fact; the spirit of Christianity is better preserved in the Catholic Church, if only in a perverse form.[196]

[195]    I say that it has taught tolerance in the course of time. At its inception Protestantism was intolerant of Catholics, but it gradually became tolerant and must become even more tolerant. (One must not confuse intolerance with indifference!)

[196]    Eiler, *Meine Wanderungen durch's Leben*, 1857, II, p. 266.

The relationship between Protestantism and knowledge was still intimate so that the Reformation represented nothing exclusive; and many more new, and still more innovative, reforms must occur with the advance of knowledge. *Protestantism accepted the modern principle of progress on its own merits.*[197]

If we inquire as to *the relationship of Protestantism with the state,* then the following is indicated: since Protestantism has no priesthood in principle to organize it, it allowed secular organization of the state to develop, and Protestantism utilized to the fullest extent for its ecclesiastical affairs that which proved necessary for each belief. On the other hand, the Protestant state can use religion for its ends, and it can lead to a Caesarism of the most tragic kind, as for example, in several German states. By this means Protestantism developed individualism more than Catholicism, and it also made politics ripen. Great political reforms were thus more easily accomplished in Protestant nations than in Catholic nations. The reformed church, with its democratic organization, is an arduous training ground for political life. The Catholic principle of authority suppressed every reform; in the intellectual sphere, this led to skepticism; in life, to indifference or to violent outbreaks. The Catholic peoples thus developed more by leaps, through great revolutions, while the Protestant peoples developed, on the whole, more gradually and more peacefully. Consequently, Protestantism led more easily in all spheres to freedom and equality.

9. In the first century of the Reformation, religious and spiritual life was strong and healthy, even in the aforementioned matter. By constant strife with Rome and within itself, the foundation of the new institution was laid.

Under the influence of free inquiry the principles of the new scientific method of Bacon and Descartes were developed, and Protestantism soon opened the doors and gateways to modern enlightenment. Deism developed in England and rationalism in

[197]    No more is required if the statement of the text can be positively demonstrated, for it points to the fact, as well as the basic principle of Protestantism, that the Reformation had quickly established all accepted theologies of justification by faith.

Germany; in Germany, up to the end of the previous century, all theological chairs were occupied, for the most part, by rationalists.

In opposition to a superficial rationalism and a sterile orthodoxy, movements arose in all Protestant countries which aimed at an intensification of religious life; thus, Pietism in Germany, Methodism in England. With these belong mysticism and visionaries, as for example, the Moravian Brethren. The French Revolution, and even more the general destruction which the Enlightenment brought with it, forced on Protestantism the lesson that it must tend to the truths of religious life, and thus we find in this century a renewed religious activity that parallels the activity of the Catholic Church.

At present, Protestants have more clearly perceived that their major problem is not in the war with Rome, that it is not the question of the rightness or wrongness of this or that sect, but that it is the dilemma of the modern state of religiosity. Accordingly, an internal evangelical movement has developed in all Protestant nations.[198] The Protestants perceive that their system of genuine religious individualism is harmonious and that individual sects must work beside and with one another. The practice of religion has been emphasized, while apologists theorize about the strength of its demands.

But the last fact characterizes the drawback of illustrations. As in the Catholic world, so also in the Protestant world, the largest part of the educated classes are nonbelievers. Strauss, with laudable frankness in his investigation of German Protestantism, has articulated this point. A division remains between the Catholic and Protestant nonbelievers, a difference to the degree that it is necessarily proved by the existence of both systems. No priestly order exists in Protestantism, no grand church organization from whose influence the nonbelieving Catholic withdraws only with difficulty. Protestants generally are more plastic and, in like man-

---

[198] Since the founding of the British and Foreign Bible Association at London in 1804, more than 700 million Bibles and New Testaments in over 200 languages have been disseminated.

ner, are more easily emancipated than the Catholics.[199] In most Protestant countries popular education is better than in Catholic countries; thus, even in the present state of culture, irreligiosity is more widespread in united Protestant countries than in the nonbelieving Catholic countries. The result is the high suicide frequency evidenced by these nations. There is a low suicide frequency where religiosity is still apparent, as in corresponding Catholic countries.

10. Germany, the homeland of Luther, presents a tragic picture of the religious life. The Reformation had been only partially stabilized when the general enlightenment touched this nation. And it is rational theology itself which sows disbelief and destroys Christianity. Rationalism ruled the academic studies of the preceding century, and theology was sympathetic to the enlightened tendency of the Wolffian school, with Lessing, etc. Although the positive the-

[199]    Following Brachelli, in 1876 the following European nations had one secular priest for the indicated number of Catholics:

| Italy | 267 | France | 823 |
|---|---|---|---|
| Spain | 419 | Belgium | 1050 |
| Portugal | 736 | Austria-Hungary | 1144 |
| Switzerland | 540 | Austria | 1143 |
| Luxemburg | 571 | Hungary | 1145 |
| Holland | 680 | Russia | 1200 |
| Germany | 812 | Great Britain, Ireland | 1320 |

For the Greek-Oriental Christian Church one secular priest appears among:

| Greece | 350 |
|---|---|
| Rumania | 420 |
| Austria-Hungary | 884 |
| Russia | 1060 |
| Serbia | 1900 |

For the Protestants one minister appears among:

| France | 794 | Switzerland | 1440 |
|---|---|---|---|
| England, Ireland | 908 | Germany | 1600 |
| Hungary | 932 | Sweden, Norway | 1714 |
| Holland | 1100 | Austria | 1734 |
| Denmark | 1300 | Finland | 2268 |

ology of popular religions forsook rationalism, disbelief was also widespread among the people, so that the truth of Strauss's statement about the denominations of German Protestantism is clearly seen.

Bureaucracy produces corruption, and today it seeks to use the small churches for its ends. Despite this Protestantism shall lead to freedom; Germany has not, up to now, become politically free, for the uncounted princes and princesses who have ruled the people for some time use the situation to make themselves independent of the king, patronizing the new teachers and making the preachers into their functionaries. That is the case generally in almost all Lutheran countries.

Philosophy since Kant is decidedly anti-Christian. Materialism has gathered a large number of adherents in its maiden years, and each day new offspring are born to what in Germany is called "Philosophy," even if it is only a philosophy of the passing times or something analogous. In no country has the antipathy against Christianity been made so apparent. Nowhere has the destruction of religion been carried out so systematically as in Germany. All kinds of materials were used—writings, lectures, and speeches— to assail positive religious faith, to discredit it, to rob it of its worth:

So strong an expression of contempt for God and His Word, of alienation from Christ and His Crown, of hate against the Church and its institutions, has rarely been made. If it is only a new outbreak of Brehm's animal life, it has been an evil and malicious invective against the Christian faith, and it is not only in the Social Democrat's press that the attack on Christianity has been permitted, to a certain extent with the consideration of the state authorities. There are few dignitaries, whose public lives are filled with uncertainty, who have not been brought into alliances with the divergent religious factions. Religious opponents struggle everywhere with one another as if they lived in different worlds.[200]

Christianity disappeared, but the minority had something to

[200]    Prof. Cremer in his report on the evangelical religious life in Germany contained in the *Seventh General Assembly of the Evangelical Alliance*. Cremer also bewails the inadequacies of theology.

take its place. The consequence of this condition was a premature, sickly flight from life, which appeared at first in the sphere of poetry. Goethe's *Werther* is the first great artistic expression of this state of mind. Goethe extricated himself from melancholy and, in his *Faust*, made the half-education of his time into a form of religion. But what Goethe believed was sufficient only for a minority; the great mass of people were not moved by it for a considerable period of time. The offspring of Goethe (and Schiller)—the Romantics—sought natural and moral foundations; some were mentally ill and gave themselves to death, and others sought, because they were appalled by Protestant rationalism and dogmatic orthodoxy, a desired peace of soul in Catholicism, and willingly dedicated their minds and skills to the reaction.[201]

The newest frame of mind is indicated by the pessimistic philosophy and the numerous converts to modern Buddhism.

"Shall it be very incorrect," asks Pfleiderer, "not so much undervaluating the by no means thoughtless modern pessimism, to see it, at its best, *as the morning-after blues of the German enlightenment, because its semi-defeatist nature inaugurated the deep influence of the super-refinement of the last half century, especially in religious-ethical aims.*"[202]

---

[201]    The spiritual aims of the Romantics are very well defined in Brandes, *Die Hauptströmungen der Literatur des 19. Jahrhunderts* (German trans. Strodtmann) 1873, I and II. The results of this excellent analysis agree in general with our interpretation of the modern development and, when seen from this point of view, the characteristics of the movement fall into their proper perspective. The Romantics are to me the poetic result of the general restlessness and lawlessness, the psychotic caricature of the promethean struggles of Goethe's *Faust*, and the melancholy continuation of the sentimental discontent from Rousseau to the "ancient Christian humanity" proposed by Schiller. The psychological analysis of the cause and motive of suicide offers the principles for the understanding of the Romantics and, in general, the sickly poetry of the present time. (Concerning the connection of the German Romantics with Goethe and Schiller—this connection is important for cultural history—see Hettner, *Die romantische Schule in ihrem inneren Zusammenhang mit Goethe und Schiller,* 1850; cf. Brandes, 1, c, II, p. 26 ff.)

[202]    E. Pfleiderer, *Der moderne Pessimismus,* p. 106 (*Deutsche Zeit und Streitfragen,* Fr. v. Holtzendorf and W. Oncken, Heft 54 and 55.) Cf. Sully, *Pessimism: A History and Criticism,* 1877, p. 449.

Surely modern pessimism is nothing other than the philo-sophical expression of the modern weariness with life, a theory of suicide which makes it necessary for Germans, in whose hearts lie the weal of its people, to seek to answer the question *why even an educated Germany, Protestant Germany, had succumbed to philo-sophic, systematic expressions of the weariness with life.*

Matters were better with the Protestant majority in Germany than with the Catholic minority in Germany.[203]

In the continuing war against Protestantism, Catholic Germany had refined its faith so much that one must now view German Ca-tholicism as indisputably more attractive. The Protestant develop-ment has not raised obstacles for German Catholics; the clergy is moral, and compared to the Austrian, shows vigor. Theology bloomed and continues to grow in Germany, while for us, an almost completely Catholic country, theological knowledge is almost non-existent. Compared to his Protestant brothers, the German Catholic enjoys a significantly high degree of moral stamina and internal religiosity.

In the era of general reaction, the Catholic Church in Germany was greatly strengthened, and many Protestants sought to satisfy their religious needs in it.[204] Bavaria remained for a long time the privileged central seat of Ultramontanism.

The last council also demonstrates that a large segment of the Catholics in Germany are no longer satisfied with the Papacy, and it resulted in the Old Catholic secession under the guidance of Döllinger, Frederick, Michelis, and others. This movement is still much too weak to break the power of Rome in Germany. On the contrary, Rome strengthened its position in the present strife be-tween Ultramontanism and the government, and that so much more because the government is basically reactionary.

11. In Denmark, the Reformation has provided meager re-

---

[203]    In Germany there are about 25 million Protestants and about 14 million Catholics; to be sure:

in the North 70.93% Protestants, 27.26% Catholics
in the South 37.35% Protestants, 61.01% Catholics

[204]    Among the prominent converts were: Stolberg, Schlegel, A. H. Müller, C. L. Haller, and others.

sults for political foundations. Crown and nobles use the church for their ends, doing nothing for the people either in intellectual or religious-moral matters. Since the Reformation, Denmark has been guided by German theology and religious literature, but it was rationalism in particular which found sympathy with the ministers and the masses of people. Denmark is at present very irreligious. The clergy is without education or morals and is generally intellectually decadent and stagnant. Opposition to rationalism has been raised (led by Grundtvig), but this opposition emphasizes national rather than religious elements and does theology no great service.[205]

The fortunes of the German Province of Schleswig-Holstein have been pitiful. For some time after the Revolution of 1848, the country was systematically oppressed and also deprived of its pastoral offices. It was by this means that the German pastors were removed and were replaced by Danish clergymen. The religious condition was, as a consequence of such brutality, much worse, if possible, than in Denmark itself.[206]

12. The religious conditions in the two other Scandinavian

---

[205]    The intolerant treatment afforded the spiritually rich Brandes at the University of Copenhagen for his role in the strife of the Freethinkers vs. the Orthodox (he refutes Rasmus Nielsen's position, in an essay "Über den Dualismus in unserer neuesten Philosophie," that faith has absolutely nothing to do with knowledge and defends in his periodical writings the freedom of thought against every tutor and ward, especially in his much cited principal writings on the main currents of the nineteenth century) does not permit an inner, religious life, but only the barren orthodoxy guarded by intolerance.

[206]    If what the Schleswig pastor Petersen says about Danish decadence, immorality, and disbelief is only half true, then Denmark is the most irreligious nation in Europe. V. Petersen, *Erlebnisse eines Schleswigsten Predigers*, 1856—there were only 6000 faithful church members in Copenhagen in 1859 in a population of 150,000. In Altona a single church suffices for a population of 45,000. Sore is the need for preachers: In Schleswig there are parishes with 13,000 inhabitants scattered for miles and only two preachers; Holstein, in 1861, had only 192 preachers for its 544,419 inhabitants, and, moreover, not infrequently two or three preachers were stationed at one and the same church. This need for preachers was and still is felt in all Scandinavian nations. Cf. Forester, *Norway*, 1848 and 1849, p. 309.

countries, Sweden and Norway, are much better than in Denmark.

In Sweden, Lutheranism is preserved in its purity. The people are religious and the clergy have great power; Sweden was the first in recent times to understand rationalism. The rigid orthodoxy began to join itself to the theological advance of the new age until recently, and the internal churchly life remained peaceful and vital. It has turned its special attention to the extirpation of the Swedish national evil, drunkenness.

Norway has, on the one hand, similarities to Sweden and, on the other hand, similarities to Denmark. Danish rationalism has made great advances here, but the enlightenment is similar to the civilized countries of the continent and is therefore of little danger. The people are religious and the clergy are strong.[207]

13. Up to this point we have discussed the Lutheran peoples, and we turn now to a discussion of the Reformed Church.

Calvinism sought—its dogmatic views are suitable—to fashion life sternly, austerely, and legally in all its relationships. The teaching of predestination, which was not logically related to its consequences and a singularly accurate determinism, necessarily brought forth a great moral austerity. For only unconditional conformity to the God-given laws, only unconditional submission face-to-face with the Absolute Lawgiver, guaranteed the certitude that the individual would not be predestined to eternal damnation.[208] The organization of the church is democratic, the separation of the laity and clergy has been suspended, religion and church are rigorously separated, every formalism is forbidden and the results are evident in the life of the church.

---

[207]     Kloeden, *Über die Stellung der Gebildeten in Norwegen*, loc. cit. III, p. 378.

[208]     The characterizations by Buckle of the somberness of the Scottish character are certainly overdrawn, to the extent that not all the followers of Calvin conceived life so seriously as those from whom Buckle has sketched his picture. But it is correct to the degree that Calvinism resulted in a serious mood of life by its energetic preaching of morality. (It would be interesting to study accurately the effects of various teachings; one should achieve noteworthy results. Where, for example, Methodism is widespread, there should also be a change of countenance; one should find there a crowd of sterner and joyless faces. *Quarterly Review*, IV, p. 503).

The Reformed people are, with the exception of the Swiss, the most religious of the Protestant nations at present. What Spain and Portugal are to the Catholic world, the Reformed countries are for the Protestant world.

We now begin our survey with the homeland of Calvinism.

Switzerland, following England the most industrious and the most industrialized country in Europe, is irreligious to the highest degree. In Geneva, the cradle of Calvinism, religion is almost unknown.[209] On the whole, as the modern enlightenment progressed, theology and the masses moved closer to atheism. Democracy also had its destructive effects. The democratic church organization resulted, it must be admitted, as a consequence of the Protestant and especially the Calvinist constitutional principles, and can be regarded as an ideal for ecclesiastical organization; democratic development must proceed, but, as with every freedom, must not be misused. In Switzerland, many regions have changed from a democratic to an oligarchic organization, and this is a major social problem for church and state. The masses have also become irreligious.

The report on the religious-spiritual condition of Protestant Switzerland, delivered in 1856 to the convention of the Evangelical Alliance in Paris by the Rev. Güder, was very depressing. His report of the present condition was sound but sad.[210] The masses have become irreligious and immoral and are less hesitant to openly confess their disbelief. The system in which religious freedoms were easily obtained served as a cloak for all kinds of vulgarity. Church attendance generally decreased; the baptized and the spiritually ordained are understood to be in decline; religious instruction is not allowed in the public schools;[211] in short, educated and uneducated are irreligious.[212]

---

[209]  Thus did the *Saturday Review* express itself, 1859, Oct., p. 421.

[210]  *Berichte und Reden*, p. 23 ff.

[211]  No religious instruction is provided in fifty schools in Zurich already and, in addition, in advanced seminar courses. (Would I err, if I regarded Scherr's pettifogging literary profession as a standard of Swiss higher "education"?)

[212]  The reintroduction of capital punishment is regarded as symptomatic of the people's opposition to the desires of their rulers.

As expected, unbelief called forth a reaction in Switzerland, sectarian habits blossomed, English Methodism won many converts—particularly in French Switzerland—and those spiritually oriented organized free churches and communions, etc. But all of this was not enough to stem the spread of irreligiosity and its evil consequences.

The Catholic population of Switzerland is religious and decidedly more spiritual than the Protestant population.[213] As a suppressed minority, they preserved their religiosity to a high degree and owed, as is true at all times, their many moral victories over the Protestants to their hierarchic organization.[214] The Jesuits so educated the people that in the war for separation of 1847, they approached an art in the method of conducting religious warfare.[215] Through the long and ineffectual search for approved revision of organizational bonds, the power of the Church was first broken in 1874 and the powerful Old Catholic Movement, which in Switzerland and especially in Geneva had found many converts, showed that the Catholic people did not cling to their church in times of crisis as fervently as in previous times.[216]

14. Tiny and peaceful Holland offers odd characteristics in its religious situation, as in everything else.

The Lutheran view was known very early in this industrious country, and a large number of its inhabitants somewhat later were received into the Reformed Church, having to endure the trial by

---

[213]    Of the twenty-two Cantons, only three are close to complete reform, twelve are mixed, and seven Catholic. Overall there are one and a half million Reformed and 980,000 Catholics.

[214]    Geneva, the Rome of Calvinism, which had no Catholic population until the French Revolution, and where the celebration of the mass was forbidden under penalty of death to every Catholic priest until 1793, is now the seat of a Bishop and has more Catholic than Reformed inhabitants.

[215]    Many have wanted to present the war for separatism as a religious war. But the situation did not involve the conflict of truly religious convictions, as, somewhat, in the Thirty Years War, but rather involved purely ecclesiastical affairs. It was a war of the federal government against clerical Ultramontanism. Such a rapid settlement of the disputes would not have been possible in a religious war.

[216]    The well-known ex-Carmelite P. Hyacinthe was chosen in 1873 as a pastor in Geneva and also two other ex-Catholics.

fire of their beliefs against the Inquisition of the cruel Phillip. The ecclesiastics were also struggling with political dissenters, and Hollanders have been the bitterest enemies of the Papacy since that time. Religious freedom, granted to all inhabitants—Descartes, Spinoza, and others found freedom in Holland—brought rationalism to the churches and the enlightenment was deeply rooted. The masses of the people have nevertheless remained religious and have sought the necessary satisfaction of their religious needs outside the church.[217] The peaceful life of the separate churches united in the national church speaks for the high state of religiosity, above all in the Christian-Reformed.

The Catholic minority in Holland is religious and churchgoing to a high degree. Ultramontanism has really found its Eldorado here.[218] The Jesuits streamed in crowds through the country after 1848 and strengthened the Papal hierarchy; state law afterwards recognized absolute religious freedom.

15. The conservative spirit of the Middle Ages is still all-powerful in England, but it is steadily giving way to freedom before storms of protest. The Episcopal Church is accordingly a noteworthy synthesis of Catholicism and Protestant, of the Middle Ages and the new era.

Bacon, Hobbes, and Locke stimulated, each in his own way, the empirical method of thought to which England has remained true to the present day. Philosophy is, as in everything, separated from theology, but for the first time in recent years it has tended to a complete negation of positive religion by individual petty thinkers. By comparison with their opponents, the English deists were intellectually weak and the effect of the intolerance preached in their writings was relatively ineffectual.[219] Their articulate and philosophically organized opposition could not supress the waver-

---

[217]  One hears Protestants themselves bewail the decadence of theology, and they search for the point at which it has declined. And this is just; there are also in Holland parishes that remain purposely without a preacher because their candidates are too rationalistic. This is certainly an index of religiosity and piety.

[218]  Two-fifths of the inhabitants are Catholic.

[219]  Leslie Stephen, *History of English Thought in the Eighteenth Century*, 1877, I, p. 85 ff.

ing deistic movement, but they arrested its growth in time and then totally bogged it down.[220] However, it has become effective since then and has prepared the modern enlightenment.

Of a somewhat different nature was the effect of the English moralists, that great group of philosophers who sought to give theological ethics a new and different base. While the deists, seeking a foundation for natural religion, focused their attacks on the theoretical aspects of Christianity, the moralists demonstrated that an ethic is possible without positive religion and attacked, many times without wishing to, the central principles of popular religion for the masses.

The Christianity of the philosopher David Hume was truly distinctive and, to a high degree, malign. His epistemological-theoretical skepticism had to make allusions to religion, for if a knowledge of cause is not possible, then one has disproved theism directly and has indirectly disproved the basis of Christianity, and his views on the truths of religion are outspoken. In his superb essay concerning religion, he came to the conclusion that the poor order of the world completely excluded the hypothesis of God, that one could only reasonably conclude that nature was ruled throughout by chance. Masterful and bitter are his descriptions of the evils of this world. Schopenhauer has not produced anything more critical through his pessimism. But Hume is not a pessimist and his definitive position might be capsuled: one should accept the world as it is and not ask of it Why, Wherefore and To What Purpose? His exalted frame of mind leads to the conclusion that he used skepticism only as a means to a rational, postive world-view.[221] He is entirely indifferent as to whether man commits suicide or not. Life or death has no more meaning in this world than life or death in another world.[222]

---

[220]     Deserving of note is the fact that Blount, one of the deists, committed suicide (1693); he defended suicide as morally permissible in an essay on suicide.

[221]     Comte was certainly stimulated in the fundamental thoughts of his positive philosophy by Hume's conception of causality. Cf. *Phil. positive*, VI, p. 259.

[222]     Hume's "Essay on Suicide" is interesting for the histo suicide tendency. Hume himself had it suppressed, and it was

The Enlightenment, anti-ecclesiasticism and irreligiosity became even stronger after Hume lived and wrote despite the strivings of Christianity to maintain the influences of religion in public
and private life. Toward the end of the eighteenth century, the
French enlighteners became known in England, and the church did
not survive for long. Thomas Paine thus stands as a camp-follower
of deism. Of significance is the fact that Paine, a man of the people and himself unschooled and unlearned, brought to expression
the dissatisfaction of the masses with the existing religion. His
*Age of Reason* (1793–1807) is shallow and unphilosophical by our
standards, but it remains a sad commentary that the uneducated
can and must themselves define the inadequacy of the existing
church for positive religion when the educated classes do not fulfill
their duties.[223]

---

after his death. There was continued hesitancy to treat the subject freely
and publicly for somewhat more than 100 years. As suicide was committed
more frequently, the subject commanded more general attention, and
writings concerning it became more and more common. Concerning the
history of Hume's "Essay on Suicide," cf. *Essays* (Green-Grose's ed.), I,
p. 70.

[223]    Winslow reports that people committed suicide, to whom the
thought had not previously occurred, after they had read the book.—
Paine's book is typical of many ill-defined superficial, anti-Christian books.
It is written with great enthusiasm in a revolutionary mood, which is to be
expected of a man who took part in the American and French Revolutions. Paine placed his book—as he has told us—upon the altar of the
world. He wrote against Christianity because nothing in favor of the
Omnipotent is as dishonorable as it, but he was afraid that humanity and
genuine theology would not find a common ground without the decline of
superstition and the overthrow of the false systems of existent morality.
Therefore, his book is directed not less against atheism than it is against
Christianity. Paine believed in God and in the immortality of the soul, but
he did not believe in the Judaic, Roman, Greek, Turkish, or Protestant
Church. His church was to him his own thoughts and convictions. In sum,
he is a deist to whom natural science is the genuine theology. The Bible
contained little truth for the deists, rather they are atheistic. The teaching of revelation is mere humbug; there is only one old book which merits
general belief: Euclid's *Elements of Geometry*. (Paine was reared as a
Quaker, which he held to be relatively the best Christian sect. When he
was seven or eight years old, he heard one of his relatives preaching on the

Irreligiosity has continued to spread in our century not in the coarse manner of previous eras, but more calmly, more prudently, with consideration in most cases for placing something new in place of what has been destroyed. Typical in this respect is John Stuart Mill. He abandons popular religion as did Comte. Without spite, but only in the pure pursuit of truth, does he criticize the basis of Christianity, acknowledging the good in it but desiring, because he does not accept it as the truth, to replace it with utilitarianism as a religion. Mill, who because of his entirely proper education never had a religious need—he tells us this in his autobiography—wished that his ethical system had become a popular religion. It is interesting to compare Mill's struggles with those of Comte: the nonbelieving Englishman desired freedom; the nonbelieving Frenchman, an intellectual aristocracy. The former is certainly Protestant, the latter Catholic, and there are only these two ways by which a man can arrive at a definite peace of mind.

But there are and were blind and passionate enemies of Christianity. Byron's melancholy poetry is just such an expression of the modern spirit of negation, imploring the dissatisfied elements in their titanic struggle against authority to endure the torments and anguish of a self-chained Prometheus.[224] But Byron's ravings, because it is just raving, did not have the lasting effect of some of Goethe's artistic works.

---

salvation of humanity through the death of the Son of God; the contradiction of this doctrine displeased him so much that he became from then on an embittered foe of Christianity; henceforth he sought to refute it, as he pitilessly undertook the opposition of the Bible and that of his own irrational views, clothing them with every piety. *The Age of Reason, Being an Investigation of True and Fabulous Theology* (German: *Untersuchungen über wahre und fabelhafte Theologie*, 1794) I, pp. 25–28, 94, 101, 103, 104, 195; II, p. 9; cf. I, p. 139 ff.

[224]    One can understand Byron and Shelley's passionate state if one remembers that the Anglican Church retains the Roman hierarchy, with its disciplining of minds, and that it was joined to the principle of reform in a peculiar way. The striving of this English revolutionary is characterized by a line which he wrote in the guest book in the Chamounithale: "I am a lover of man, and a believer in the power of the people, and an atheist."

Alarmed by the prevailing flight from belief, various religious sects developed large-scale activities in this century, but disbelief and a stifling orthodoxy had already developed in the previous century, in contrast to Wesley's electrifying example of a depth of religious feeling.

Although theoretically differing in practice, the various sects work peacefully alongside one another. Their inner missionary activity is stressed. In the streets, in the taverns, and in infamous locales, the gospel is preached to the profligate. Preachers bring the good news to cabmen, sailors, and others. The doctor and the university professor give instruction in Sunday School next to the Lord Chancellor—how many doctors among us are religious or at all spiritual? English religiosity strikes us as insipid, "and although it bears fruit for the whole it is really only hypocrisy, etc."; consideration is not given to the improbability that an entire people should somehow deceive itself for centuries.[225] Thus external missionary activity, like the inner, is superb in England.

The state church has often been reproached as really only existing for the educated, aristocratic, and wealthy classes. It is supposed to have no heart and no understanding for the poor man, the worker. The reproach is many times justified. But it is quite evident that the educated themselves are spiritual and religious; further consideration must be given the fact that the destiny of a country, in general, rests in the hands of the educated and the well-to-do classes, and that a dozen people hold the major share of responsibility in a nation. But, then, one should not forget the numerous dissenters who for the most part rectify the mistakes which the state church commits.[226]

Recapitulating what has been said, the following overall picture of the spiritual life of England results. The people are religious

[225]    What would an Austrian say if he saw the International Exposition opened and closed with religious ceremonies, as in London?

[226]    The fact that so many aristocrats and preachers have converted to Catholicism since the 1840's may be evidence of a shortcoming in the Anglican Church; it has not been inimicable but favorable to the development of the suicide tendency.

in England, the educated and the uneducated to the same degree.[227]
Every Englishman sees religion as a more positive basis, the single
basis, of the social and political success of his nation. The Protestant principle of freedom leads to tolerance in the course of its development, and, as a result of this, religion is made a truly heartfelt
activity. In no European country has secular literature sustained
such an exalted and religious spirit as in England; whether Christian or non-Christian, everyone respects the institutions and convictions which are sacred to millions of their fellow citizens. For
this reason, the modern incompleteness is found far less in England
than in the other civilized countries of the continent, and the suicide tendency is therefore also very small compared with other
countries. Thousands of private associations concern themselves
with mental and physical welfare and the sufferings of the citizens,
and so it happens that dissatisfaction with life is nipped in the bud.

16. In order to know the religious conditions of "the classical
country of the Bible" more accurately, we must, though only
briefly, cast a glance at Scotland and Ireland.

The religious-spiritual conditions of Scotland are known to us
through Buckle's famous presentation of Scottish civilization. In
Austria it is believed that the character of the Scottish people is
darkened by their religion. We deride the power of the clergy and

[227]    In London, in 1865, there were:

|  | Clergy | Churches (Chapels) | Seats |
|---|---|---|---|
| State Church | 600 | 553 | 512,067 |
| Congregationalist | 291 | 174 | 130,611 |
| Baptist | 101 | 173 | 87,559 |
| Methodist | 180 | 202 | 81,773 |
| Presbyterian | 25 | 29 | 22,928 |
| Others | 160 | 185 | 82,957 |
|  | 1357 | 1316 | 917,895 |

In England and Scotland there were (for 24,363,483) 36,200 clergymen and 34,700 churches and chapels; one clergyman per 673 persons.

In England no biblical character may be portrayed on the stage; Austrians have farcical comedies, such as "Der besoffene Herrgott" and others.

even more the inquisitorial intolerance and bigotry of the nation.

But the situation is not all bad, and, if one turns from the shadowy side, the bright side can also be seen.

To be sure, strict Calvinism among the Scottish has engendered a certain austerity and dourness, such that it has protected the people from becoming frivolous and superficial.[228] The Scots were and are intolerant, and this is decidedly a great defect, but, while their intolerance is the result of a fixed and active conviction, other nations are just as intolerant without having fixed and active convictions. The power of the clergy is great, but is it worse than the power which, for example, is exercised among us in Austria by certain daily newspapers?

The fact is that the people of Scotland are thoroughly religious and they therefore direct their minds more to ideal things than other irreligious peoples; but the antipathy to such religiosity usually springs from indifference, and such a position is thus completely unqualified to judge it. Consider the splendid establishment of the free church! Dissatisfied with the patronage which is repugnant to the Presbyterian spirit of Calvinism, but which was again established in Scotland under Queen Anne (1712), a part of the inhabitants left the Scottish Church (1843), maintaining, however, exactly the same teaching, and organizing their own church with the constitution they desired. In less than twenty years about 900 churches and subsidiary buildings were built; schools were established, a university was founded, and they surpassed themselves in every respect in Christian works. Is that to be despised? No! A

[228]   When Döllinger reproachfully emphasizes that in the Scottish Church there is no organ, no altar, no cross, no picture, no light, that the worship service is lacking in every symbol, that the funeral is no religious act, etc., his censure is made from the Catholic point of view, and he should first show proof that the Catholic ceremonial is any better. But this is precisely the difference between Catholicism and Protestantism, especially the Reformed, that religion is to be sought not in externals but inwardly; the former is undoubtedly more effective for the masses, but the latter is more genuine and exalted and therefore establishes much more conviction and inwardness of feeling, which Catholicism, in any case, does not promote.

people who have a mind for such works, who are able to develop such energy, are to be envied. And if many mistakes are made among their many accomplishments, they are not to be blamed, for it is human to err and errors appear everywhere and among all peoples at present.

In accordance with their strict religious sense, Scottish literature is also moral to the highest degree, is serious and genuine. And the Scottish have done much for the modern enlightenment! This is very important to us: despite their religiosity and spirituality a people can take part to a large degree in the mental labor of civilization, creating a solid and complete edifice and not something half-finished and shallow. For this reason one cannot say that the low suicide frequency of Spain, for example, is due to a lack of education and not religiosity, because we see that Scotland, without doubt one of the most civilized countries on earth, shows a small suicide frequency despite all its education and intellectual activities. It is their religiosity which gives to this people the necessary support for the dangers of life.

For our explanation of the social phenomenon of suicide, we must especially assert one more peculiarity of Scotland. The Scottish are given to a high degree to drink.[229] Now we know that

---

229    How the Scottish people attempt to explain away this vice may be illustrated by the following fact, which is also characteristic of them. The church has raised the question whether grape juice should not be used in Holy Communion instead of wine, so that the sacrament doesn't contribute to the spread of drunkenness.

In 1874, the whisky consumed in Great Britain was: 29,821,574 gallons. Of this, the per capita share was:

| | |
|---|---|
| England | 0.699 gallons |
| Ireland | 1.264 gallons |
| Scotland | 1.961 gallons |

The per capita share of beer was:

| | |
|---|---|
| England | 43.056 gallons |
| Ireland | 14.238 gallons |
| Scotland | 12.312 gallons |

drunkenness effects a strong disposition to suicide, but, because the suicide tendency is weak in Scotland, despite the vice of drunkenness, there must surely be a factor which arrests this deleterious force, and this factor is nothing other than religiosity and attachment to the church, which here, directly and indirectly, has a beneficial effect in impeding suicide.

The members of the Catholic Church in Great Britain are also very spiritual and religious. The unjust suppression of Catholicism, which was unbelievably strenuous, especially in Ireland, and which will always remain a blemish on English Protestantism, has kept Catholic determination alive.[230] But this is not the only factor. In most recent times, the Catholic Church has dealt the Anglican Church some hard blows, converting very many of the educated, aristocrats, and clergy to Catholicism. As a result of this, many people have predicted a complete Romanization of England.[231]

17. Opinion of intellectual life in the United States of North America, that is, the opinion shared by our educated people, is of a very low level. The country is usually described as a machine shop *en gros*: the ideal, the beautiful, and the sublime are said to be totally absent, and the bands of cheats and swindlers who have written about America have portrayed only an "Uncle Tom's Cabin" or the redskin with his tomahawk and scalps as subjects of interest.

The people of America are certainly very "practical," but it is

---

Spiritous liquors in general, domestic and foreign, (1876) per capita:

|  |  |
|---|---|
| England | 1.114 gallons |
| Ireland | 1.384 gallons |
| Scotland | 2.346 gallons |

Very little wine is consumed in Scotland and this only by the wealthier classes.

230    The fact that the Old Catholic movement, which found sympathy in all Catholic countries, passes over England without leaving a trace also suggests, among other things, that English Catholics have great religiosity.

231    From 1840–52, 92 members of the University of Oxford converted to Catholicism, 42 members of Cambridge University; up to 1867, 867 members of the most distinguished families converted to Catholicism, and of these 243 were clergymen.

not true that the ideal and the sublime are not cultivated. The American has no mind for a philosophical system à la Hegel, not as though philosophy had no footing at all in America, but simply because religion satisfies the needs of the majority.[232] The Puritanism of the first colonists endures among the American people even today. Swiss Calvinism, as it has been modified in Holland, England, and Scotland, is the peculiar source of their national character and of the social institutions of the country.[233] There is perfect religious freedom in America; not tolerance, as in the progressive nations of Europe, but complete, absolute freedom. There is no state or national church. For this reason there are no "sects" in America, but only "denominations." Religion has really become an object of feeling. Although separated by many theoretical views, in practice a much greater unity than exists in national churches dominates the numerous denominations. Protestantism has developed most naturally and most attractively in America; the principle of free inquiry within the Bible is almost completely fulfilled and leads to religious individualism.[234] But the unanimity naturally

[232]    The religiosity and attachment to religion in America may be easily measured by (a) the constant appearance of new denominations; (b) the famous "revivals" of the last decade; (c) the many-sided internal and external missionary activities; and (d) the number and increase of Sunday Schools. There were, in 1879, at least 82,261 Sunday Schools, with 886,328 teachers and 6,623,124 pupils; whoever has even an approximately correct conception of the nature and significance of the Protestant Sunday School knows what an institution so widely established signifies for religious conditions in America. Cf. *Sunday School Chronicle*, July, 1880.

[233]    Cf. Bancroft, *History of the United States of North America*, German trans., Kretzhmar II, pp. 400 ff.

[234]    To give the reader an approximate picture of American denominationalism, I present the following estimates concerning the number of churches and chapels (synagogues) in the City of New York in 1878:

| | |
|---|---|
| Baptist | 46 |
| Congregational | 9 |
| Quaker | 5 |
| Greek | 1 |
| Jewish | 23 |
| Lutheran | 23 |
| Methodist (Episcopal) | 58 |

appears from the inside out, not by imposition of an external authority.

The great religiosity of Americans appears in the right light only if one considers the following: with absolute freedom of thought, which dominates in all fields, intellectual anarchy must be especially high in just those lands where there are so many foreign elements, unless some authority comes forth and curbs the people. This authority is religion, and thus freedom of thought, as Scaff excellently remarked in his last report on American Christianity, does not spur a profession of views, as in Germany, but more thinkers.

Church and state are absolutely separated; no advantage can be taken of attachment to the church and religiosity for the purposes of government. But those who govern are no less religious than the governed, and so the true relationship between church and state results of itself. This relationship leaves Europeans with much remaining to create, and we have already, in this respect, heard innumerable proposals and much advice; the problem remains unsolved because in most every European nation the church (even among Protestants) has a hierarchy, and those who govern—and this is especially important—are not attached to the church and are irreligious. The question of the relationship between church and state can be solved in the same simple manner as the question

| | |
|---|---:|
| Methodist (African-Episcopal) | 8 |
| Methodist (Free) | 2 |
| Moravian Brethren | 2 |
| Presbyterian | 65 |
| Presbyterian (United) | 10 |
| Presbyterian (Reformed) | 6 |
| Episcopal | 85 |
| Episcopal (Reformed) | 2 |
| Reformed | 28 |
| Roman Catholic | 56 |
| United | 18 |
| Unitarian | 4 |
| Universal | 6 |
| Others | 39 |
| Total | 496 |

so often raised of the relationship between art and morality: art has no moral purpose, but the artist should be moral; those who govern have no ecclesiastical purposes, but they should be religious. In America the question has been solved naturally and simply in this manner.[235]

The absolute separation of church and state has not hurt the republic; free government does not need the protection of the clergy because it rests on the solid foundation of religion. If that were not the case, a nation with universal suffrage, with absolute political freedom, could not maintain itself, because "despotism," Tocqueville correctly says, "may always govern without religion, but freedom cannot."

Finally, if one considers that America has no military forces at all whose bayonets can be used in times of peace for the maintenance of internal order, as in Europe, and if one considers in addition to this that America is receiving many foreign immigrants and, only too often, anarchical elements among its immigrants, one must admire the solid structure on which the starry banner of the Union has been planted so firmly. Disturbances, as in 1877 and other years, disappear when one compares them with the evils which threaten us, and which we are able to bear only because we are accustomed to them.

The low suicide frequency is associated with the unified worldview and great religiosity. With great political, commercial, and religious tumult, mental illness is certainly strongly widespread, but suicide seldom appears because of great religiosity; de Tocqueville has already correctly recognized the relationship between both these partial phenomena of modern civilization.[236] The fact that the free, cultivated, energetic and active American people have a low suicide tendency despite its celebrated tensions, no less than the low suicide frequency of England and especially Scotland,

---

235    I remember that the absolute division of church and state was accomplished only since 1783, and only after a lengthy independence.

236    *De la Démocratie en Amérique* (14th ed.), III, p. 224: "The Americans do not commit suicide, however disturbed they may be, because religion protects them from such an act—their will resists, but their reason often weakens."

verifies our explanation of the social mass phenomenon of suicide.

But it is interesting to note that the Germans in America also show the largest number of suicides, as it is the Germans there who preach atheism and irreligiosity most publicly.[237]

18. The Greek Church is based upon the same principles as the Roman, but between both, especially since the decisive schism,

[237]   The statistical evidence concerning the country of birth of suicides in New York in 1877 indicates:

| Norway | 1 | Belgium | 1 |
|---|---|---|---|
| Austria | 2 | China | 1 |
| Poland | 1 | Cuba | 2 |
| Scotland | 2 | Germany | 59 |
| South America | 1 | England | 6 |
| Sweden | 3 | France | 2 |
| United States | 44 | Holland | 1 |
| Wales | 1 | Ireland | 17 |
| Unknown | 4 | | |

Total     148

If one compares the most numerous nationalities entering New York, Americans, Irish, and Germans, the last shows a decisively high suicide frequency.

Balbi made the following account in 1827: Suicides per million inhabitants:

| New York | 128 |
|---|---|
| Boston | 80 |
| Philadelphia | 84 |
| Baltimore | 73 |

From the State of Massachusetts, we have the following data:

| Year | Suicides | Year | Suicides |
|---|---|---|---|
| 1859 | 83 | 1868 | 88 |
| 1860 | 113 | 1869 | 92 |
| 1861 | 92 | 1870 | 91 |
| 1862 | 92 | 1871 | 122 |
| 1863 | 67 | 1872 | 117 |
| 1866 | 73 | 1873 | 117 |
| 1867 | 75 | 1874 | 115 |
| | | 1875 | 159 |

According to the census figures of 1870, there were 1060 (by another calculation, 1360) suicides in the United States in this same year.

great differences have appeared, due especially to the differences between Byzantine and Roman, between East and West. Both churches are now an organic unit.[238]

An unconditional belief in authority dominates in both churches, but while in the West, despite all authority, a certain degree of education cannot be arrested, the Eastern Church remains static, like most social institutions of the East. The Roman Church became a world church and conflicts between secular and spiritual authority resulted in different nations. The Greek Church, restricted to the East, became the state and national church in particular nations and, as a result, was used only too often as a kind of police instrument by the various dynasties. The Turkish government recognizes itself as the arbiter of ecclesiastical disputes.[239] Caesaropapism also exists in many Protestant countries, but there is a world of difference between it and the Greek: the principles of both churches remain fundamentally different, but then the systems of government in the Protestant nations are better than in the Greek despotisms.

In most Greek national churches almost no theological literature has been produced in recent times. The clergy is just as uneducated as the people. But the people are faithful, are closely attached to the church, and are very religious in their own way. The foreign rule of Turk and Tartar and the protracted wars against them have increased their Christian consciousness. In general, the unified Christian world-view is still dominant; for this reason the people enjoy life; there is no pessimism and no morbid suicide tendency.

The same is generally valid for all Greek national churches. Only Russia constitutes a distinct exception, and we therefore want to examine briefly the spiritual situation in this country.

The large mass of the Russian people, ignorant and lacking in education, are implacably religious and attached to the church; for

[238]    Cf. chapter 5, pt. 1, nos. 6 and 7. Fallmerayer, *Fragmente aus dem Oriente*, 2nd ed., 1877; we also refer the reader to the parallels which the author draws between the Byzantine culture and the Islamic culture. Cf. pp. 206, 209, 211.
[239]    Döllinger, loc. cit., p. 162.

the Russian peasant, the last war against the Turks was a truly religious war.

The clergy, like the people, are uneducated, devoid of theological or other knowledge. The state church is a national church in the strictest sense of the word; no sects are recognized within the Orthodox Church. The Russian may believe what he wants; he belongs to the state church and cannot leave it so long as he is in Russia.[240] The remaining denominations are tolerated, but pains are taken to disseminate Russian Orthodoxy among the unorthodox. The Catholics are treated worst in Poland.[241]

Such is the spiritual condition of the people in Russia, but the situation is entirely different among the "educated"! Since the strenuous reforms of Peter the Great, the free air of European civilization has blown into the calm atmosphere of Russia and has produced that condition which is described by the characteristic name of nihilism. Russia offers a very distinct example of the *Kulturkampf*, of the concomitant repulsing of free inquiry and the belief in authority. The enlightenment has not developed organically from the spirit of the people, but rather is forcefully imposed on the people. However, as we have already seen, sudden acquaintance with a culture which is too high leads to the destruction of the lower culture.[242] Russian nihilism is distinguished less in kind than in degree from the half-education which one finds in all of Europe; the mixture of complete opposites makes a glaring color. The Russian malady is the sickness of the whole world, but the Russians suffer from it to a much higher degree than does the rest of the world. The Greek Orthodoxy of Russia has been disintegrated by the free German Protestantism; that is all. The more the people have become accustomed to the leadership of the church, the more unstable they become when their moral support is taken away, and thus Russian nihilism is modern instability par excellence; it is the coarsest type of instability in the world. The malady, which Pushkin seeks to understand, and which he, comparing it with the

240 There may be de facto at least ten million Raskolniks (dissenters).
241 Children of mixed parentage must become Orthodox.
242 Excellent ideas about the Russian situation are to be found in the book: *Zemlja i wolja*, 1868; especially p. 139 ff. In addition, the reading of the works of Turgenev is best for a study of Russian nihilism.

English spleen, portrays as "Russian melancholy," a melancholy which always turns more and more from life, is nothing but weariness with life, appearing as the result of irreligiosity. Whoever discards the whole and the ideal finds life trite, dull, boring, and desperate. The educated Russians, however, trample upon the ideals of their childhood and the ideals of their people, and so they show us the disconsolate character of an Onegin, Pechorin, Nezhdanov, and, in the best case, a Lenski.

Lermontov, in his *The Hero of Our Time*, delineates the difference between the older and faithful generation and the younger and unfaithful:

What power of will made them hold the conviction that all of heaven, with its innumerable inhabitants, looked down on them from above with mute, but unchanging sympathy! . . . But we, their sad descendants, roam about the earth without convictions and without pride, without satisfaction and without any other fear than that involuntary anxiety which oppresses the heart with thoughts of the inevitable end —we are no longer capable of great sacrifice, neither for the welfare of mankind nor even for our own happiness, because we are convinced that this happiness is impossible—and so we vacillate indifferently from doubt to doubt, as our forefathers threw themselves from one deception into another, without having, like them, either hope or even that powerful, if also indefinite, enjoyment which accompanies the strong in their struggles with their fellow men or against their fate. . . . Voltaire, Byron, and Schopenhauer are the new gospel for the Russians; dissatisfied with themselves and all social institutions, the modern youth of Russia turn their bitterness against themselves and the authority of church and state which restricts them—dreadful Russia![243]

[243]    I have not been able to procure official data concerning the suicide frequency in Russia, yet we can deduce with certainty that many suicides must occur among the "nihilists." The newspapers often provide notice of them. The little material for induction is as follows:

| | | |
|---|---|---|
| 1826–30 | ............ | 1163 suicides |
| 1833–41 | ............ | 1484 suicides |
| 1875 | ............ | 1771 suicides |

Kolb gives 1113 cases for six governments (St. Petersburg, Moscow, Odessa, Kazan, Kharkov, Saratov). (That would be 110 per million inhabitants, while according to the estimate above for 1875, there would be only 30 per million.)

THE NON-CHRISTIAN PEOPLES. 19. What is valid for the Christian peoples also holds for the non-Christian peoples, especially those who participate in the modern labor of civilization. The non-Christian peoples are also happy and enjoy life if they have a unified world-view, if their intellectual cultivation is in harmony with their inner life, if they are, in a word, religious. This depends not so very much on the goodness and elevation of the religion as it does on the degree to which religion is really an object of feeling and is a genuine means of satisfaction and fulfillment for the people. A faithful Jew or Mohammedan finds just as strong a support in his faith as the faithful Christian. All three find peace for their souls amidst gloom; the effect of all three can be the same despite the qualitative differences of the effective causes.

Let us first consider the Jews.

The philosophers, no less than the common people, have long racked their brains over the "cosmopolitan race" of the Jews, and yet the history of this most remarkable people has not yet been written. We are interested here only in the living faith in God of this people. The Old Testament reveals how strongly theism had been planted in the hearts of the Jews by those responsible for their intellectual and moral leadership. It is quite amazing how these people amidst their terrible troubles—there is hardly any more unfortunate people than the Jews—always found new hopes and new faith in their God.

The Jews have endured the many oppressions to which they have been exposed as a result of their religion, which, as Gibbon has rightly remarked, is wonderfully adapted for defense but has never been directed to conquest. Persecuted and despised, the Jewish people cling to the religion of their fathers and have distinguished themselves by a joy in life and a practical optimism which does not allow the development of the morbid suicide tendency. Their great moderation also has a favorable effect in the same sense.[244]

[244]    Suicide appears among the Jews, as an exception to the general rule, during times of severe persecution. In their sacred literature, which includes a history of more than ten thousand years, there are found ten examples of suicide at most.

But religious indifference, skepticism, and unbelief are also prevalent among the Jews, especially among the educated. And it cannot be otherwise; living with and among irreligious Christians, they take an active part in modern intellectual activities, and therefore show, especially in the cities, the same characteristics as the Christians with respect to religion. Heine, the poet of naked skepticism, was a Jew.

Mohammedanism is not favorable to the development of the tendency to suicide. Moslem theism has the same favorable effect as among the Jews; their fatalism also has an exceptionally favorable contributory effect. One can clearly see in contemporary political events in Turkey, in the entire life of the people, how a method of "from failure to failure" has developed. There is probably no strictly consistent fatalism in general, but the Koran in any case has developed a maximum of fatalistic indifference among its adherents. It thus is understandable that suicide is seldom committed by faithful Mohammedans, but in more recent times it appears more frequently among the European Turks and the Egyptians, no doubt because the influence of European culture has produced an incompleteness in these countries comparable to Russian nihilism.[245]

In contrast to the two monotheistic religions considered, pantheistic Buddhism is the religion peculiar to suicide, appropriate to self-slaughter, and it is certainly remarkable that such a religion has the largest body of adherents.[246]

The teaching of Nirvana leads directly to asceticism, to moral suicide, and finally to the giving up of life itself.[247] Brahmanism

---

[245]     How little practical politicians understand sociology is clearly seen by the demands they make; they seek a parliament and similar institutions without proper preparation and social adjustment. These gentlemen surely do not see that the people will only be destroyed by such institutions.

[246]     Concerning the atonements of the Brahmans, cf. Duckner, *Geschichte des Altertums*, III, p. 135 ff; concerning the effects of Buddhism, ibid., p. 265 ff. For the judgment on pantheism, p. 425.

[247]     Buddha himself cast aside the traditional ideas of divinity, but he was not atheistic. As is well known, Schopenhauer has praised the atheistic views of Buddha, but I do not believe that Buddhistic popular religion was atheistic. Buddha may have cast aside the ideas of divinity as he found

is also very favorable to the development of the suicide tendency, for reasons similar to Buddhism. It is pantheistic mysticism which has always favored religious suicide. Antiquity already knew the so-called gymnosophists, who in their belief in metempsychosis saw death as a desirable transformation, and who frequently committed suicide en masse.[248]

Concerning the effects of the remaining religions there is little specifically to be said. In general, what was previously noted also has valid applications here. As far as the religions of primitive peoples are concerned, we know that primitive peoples seldom commit suicide, and evidence the morbid suicide tendency only under very definite abnormal conditions.

20. This concise analysis of the religious conditions of civilized peoples verifies the result of our investigation. For those people who are irreligious, suicide frequency is very high. The suicide tendency is not found among religious peoples, at least not in any significant degree. This rather significant agreement of the results of sociological research on the religiosity and spirituality of the various nations (from which we have made inductions in chap. 2 using the statistics on suicide) is explained not accidentally but necessarily by the significance of religion (and church) in the collective life of the people.

Such an agreement allows no room for conjecture; the suicide tendency was brought about through civilization, and must therefore make its appearance in all places where one finds great intellectual activity, while it cannot arise where there is intellectual stagnancy. Simple reflection, on the other hand, tells us that it is not known why intellectual activity must lead necessarily to suicide. And, investigating the causes and motives of suicide, one finds in fact that it is not intellectual activity but moral half-educa-

---

them, but that is only the negative side of Buddhism, the negative side of his Protestantism in contrast to Brahmanism. The positive side consists in a new moral teaching and in an elevated pantheism that eventually led to the superstitions found among contemporary Buddhists.

[248]    Such a gymnosophist burned himself to death publicly before the eyes of Alexander; another did it before Augustus. Plutarch, *Vita Alexandri*; *Diodorus Sic.*, Bibl., lib. XVII.

tion which positively produces suicide. Not the educated and the over-educated commit it, but the half-educated, whose morality and religiosity are deficient. That suicide is also committed by good men and individuals who are truly educated proves nothing. We know how suicide in particular is related as a partial phenomenon to the tensions of modern society. But it can easily happen in the present condition of general tumult that a sound man can despair of life and deliver himself unto death; however, in spite of everything, such cases seldom appear.

Upon closer analysis, the aforementioned agreement is refuted through a simple statistical induction. It is not true that the suicide tendency appears most frequently in the most educated nations; in England and America, the two most educated and most industrialized nations, suicide appears much less frequently than in uneducated Spain or in other nations.[249] And, further, mental illness appears frequently in America as a consequence of the overwhelming physical and mental strain. Drunkenness is very high in Scotland, but, despite these conditions, the suicide tendency in these nations is low. But this proves more strikingly that where the suicide tendency is generally low, one and the same cause must exist which arrests the appearance and development of a morbid flight from life. And that cause is religiosity.

The parallelism of the above-described irreligiosity and nonspirituality with the intensity of the suicide tendency may be illustrated by the following data:[250]

[249]    Suicide frequently appears among barbarians if they are disturbed in their existence by white men.

[250]    Protestant Germany (Saxony, Prussia), Denmark, France, and Austria (only the German and German-Czech countries), the most educated but also most irreligious nations, show the highest suicide frequency, and some, like Austria, show an increase in suicide frequency. (The rapid climb probably indicates a latent irreligiosity.) On the other hand, the religious nations, whether educated or uneducated, have a low suicide tendency: England, United States, Italy (Spain, Portugal). The parallel could hardly be greater, considering the nature of the phenomenon which is affected by innumerable smaller or larger simultaneous and proximate causes. If in fact only the most educated nations show the highest suicide frequency, then investigation of each individual case should give practical

Suicides per one million inhabitants (1871–75):

| | | | |
|---|---|---|---|
| Saxony | 299 | Massachusetts | 82(?) |
| Denmark | 258 | Sweden | 81 |
| France | 150 | Norway | 73 |
| Prussia | 134 | Belgium | 68 |
| Austria | 120 | England, Wales | 65 |
| Lower Austria | 271 | Holland | 40(?) |
| Bohemia | 161 | Italy | 34 |
| Moravia, Silesia | 155 | Scotland | 31 |
| Tyrol, Vorarlberg | 77 | Russia | 30 |
| Bavaria | 90 | | |

Suicides per 10,000 inhabitants in major cities of the world (1876–78):

| | | | |
|---|---|---|---|
| Leipzig | 4.87 | Prague (1878) | 3.01 |
| Breslau | 3.69 | Vienna | 2.85 |
| Dresden | 3.65 | Berlin | 2.78 |
| Paris | 3.59 | Munich | 1.76 |
| Brussels | 3.53 | New York | 1.48 |
| Frankfort | 3.40 | London | 0.84 |
| (on the Main River) | | | |

That there are religions which favor suicide proves nothing against those religions which are inimicable to suicide, just as the Stoic philosophy, which had given the stamp of dogma to suicide, proves nothing against the remaining philosophical systems. There are good and bad religions, because there generally are good and bad life- and world-outlooks, and it is the task of true education to distinguish the true from the false. The monotheistic religions were

---

evidence for our interpretation: not education itself, but only a certain type of education leads to suicide. Compare especially (*Daten*, pp. 43 ff., 132 ff.) wealthy France with impoverished Ireland; the educated and industrious lands of Saxony, the Rhineland, and Scotland; immense London with Vienna or Berlin; New York, which has the most fluctuating population of all great cities, with Hamburg; Leipzig or Prague with the not much larger Edinburgh, or with Glasgow, which is at least twice as large, etc.

In these and similar comparisons, which every reader can make for himself, the efficacy and strength of the numerous causes of suicide which we have discovered must naturally be considered carefully, and the few apparent exceptions perceived.

and are decidedly favorable to life; they are, especially living in concord with themselves, the flowers of the great tree of mankind's religions and, so far as history can be followed as a teacher, are destined in addition to lead the civilized peoples to an ever higher and higher perfection.[251]

The periodical appearance of the morbid suicide tendency is always paralleled by a rising irreligiosity among the people, and since we have said that the suicide tendency prospers in an advancing civilization, we have used the word civilization in its broadest sense. Only in an advancing civilization is the irreligious half-education present; civilization is not synonomous with true, good, moral education and conditions for all individuals.

The irreligiosity of the Christian peoples is especially explained by a similar advance of civilization, as it occurred in analogous ways among ancient cultural groups. Catholicism of the Middle Ages was concerned in its wisdom with the final end of man toward which mankind strived. It founded a unified world-view and through it gave to its converts peace of soul, upon which the true happiness of man depends. But the Catholic world-view is only one representation of that which mankind has hoped and striven to attain. Therefore, the old order had to yield to a new. This transition from the old to the new led to Protestantism, which it continued to suppress and which in the end led to the strife be-

251    From a sociological point of view, this psychological effect of monotheism is highly interesting. Considered purely logically, monotheism not only brings unity and order to the world, but also to the mind, and it is therefore not accidental that it emerged of necessity from polytheism in the course of time. It preserves thought against the fantasies to which pantheism and polytheism lead, and it therefore maintains a strong and healthy mind. It also completely satisfies the religious, moral, and esthetic-poetic needs. When Comte asserted that only polytheism satisfies the genuine religious need, he was simply wrong. Comte thought more about poetic feeling, but forgot the considerable exalted poetry of monotheism. Reading the Psalms of David, Plato, Dante, and the religious poets, one does not find monotheism unpoetic. Finally, there is the favorable effect of its intrinsic, although logically not absolutely necessary, connection with the belief in immortality. Our investigation clearly indicates to us what God is to man: "An inexpressible sigh lying at the base of the soul (Sebastian Frank von Wörth)."

tween knowledge and belief and prepared the way for the new
order of society. Besides its negative, disintegrating elements
and where in specific circumstances it lost its positive elements,
Protestantism evoked a great suicide tendency, which we must
comprehend as the surest index of a great and powerful time of
transition.[252] The suicide tendency and state of tension, philosophical pessimism, the sentimental laments of our poets—all of these
are the expression of the same fact: the yearning for peace. I must
repeat the thought of an English clergyman from his Protestant
standpoint in opposition to Rome at the end of my research on the
causes of the modern suicide tendency: "We are tired of strife."

[252]    One is not allowed to assert against our understanding of the Middle Ages that suicide also appeared during this time. The suicide tendency
was not so generally widespread as it is today, and there certainly was no
morbid suicide tendency. If anything distinguished the Middle Ages (cf.
Lecky, II, p. 40) it was that suicide frequently appeared in the final and
most corrupt era of the West Gothic Kingdoms in Spain, which was a stage
of decline, and was confined to a small group of men—which, when compared to the rest of the Middle Ages, reveals its sinister characteristics.

Preventitive
Treatment

# 6

# TOWARD A REMEDY FOR THE

# MODERN SUICIDE TENDENCY

1. IN THE PRECEDING RESEARCH we have furnished a diagnosis of the social illness of our time; the therapeutic must obviously fit the diagnosis, and will consist of the removal of the causes which condition the evil.

The social therapeutic must proceed as does the medical: first attempt to alleviate the existing malady, but then—and this is more important—seek to prevent its genesis. Once any malady is firmly rooted, no therapy is usually of much avail. Sociologists, ethicists, and medical doctors are gradually coming to the conclusion that the true task of all practical disciplines consists in hygienic prophylaxis. The times have passed in which one expected, or could expect, the curing of all evils by decree; particularly ineffective would be laws regarding a social evil of the nature of the modern suicide tendency.[253]

2. Man must above all become healthy, physically and mor-

[253] There are, with justice, no laws against suicide in most modern legal systems. But it cannot be said therefore that, in special cases, an indirect or direct prohibition could not be effective; thus, for example, one general order of Napoleon's, in which suicide by soldiers would be treated as cowardice, was effective; and a young woman in Marseille was dissuaded from suicide by the threat that her body would be displayed in public should she choose such a means of death. (Cf. Beccaria, *Traité des délits et des peines*, no. 32; von Wächter, *Revision der Lehre vom Selbstmord*, Neues Archivs, 1829; cf. Meyer, *Lehrbuch des deutschen Strafrechtes*, 1875, no. 82. Concerning the character of the ancient world, cf. Becker, *Charikles*, edited by Göll, III, p. 164).

ally; we must accustom ourselves to unqualified obedience to the established prophylactic rules of modern science.

Science gives us the means at hand to protect ourselves from the harmful effects of nature. It teaches us how we can shape to our advantage all the conditions we studied in the chapters on bodily organization, general societal conditions and psychoses. Why do we not so shape them? Because we do not want to.

3. Nearly all theoreticians and practitioners seek to alleviate the evils of modern society through economic and political reforms. General attention is certainly fastened on these efforts, and very much is generally expected of them, but I am not able to share these hopes. The political and economic conditions of a people are only the external manifestations of the inner spiritual life; they are conditioned by this spiritual life, upon which the physician must therefore focus his attention. Often the programs and quarrels of our parliament, our politicians, and our national economists appear to me remarkably petty and vain. In any event, political and economic concessions and major or minor reforms will not rescue society. A morsel of justice and money, more or less, will not put an end to the pessimistic weariness with life.

I can cite as my opinion on this, which will appear highly heretical to all practical politicians, a magnificent example from history: Christ. The Roman world in the time of Christ was pretty much in the same desperate frame of mind as contemporary society. Then, as now, a morbid suicide tendency ruled; men were dissatisfied and unhappy; yearning for a redeemer was widespread. Who redeemed mankind? No politician, no national economist, no socialist or demagogue. It is truly magnificent to see how Christ, in such politically and socially agitated times as those, abstained from all politics. How easy it would have been for Him to win converts by political and social incitements! But He insisted upon the ennobling of character; He insisted upon the intensification of religious feeling; He desired that men become good, for He knew that only then would they find peace for their souls.

We, too, shall find the desired peace for our souls when we have become good.[254]

[254]    It is to be understood that the enduring oppressive need and the depressive misery which exists must be removed. I do not flatter myself as

4. Since the modern suicide tendency is ultimately the product of increasing irreligiosity, the malady can only be completely healed if the irreligiosity and its accompanying "half-ness" are arrested. We must step outside ourselves. We must stop grubbing in our innards and cease to use our understanding as the executioner of our hearts. We must find interests in the external world and in society. We must learn to give of ourselves: we lack true and genuine love. Certainly we believe that we are able to love, that we are capable of the most delicate feelings, but that is not true. Morbid sentimentality is not identical with true, genuine, warm, vital, and original feeling. *If one wants to remove the morbid suicide tendency, he should develop in man the capacity for the harmonious and thorough cultivation of ideas and feelings, imbue them with power and energy, and give them a moral basis.*

Some investigators, Renan, Treitschke, and others, believe the people should be brought up to be religious, while the educated should be allowed to remain free. But that is to sanction the existing "half-ness," and is happening anyway. Should one perhaps create a strictly distinct aristocracy of education? Where does this education begin, and where does it leave off?

More consistent are those who, with their denial of positive religion, postulate only a unified scientific world-view. The question, however, is whether religion can and should be dismissed so quickly. I believe man needs religion to live as much as he needs air to breathe. Historical development also indicates that concurrent with the development of thought there is a corresponding development of religious-moral life and feeling. Comte commits a gross error in his positive philosophy when he allows progress in the religious sphere only to a certain point, and from there on simply casts aside all religious life.

---

capable of assuaging everyone who is hungry with a moral sermon: I speak on the definitive solution of social problems.

For example, charitable treatment of the poor will suppress the suicide tendency; as Casper points out: in a French Protestant colony of 6000 souls only three suicides occurred because of the excellent charitable organization for the needy. —One other example: Magendie once found himself in such great need that he no longer wished to live; then, at the critical moment, an officer of the court arrived with a report that Magendie had inherited 20,000 francs—and his excellent health was restored.

Many find in art, especially certain styles, a substitute for religion, and so believe art will rescue modern society. But this is equally false. A refined, esthetic enjoyment of art is as incapable of making the problems of life endurable as is an aristocracy of science. The creative artist, especially the great artist, is surely expressing the same thing as the founder of a religion, but the seeing or hearing of a work of art does not replace sympathy for or appreciation of its universal religious content. A shallow view of life is revealed by the belief that the riddle of the universe can be concertized away from mind and heart. Art may always enter the service of religion but is unable to replace it.

We need a religion; we need to be religious.

The thought comes to mind of regarding Christianity as the saving religion. But what form of Christianity? This is a difficult question to answer. If humanity could become strictly Catholic, the suicide tendency would certainly disappear. For Catholicism, by virtue of its Church organization, could most easily, quickly and effectively create universal acceptance for a unified world outlook. But the course of history cannot be ignored; the Reformation would again break out, just as it did before. Moreover, it is not only a matter of removing the suicide tendency, but removing it by the proper means. For us, however, Catholicism has become impossible. Should we then become Protestants? So far as we deny Catholicism, we are already Protestants; but the question remains, whether and in what form we can remain Christian.

"I believe from the depths of my soul, after the most mature reflection, that the teaching of Christ, cleansed of priestly adulteration and properly understood in its expression according to our own limitations, is the most perfect system I can think of for affording world peace and joy most quickly, most powerfully, most surely, and to the greatest number of people."[255] I also believe that any one of the many Protestant sects could be the desired religion; but, to the extent that they should have to accommodate themselves to progressive times, these Christian sects would really bring about a new religion.

[255]    Lichtenberg.

It is as if our era were made for a new religion. Just as at the time of the Roman Empire, society has been shaken to its foundations: men feel unhappy; dissatisfaction and the wish for a savior is widespread. But especially favorable for the spread of the new teaching in the Roman Empire were the general nervousness and pathological agitations which are also characteristic of our society. Like all religions, the new teaching would take more a psychological than a logical path to its victorious end. Since religion, although in truly Protestant fashion a matter for the individual, must nevertheless at the same time be a popular religion through which the hearts of all men without exception would be united, this would not, then, permit its theoretical component to ascend the heights of intellectual accomplishment. I think rather that this religion, like the Catholicism of the Middle Ages, could inaugurate a new and better Middle Ages, after which a new period of free thought would begin again, until at last, through alternating periods of belief and disbelief, "one flock and one shepherd" would appear. Or it may happen quite differently. The historical development of man is, in proportion to the time which humanity has yet to live, so short that our conclusions as to the future can be made only with great caution and reserve. It is possible that a new upswing of religious feeling would take place without ecclesiastical unification. Perhaps the Congregational or some similar method and organization could even bring to a definitive conclusion and stabilize that religious individualism to which Protestantism has so far attained.

5. I am afraid that the conclusions at which we have arrived will not be satisfying to many of my readers. Perhaps some will see in me a fatalist: how shall the social therapeutic be possible if the organization of a new religion must be awaited? What can the individual do if, as was indicated, the morbid suicide tendency at certain times naturally and periodically develops?

I admit that I am definitely a determinist, but I reject even more definitely the reproach of fatalism; indeterminism would lead to fatalistic views, but no trace of this outlook is to be found in this book.

That we must die, that death is a physical necessity, a natural law, is well known; but it is not a natural law that we must die perchance by poisoning. If someone commits suicide, he obeys no natural law, but chooses death as a consequence of secondary laws which, under other circumstances, prevent suicide; the good and the bad, the useful and the pernicious, men do according to the same laws, which obviously are no ultimate law but the interaction of many laws. One who has taken poison can save himself through an antidote; only for natural death does no cure exist.

Much of what happens to us certainly happens of necessity, without our cooperation. Man is linked to his immediate and more distant environment by thousands and thousands of threads, and to a certain extent is independent of it. But man is no blind product of the forces of nature; we do not depend completely and exclusively on the external world. Our consciousness faces the external world, a psychological whole which perceives the external world according to its own laws. It is a psychological totality endowed with memory and recall. Every simple and complex effect of the external world are equally independent; our relation to it is that of reciprocity, not simple dependence. Knowledge gives us the power to intervene in the causal relationship; we can set certain purposes as ideals, and we are able to choose the appropriate means. But because we always follow the strongest motive, we are not blind, because other motives also affect us. We reflect before our decision, choosing and seeking those means which best suit our purpose. The choice itself is the result of our character, but this we form ourselves for the most part. We are just as responsible for a malformed will as we are for inadequate logical operations of thought; like the intellect, the will must be trained and educated. And only because it is determined is it capable of training and education: we form our will through our appetites, tendencies, dislikes, habits, and guiding principles. One can certainly not develop will out of will alone; one cannot simply cast out of himself a malformed will. But we can modify our present will by education, by self-discipline, as it is modified by the education which comes to us from others. We can employ all dispositions, habits, and traits of character which we know from experience must lead to certain results under certain conditions.

The indeterminist cannot do this; rules and guides for action are for him completely unnecessary and superfluous, since he cannot know at all whether he will later be able to adhere to them: his will cannot be determined, so he uses no leading, determining principles. According to indeterminism, man is an idle spectator of that which happens in him; he is the inactive stage on which actions proceed in and with him. The connection between subject and action is broken, the chain that binds act and actor snapped. Thus, if the will is indeterminate, we are also entirely lacking in responsibility for our will and its corresponding actions; all training and education of the will is impossible, and no one can be led to virtue. The indeterminist does not need to avoid immorality, does not need to strengthen his will, since he has no assurance that future action will be thus improved, and since his will appears in him in any case without any causes. Today he acts in one way, tomorrow in another way; he has no control over such action precisely because his will is indeterminate. The indeterminist therefore does not punish, because he knows he has no right to punish; if punishment has the purpose of improving or discouraging behavior, what basis has the indeterminist for punishment? For him there are no purposes at all. How can the fear of punishment, the memory of unpleasant correction, act as motives to prevent the same or a similar act? If the will were indeterminate, then punishment is certainly unnecessary and superfluous, for a moral chaos, a blind fate, prevails. Humanity has nothing to strive for, since, according to the teaching of indeterminism, a foreknowledge of that which men aspire to is impossible. Since the law of causality has been abrogated, a prediction of things to come is impossible. Social reforms are not possible, because they are superfluous; there is no science of sociology, because no rules can be established for the indeterminate appearance of the will of man.

It is evident that an ethics, a sociology, or any science is possible only from a deterministic standpoint, and if the word "freedom" is to be employed at all, it can only be used by the determinist. Only the determinist can, by virtue of his teaching, attain the freedom of ethical perfection. He is capable of reaching a state in which he always prefers the better, when he has recognized it. Only for the determinist is holiness a goal to be strived for, only for him is there a striving toward the freedom of perfection.[256]

In contrast to this true interpretation of determinism, various false and unclear views have been entertained, both about the teaching itself and its opposite. Typically, the determinists themselves have brought discredit to their teaching, in that they were not always in a position to refute the charges of fatalism and its attendant consequences brought against them. Indeed, the determinists were often practically fatalists.

The statisticians in particular have not realized that foreknowledge of many social phenomena not only does not lead to fatalism, but is rather the sole means to fight fatalism, for only through advance knowledge can we bring our activities into conformity with what is to come. If we learn that 3,000 men in a certain country have previously committed suicide in one year, we correctly infer that approximately as many will die the following year. This conclusion, however, assumes that the same circumstances will persist. But nothing forces society to remain in the same state. It can, if it so desires, alter its conditions in such a way that suicides are no longer committed. Statistics does not arrive at natural laws by the simple enumeration of suicides, murders, etc., but only at secondary—empirical and derived—laws. These and similar crimes do not have to occur, but they do occur as a result of conditions which at present exist, but which have not and will not always exist. Therefore the number of suicides fluctuates from year to year, and the statistical evidence, in accordance with the

256   The word "freedom" will probably be understood in the same sense as indeterminism, but with great injustice. We connect the idea of freedom with an idea of true strength; but indeterminism robs us of such strength and the outer world, on the whole, will appear contingent on the will. Where freedom exists, a true, complementary, responsibility also exists; but it exists only with determinism. We have power over our inner dispositions which the will determines; we are masters of our future; we may counsel ourselves to reflect upon the freedom of choice we possess. We have freedom; through the good becoming defined as good, the good can be cherished by us and we can attain the exalted state of freedom of moral perfection.

workings of secondary causes, does not show any terrible "constancy."[257]

Perhaps these very fluctuations might cause alarm to some, who would find in the statistical data a proof of indeterminism, and, in consequence, of fatalism. One could conclude from the uncertainty of prediction that there existed an objective chance and therefore an objective indeterminateness, the necessary consequence of which would have to be fatalism.

One may not consider subjective chance as objective, however, nor mistake subjective probability for the mathematical variety. At the moment there are still many barriers to our knowledge; we still know too little to be able to predict with certainty; *but the meagerness of man's knowledge may not be viewed as a universally valid objective law.* We are not yet able to survey the causal connections of social phenomena; thus it is our ignorance that alarms us, not our knowledge. It is our problem to pierce ever more deeply into the total mechanism of the universe, through unceasing labors, until we finally grasp how the whole affects man. Only through precise knowledge of the universe and its effects on man, and of the laws that govern the psychical phenomena of man, are we in a position to achieve freedom and perfection through active intervention in the course of mankind's development. The complex combination of agents affecting mankind is indeed great and almost incalculable. In spite of this, they are amenable to scientific analy-

---

[257]     Quetelet so often indicates, among other things, the constancy of the suicide index; but a look at the suicide reports over long periods suffices to show that no constancy can be found.

Quetelet emphatically says: "It is a budget which one pays with frightening regularity, it is that of prisons, of criminal convictions, and of social tensions...."

In Germany, A. Wagner has made this outlook known in his excellent statistical work concerning the conformity to law of seemingly anarchic human affairs. But the public was alarmed by Buckle, who, on the basis of Quetelet's work and others, has spread unclear ideas of determinism.

Against these false definitions of problems, Drobisch has applied himself quite firmly and with great success in his publication: *Die moralische Statistik und die menschliche Willensfreiheit*, 1867.

sis, which shows that the actions of man do not occur without his cooperation; that while the will of man is determined, it is not for that reason unfree. So far as we are able to anayze the causes and motives of acts of will, we are able approximately to measure the effects of individual factors, and, on the basis of this measurement, we are able to direct our whole lives in such a way that we can happily and successfully accomplish the realization of ethical ideals. Like every disease, the modern suicide tendency can also be cured by insightful effort.

6. Perhaps the reader further expects a detailed guide for a therapeutic of the suicide tendency. It may be objected that our central rule is too general, that in practice one needs more particular statements appropriate to individual cases.

The complaint is justified, but the criticism of generality applies not only to this, but to every sociological work involving a therapy for social conditions. The theoretician cannot possibly consider all particular cases, especially in problems of such large scale, and must therefore leave it to the practitioner to apply the general rule to the special case. We have done what we could: we have tried to set forth the individual causes of suicide with all possible care, and we can therefore ask of a therapeutic that it remove these causes.

This lack of particular rules may actually be most noticeable in what is most important: the establishment of a unified worldview, the removal of "half-ness," and the ending of the terrible *Kulturkampf*. But even with the best intentions I am scarcely able to propose more than two prescriptions, which have long been stated by outstanding thinkers. "You who are more clever than the rest, who wait fretting and impatient on the final page of the primer [the Bible], take care!" Lessing warns in his *The Education of the Human Race*. "Take care that you do not let your less able classmates notice what you are beginning to sense, or even see! Until these less able fellows of yours have caught up with you, it is better that you should return again to this primer and examine whether that which you now consider only applications of methods, didactic devices, are not also something more." If men did not transgress against this rule, there would be no *Kultur-*

*kampf,* no suicide tendency. On their way from primitive bar-. barism to education and true enlightenment, mankind must pass through innumerable intermediate stages. If it were possible to guide the great masses systematically, logically, step by step from the simple to the complex, from the easy to the difficult, from error to truth, from naïve conviction to conscious insight, there would be no struggle between conflicting views, no "half-ness," and every new accomplishment would represent the consistent development of previous stages of culture.

But because this principle is so sharply ignored, the question arises of how to proceed in these cases. We cannot and will not go backwards; therefore we must press forward, if we do not wish to stand still. Alexis de Tocqueville says:

When the religious views of the people have once been shaken, there is no greater despair, but one must promote enlightenment at any cost, because, although an enlightened and skeptical people may indulge in a tragic view of life, there is nothing more terrible than a nation at the same time ignorant, coarse, and unfaithful.

I have nothing further to add, and I wish only that my book may move the reader to reflection, for it is the problem of the writer in the social sphere, if anywhere, not to offer the reader final answers, but rather to move him to thought and—to action.

*Appendix*

*Masaryk's Detailed Table of Contents*

## Part II

General Societal Conditions
1. The census in relation to the frequency of suicide. Absolute and relative population. Overpopulation. Underpopulation. Suddenness of population growth. Decline in population. Emigration.
2. Married life and family life. Married, single, widow, widower, divorced, concubine. Influence of married and family life on children. Illegitimate births and the tendency to suicide.
3. Suicide among prisoners.
4. Occupation.
5. Résumé.

## Part III

Political Conditions
1. Race. Racial mixtures.
2. Nationality. Mixtures of the various nations. Renunciation of one's nationality.
3. System of government.
4. Political crises, revolutions, agitations.
5. War.
6. Militarism: universal military service.
7. Résumé.

## Part IV

Economic Conditions
1. Unsettled conditions of wealth, need, misery, poverty, riches. True and false needs.
2. Economic conditions as a cause of suicide.
3. Unusual fluctuations in wealth. Poor harvest results. Business crises (1873), gambling, lottery.
4. National wealth and suicide frequency: government debts. Currency.
5. Type of labor.
6. The development of suicide tendencies with growing national wealth. The social question.

mentary disturbances. Psychic Depression: hypochondria and melancholia. Melancholy as a proper suicide psychosis ("Suicidal Mono-mania"). States of exaltation: delirium, frenzy. Mental derangement and imbecility.

3. Classification of suicide from a psychological point of view.
4. The mental conditions of suicides. Is suicide a courageous act?

## Part II

5. Psychosis as a social malady of the present day. The causes of mental illness.
    1. Natural influences. Climate; atmospheric conditions; time of year; cosmic influence: moonlight.
    2. City and country.
    3. Age.
    4. Physical condition. Illnesses which produce psychosis. Psychic disposition (temperament).
    5. Hereditary psychosis and suicide tendency.
    6. Sex.
    7. Age, childhood.
    8. Marriage and family life. Married, single, widow, widower, divorced, illegitimate birth.
    9. Prisoners.
    10. Occupation.
    11. Relative population.
    12. Race.
    13. Nationality.
    14. System of government.
    15. Political crisis, revolution, agitation, war.
    16. Militarism.
    17. Economic conditions, wealth and want, crisis (strikes).
    18. Psychosis originates most frequently through psychic causes. Mental illness will continue to increase. Guislain on modern civilization as the cause of the general diffused psychosis.

## Part III

6. Psychosis and suicide tendency are phenomenological aspects of one and the same social process. Intellectual, moral and religious education and psychosis. Confession and psychosis.

5. The therapy for the suicide tendency requires time. Determinism is not fatalism. How indeterminism encourages suicide.

6. On the usefulness of general sociological rules for the practical treatment of a special case. Lessing's and Tocqueville's rules. Conclusion.

# Masaryk's Bibliography

Bertrand, *Traité du suicide consistant dans ses rapports avec la philosophie, la théologie, la médecine,* 1857.

Blanc, *Du suicide en France; Separatabdruck des Journaux de la Société de statistique de Paris,* 1862.

Brierre de Boismont, *Du suicide et de la folie suicide,* 2d ed., 1865.

Casper, *Über den Selbstmord und seine Zunahme in unserer Zeit,* 1825 (Beiträge zur medicinischen Statistik und Staatsarzneikunde).

Cazauvieilh, *Du suicide, de l'aliénation mentale et des crimes contre les personnes, comparés dans leurs rapports réciproques,* 1840.

Diez, *Der Selbstmord,* 1838.

Douay, *Le suicide ou la mort violent,* 1870.

Falret, *De l'hypochondrie et du suicide,* 1822.

Heyfelder, *Der Selbstmord in arzneigerichtlicher Beziehung,* 1828.

Hoffbauer, *Über die Ursachen der so sehr überhandnehmenden Selbstmorde und deren Verhütung,* 1859.

Legoyt, *Sur le suicide dans les divers états de l'Europe,* 1844.

Lisle, *Du suicide, statistique, médecine, histoire, législation,* 1856.

Morselli, *Il suicidio, saggio di statistica morale comparata,* 1879.

Müller, *Der Selbstmord,* 1859.

Osiander, *Über den Selbstmord u. s. w.,* 1813.

Petit, *Recherches statistiques sur l'étiologie du suicide,* 1850.

Plagge, *Die Quellen des Irrsinns und der Selbstmorde,* 1861.

Platter, "Über den Selbstmord in Österreich in den Jahren 1819–1872," *Statistische Monatsschrift,* 1876.

Salomon, *Welche sind die Ursachen der in neuester Zeit so sehr überhandnehmenden Selbstmorde u. s. w.,* 1861.

Sedlaczek, "Die Selbstmorde in Wien 1854–1878," *Statistische Monatsschrift,* 1879.

Tissot, *De la manie du suicide et de l'esprit de révolte, de leurs causes, et de leurs remèdes*, 1840.

Wagner, *Die Gesetzmässigkeit in den scheinbar willkürlichen menschlichen Handlungen*, 1864.

Winslow, *The Anatomy of Suicide*, 1840.